P9-ECJ-251

Ocean Realm
Diving Guide To
Underwater
Florida

BY NED DELOACH

*The most complete and up-to-date information
available about diving in Florida.*

*The offshore maps and directions used in this guide
were not designed for navigational use, but to give the
diver a general idea of the distribution of diving
locations throughout Florida.*

PUBLISHED AND DISTRIBUTED

Ocean Realm Publishing Corporation, 2333 Brickell Ave., Miami, FL 33129.
Richard H. Stewart/Publisher; Patricia Reilly/Editor; Judi Padgett/Associate Editor; Crista Fanjul/Editorial Assistant; Sharell Holverson/Contributing Editor;
Susan Glauber, Art Production.

Contributing Photographers: Richard Collins, Bill Crawford, Ned DeLoach,
Rick Frehsee, Bill George, Sue Kuntz, Tom Mount, Pat Rose, Wes Skiles, Bill
Smith, Michael Stewart, Richard Stewart, Roy Stoutamire, Steve Straatsma,
Pete Velde, Alan Williams.

Copyright © 1983 by Ned DeLoach. All rights reserved. Reproduction in whole
or in part without permission is prohibited.

BE SMART.

There may be different schools of thought, different personal preferences concerning dive equipment. But divers all agree on one thing: Quality comes first.

Quality is built into every product in the Princeton Tectonics line, from the innovative Bottom Timer™ automatic stopwatch, to the virtually indestructible, compact, waterproof Bottom Light™ to our accurate, individually calibrated gauges and handsome, precision watches. And we guarantee them all.

Don't learn the hard way. Princeton Tectonics is the educated choice in diving equipment.

PRINCETON TECTONICS

1-800-257-9080 / BOX 8057 / TRENTON, NJ 08650-0057

EDITOR'S NOTE

I came to Florida 14 years ago to dive. Why Florida? Simply because it was the place for divers to be and it still is today. Early underwater images from my land-locked youth brought me here, and I have yet to be disappointed by what I've found. Clear water, acres of living coral gardens, majestic wrecks and pristine springs all combine to offer a variety and quality of underwater beauty and adventure matched nowhere on earth.

My desire to experience the best of Florida's diving ultimately drew me to every section of the state. I soon realized that the enthusiasm generated by my discoveries was infectious and also useful to others. Feeling compelled to share these findings, I published my first guide in early 1972— *Diving and Recreational Guide to Florida Springs*.

Twelve years and eight guides later, my ongoing project has grown into the 4th edition of the *Diving Guide to Underwater Florida*. This book, with 30 chapters and over 400 listings, has been designed with much care as a complete sourcebook for those seeking to discover the best diving Florida has to offer.

The effort of compiling this guide was not mine alone. Many of our best charter boat captains and dive store operators have spent countless hours graciously sharing their experiences, observations and finds so that their personal love and excitement about Florida's underwater realm could be passed on to others.

A fear that has weighted the hearts and thoughts of each of us has been that our natural wonders would be overrun by man's incursions and lost to future generations. We well know that the battle to save our seas is never ending, but it has become evident what diligent efforts by educated, caring, understanding men and women can accomplish. Today, our guarded optimism burns brighter than a decade ago.

The very best have come forward to rationally and persistently act as guardians of our waters. Through their efforts and those of our state government, much has already been preserved. The 1974 dredging moratorium has greatly improved the water clarity in South Florida, allowing our precious living corals a chance for continued life. Costly artificial reef development programs from Pensacola to Miami have created abundant sea life where none existed before. The cessation of construction on the Cross Florida Barge Canal allowed our clear, underwater river system to flow undisturbed. Conservation organizations protecting sea turtles and manatees have won the hearts and concerns of our citizenry.

However, the reality of our hopes rests with divers and watersportsmen who, through their ever-growing awareness and efforts, are becoming the sea's most effectual ambassadors.

This book is dedicated to those who, by care and understanding, have already achieved so much, yet realize that our vigil is one that is never ending.

SCUBA SEXTANT

Reliable Underwater Navigation

This simple and reliable instrument, together with a compass and a pencil, saves you precious dive time and eliminates surfacing for directions in low visibility water * Simply plot your course as you travel and the Scuba Sextant will tell you the fastest, most direct route back to your entry point * Both beginners and advanced divers find this a simple and effective way to learn navigation.
*Look for it in your local dive shop.

- -

Send _____ Scuba Sextants at $16.50 ea.   GUARANTEED — Total enclosed $ _____

For more information or to order mail to:

SCUBA SEXTANT, INC. 3366 Perishing Rd. Columbus, Nebraska 68601

NAME		
ADDRESS		
CITY	STATE	Zip

Standard discounts available to dealers.

HOW TO USE THIS GUIDE

I have gathered information about hundreds of diving sites, but have selected for this guide only those locations I felt would offer the most to the underwater enthusiast. It is my intent that the book should give the reader an overall view of diving available in state waters, as well as helpful information about what to expect when diving a particular area.

From a list of many springs dived, I have included only those sites that are currently accessible to the public and provide the most rewarding diving experiences. Nearly all the springs listed can be reached by car; however, many are difficult to find because of their remote locations. Directions are given by highways and roads. (Many are nothing more than roughly formed sand paths.) The distances in miles and tenths of mile, which can be read on an automobile odometer, are usually given from main highway intersections or bridges.

Directions and information are also included for saltwater diving sites that do not require a boat to reach. These areas are marked "Beach Dive" after the location's name. A special listing of such dives is included in the index. Rewarding diving at such spots is rare in Florida, but there are several excellent areas on the state's southwest coast and mid-to-lower east coast. Beach diving in the Keys is almost non-existent. Reef areas are too far offshore and strong current flows between islands make bridge diving hazardous.

The maps and directions for offshore locations should only be used as general references. If you are interested in diving any of these sites, it is recommended that you first contact a local diving charter service or diving store. Many such services are included in the area chapters.

I hope that the information found in this diving guide will save you time and effort in your search for the beauty and adventure found in Florida's underwater world.

Then you'll see exactly what makes Mares pneumatic guns far superior to any conventional gun ever made.

Statistically speaking, Mares pneumatic guns pack 30% more power than 3-sling rubber guns, 60% more than 2-sling, and a whopping 150% more power than 1-sling. And they're amazingly accurate, too. Because unlike sling guns, the shaft is under power and held in-line the entire length of the barrel.

What's more, there's no sling vibration to spook fish. And no rubbers to untangle after every shot.

Most Mares guns have adjustable (high/low) power for confined or open areas. At "low power" the guns are comparatively effortless to load and better suited for close range use. Or, once

For accuracy and power, spear shaft is held in line under power the entire length of barrel.

loaded, just flip the switch and you're ready to fire at "high power."

Mares guns cost less to repair and maintain than sling guns, and they're backed by a 2-year guarantee.

Inch for inch, a Mares pneumatic gun is more powerful and accurate than any other gun its size.

To verify that, just put one to the test.

Send $2.00 today for full color Mares and SeaQuest catalogs of premium diving equipment. SeaQuest decal and emblem included.

Mares

SEAQUEST, INCORPORATED, 2151-F LAS PALMAS DRIVE, CARLSBAD, CA 92008, (619) 438-1101, IN HAWAII – RANN, INC., 2979 KOAPAKA ST., HONOLULU, HI 96819 (808) 836-3557, IN CANADA – SEAWAY MANUFACTURING LIMITED, 17919 ROAN PLACE, SURREY B.C. V3S 5K1, (604) 576-1317

TEST THE MOST POWERFUL, ACCURATE GUNS EVER MADE.

(MARES PNEUMATIC GUNS)

Contents

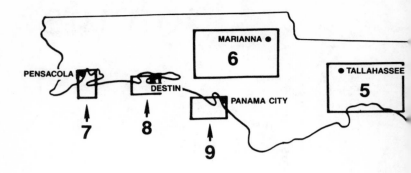

Maps

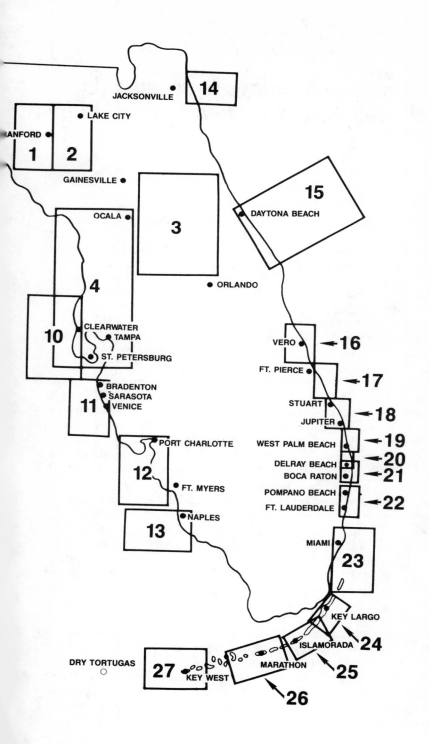

JACKSONVILLE

LAKE CITY

SANFORD

1 **2**

GAINESVILLE

OCALA

3

ORLANDO

14

15

DAYTONA BEACH

4

CLEARWATER
TAMPA

10

ST. PETERSBURG

BRADENTON
SARASOTA

11 VENICE

PORT CHARLOTTE

12

FT. MYERS

NAPLES

13

VERO ◄**16**

FT. PIERCE

◄**17**

STUART

JUPITER ◄**18**

WEST PALM BEACH ◄**19**

DELRAY BEACH ◄**20**

BOCA RATON ◄**21**

POMPANO BEACH

FT. LAUDERDALE ◄**22**

MIAMI

23

KEY LARGO

ISLAMORADA **24**

DRY TORTUGAS

27 KEY WEST

MARATHON **25**

26

Florida

A preview of things to see and do in the state's underwater wonderland.

The Florida peninsula thrusts itself southward from the continent as if attempting to form a land bridge to the clear, warm, Caribbean waters. Since the earliest days of sport diving, underwater enthusiasts have taken advantage of this geological phenomenon, traveling in pursuit of beauty and adventure. With its 1,300 miles of coastline, fronting the Atlantic on the east and the Gulf of Mexico to the west, Florida became the Mecca of this fledgling sport.

The islands of the Florida Keys were the power behind the magnet. They lured divers south, promising vast expanses of living coral gardens. By the mid-'60s, this area could boast of having the largest concentration of diving-related services found anywhere in the world.

South Florida quickly gained its reputation as America's underwater playground. The early boom spawned the development, in 1960, of the Pennekamp Coral Reef State Park, our nation's first underwater recreational area. It was established with the laudable intent of preserving the delicate ecosystem for future generations of divers.

Not until the mid-'60s did word of other diving areas within the state begin to leak out. Tales of large, clear, freshwater spring basins along the banks of the Suwannee River began to surface. Many were within a few miles of major southbound highways leading to the Keys. Florida's spring diving country had been discovered. Divers were soon flocking to the new area to experience personally the best freshwater diving in America.

The underwater topography of Florida's extensive coastal zones was a mystery to the diving public throughout most of the '60s. Though the waters *were* being explored, it was mostly by spearfishermen, who were the forerunners, and secrecy was their code. Sometimes they spent weeks in fruitless search before prosperous hunting grounds were found. Upon discovery, the location was held sacred until the bounty had been obtained. Ice chests brimming with prime snapper and grouper filets signaled the hunter's success. Spearing out their finds, they migrated farther out to sea, leaving the reefs and wrecks for the sport divers.

Just as spearfishermen were the vanguard of coastal water discoveries, cave divers were reminiscent of the 16th century conquistadors, plunging relentlessly into Florida's dense woodland, searching for cave entrances

BILL CRAWFORD

The French angel, a typical Florida reef resident.

into the aquifer (underground rivers). Harried by mosquitoes, snakes, gators, seemingly impenetrable undergrowth and shotgun-toting land-owners, the cave seekers discovered most of the springs now so popular with sport divers.

By the early '70s, divers were streaming into the state in ever-increasing numbers, eager to explore the new reefs, wrecks and springs. On any given weekend, the charter boats from Pensacola to Key West were filled. Queuing up for air fills became the norm at air stations serving the spring country. Visitors were quickly learning that the state's underwater recreational areas were as varied as they were abundant. The thrill of the last

NED DELOACH

dive could only be matched by the anticipation of hundreds of underwater sites still left to be discovered. Florida had it all—reefs, wrecks, springs, caves, rigs for diving, spearfishing, lobstering, relic hunting, shell collecting, drift diving, underwater photography, tropical collecting, treasure hunting—everything but ice diving. It was an exciting time to be a diver in Florida.

This first great era of Florida diving came to an end in 1973 with the sudden advent of the Arab oil embargo. Traffic on the interstates slowed from a steady flow to a sporadic trickle as the gas shortage became acute. Lack of fuel limited local divers to sites close to home. Keys' dive store owners still recount tales of taking undisturbed siestas on US 1 during the crunch. Within months, America had finagled enough gas from the rest of the world to get weekend traffic moving once again, but the flow to Florida was slow making a comeback.

During this period, areas outside the United States began vigorous and effective advertising campaigns to compete seriously for the American diver's vacation time. The Cayman Islands was the first Caribbean resort area to promote itself prosperously through diving. Their notable success was soon emulated by the Bahamas, Virgin Islands, Bonaire and Cozumel. Florida lagged in its promotional efforts and lost many regular visitors. Divers quickly accustomed themselves to driving to their local airport, checking in their gear, and turning their underwater adventure over to others. The others—travel agents, transport services, hotel management, charter boat captains and diving guides—did the rest. Diving suddenly changed from an expedition into a luxury tour. Breakfast was ready at nine, coordinated with the dive at ten. Fast boats made quick runs to reef locations marked by buoys. After diving two tanks, it was back to the dock by one. There was just enough time to shower before lunch. The remainder of the day was spent sipping cocktails, swapping stories and staring dreamy-eyed out to sea.

While the natural wonders and beauty of the tropical reefs couldn't be matched, something was missing for many divers.

Was it personal discovery? Coupled with the diver's innate desire to witness the natural beauty of our planet is his need for personal exploration—to discover for himself. Although divers had been guided to one of the world's most spectacular underwater settings, the thrill of discovery was absent for many. It had, unwittingly, been exchanged for convenience.

Today, more and more sport divers are putting adventure back into their diving travel. With money tight but vacation time still available, there has been a marked return to domestic diving. Florida now is welcoming back an increased number of diving visitors, ready to seek underwater adventure on their own terms.

Although the copious reefs of South Florida are still the state's stellar attraction, hundreds of locations promising underwater adventure lie along the route south. The Gulf coast of Florida's panhandle, long renowned for the visual impact of her seascapes, is one of America's favorite beach resorts. Miles of white silica sand, crowned by rolling dunes and gently lapped by clear, calm seas, form images that last for a lifetime.

Beach diving is disappointing. Shallow sand flats stretch monotonously for miles, with only an occasional sand dollar or starfish to be found. The real adventure starts a few miles out to sea. There lie the great steel shipwrecks gracing the ocean floor with their majesty. Through the years, these towering spires of steel have enticed a plethora of marine life from the open waters. Clouds of bait fish, thousands in number, drift aimlessly above, with larger fish and crustaceans holed-up in the mazes of twisted debris. Rock reefs (limestone outcroppings) and artificial reefs built from bridge and building rubble, add variety to the diving.

The summer is the "in" season for Gulf diving. Calm seas are common from April through October. During these months, the water temperature stays about 80 degrees. Water visibility averages 60 feet, with 100-foot visibility common. Spearfishermen find good hunting away from the more popular reefs and wrecks. Snapper, amberjacks and Warsaw grouper are the most plentiful game fish. Larger fish move into the area during the winter. Shelling is popular underwater and along the beaches, and many of Florida's rarest shells may be collected here.

Canoeing the Ichetucknee, a delight of Florida's spring country.

Just a few miles north of the Gulf, a radically different diving experience awaits. Cool, clear freshwater erupts from underground rivers (aquifers) forming large, calm spring pools. Commercially operated Vortex Spring, located just north of Ponce de Leon, Morrison Springs and Merrit's Mill Pond, outside the city of Marianna, are a few of the more popular and easier-to-find Panhandle springs. Underwater relic hunting is at its best in the spring-fed Chipola River and Holmes Creek, where large, prehistoric shark's teeth and arrowheads are common discoveries for patient collectors.

Emerging from the Panhandle into north-central Florida, a diver finds himself in the center of the largest grouping of diveable springs anywhere. Branford, a small community located on the east bank of the Suwannee River, has long been the gateway to spring diving. Dozens of springs and sinkholes (surface pools that are formed when the earth collapses into the aquifer) are found north and south of the town. The Peacock Slough area has one of the most popular arrays of springs. Divers enjoy over 20 different springs and sinks within a 1½-mile radius. Troy Springs, located on the west bank of the Suwannee, has a large, open basin with depths to 80 feet. The broken remains of a 19th-century steamboat lie in the sand where the spring run enters the river.

Ten miles west of Branford is Ichetucknee State Park, where over a dozen springs feed into the crystal clear Ichetucknee River. The limpid stream's two-knot current carries park visitors, on inner-tubes or snorkeling, for three miles through unspoiled woodlands.

Ginnie Springs, a commercially-operated diving and camping resort, is just a few miles south of the Ichetucknee on the banks of the Santa Fe River. Rated excellent for both diving and camping, the grounds have six springs, a beautiful riverfront, and acres of peaceful woods to explore. Dozens of diveable springs are hidden in timberlands, meadows and swamps throughout the state's central and west central regions. Many are situated in virtually inaccessible spots which require great effort, and luck, to locate.

Spring diving activities were cast a cool eye in the early '70s because of the sensational publicity surrounding the tragic drownings that occurred in Florida's water-filled caverns. 1974 was the state's worst year for fatalities, when 26 divers were lost. Today, many visitors improperly associate spring diving with cave diving, missing out on the delightful experiences found in the safe, open spring basins. In spite of the probable increase of cave divers, the number of cave deaths has sharply declined since 1974. This can be attributed to the educational efforts of the National Speleological Society's Cave Diving Section, and to other volunteer diving training agencies. Cave diving is a viable underwater activity, but only after extensive training with a qualified cave diving instructor. People interested in safe cave diving training should read the *N.S.S. Cave Diving Manual*. This 300-page manual is the newest and most complete text ever compiled. Copies may be obtained by sending $13.00 to: N.S.S. Cave Diving Section Publications, H.V. Grey, P.O. Box 575, Venice, FL 34284-0575.

Kings Bay, in Crystal River on the west coast, is one of the state's most popular diving spots. A concentration of 30 freshwater springs surface in the saltwater bay and connecting canals. Eight of these are rated as outstanding dives. Boat travel is the only way to reach all of the sites. These may be rented from one of the four fully-equipped diving concessions on the bay. The springs are little affected by wind, rain or tide, so the diving is always good, with 100+-foot visibility 'year-round.

Crystal River is also famous for its herds of sea cows (manatees) which frequent the spring's warm waters during cool winter months. Strict regulations govern, but do not restrict, access to these huge mammals, now on the state's endangered species list.

Off the southwest coast, the waters from Tampa through Naples have been regularly explored by a large contingent of active area divers for the past 25 years. Spearfishermen have scoured the bottom in all directions, locating dozens of rock-reef lines and wrecks. These locations, coupled with the largest and best-maintained artificial reef construction program in the country, have created a widespread playground for the sport diver. Recognition of the Gulf's underwater recreational potential is finally happening.

Diving off the northeast coast, from Jacksonville to Cape Canaveral, produces swashbuckling tales garnished with large fish, great wrecks and superlative adventures. Although not known for placid, clear water, the seas do settle during the spring and summer months, with visibility ranging from 20 to 60 feet. New diving charters out of Jacksonville regularly take groups to a series of wrecks and rock reefs that proliferate with sea life and color.

Discovered with a vengeance by divers of the early '70s, the southeast coastal waters from Ft. Pierce to Miami are growing still more popular a decade later. The great Gulf Stream skirts the entire length of the Keys and turns north, following the entire mass configuration. Its path constantly renews the area reefs and wrecks with warm, clear water, rich in marine life. Wild underwater panoramas, studded with sweeping fields of sea fans and gorgonia typify the bottom. Drifting effortlessly with the current, over acres of flourishing reefs, has always been the most popular and exhilarating area diving activity.

The Palm Beaches' most famous diving is done on three huge steel wrecks, intentionally sunk in a cluster just a mile and a half from the Lake Worth Inlet. State and local ordinances have protected them from spearfishermen and tropical collectors for years. This protection has allowed the wrecks (*Mizpah*, *Amarilys* and her neighboring patrol craft) to become a sea life showcase for thousands each year.

Nearly all of Florida's offshore diving requires the use of a boat. One notable exception is the first of three reef lines that run parallel with the shore from Pompano Beach through the Fort Lauderdale area. A few sections of the reef are within 100 yards of the beach. Depths range from ten to 15 feet. Visibility fluctuates daily depending on the weather. Scuba is not allowed off the beach south of Oakland Park Boulevard, but free-divers can enter the water anywhere from the beach. The reef patches along the line support interesting growths of both soft and hard corals, intermingled with sea fans and sponges. Few large game fish are found so close to shore, but multicolored tropicals are always plentiful. Many divers have grabbed their first lobster from the pockets along this reef.

The second and third reef lines are from a mile to two miles offshore. Long reef sections rise ten to 15 feet from the white sand floor. Depths vary from 40 feet on the second reef line to nearly 100 feet on the third reef. Great schools of spades, grunts, goatfish and yellowtails typify the sea life.

A boon to divers in the Miami area has been the Dade County Artificial Reef Program, administered by the Department of Environmental Resources Management (DERM). Funding by grants from the Florida Department of Natural Resources has enabled DERM to create numerous artificial reef sites in Dade County waters for the purpose of enhancing inshore and offshore fishery resources by increasing marine habitats. Currently, there are eight artificial reef sites, many of them shallow enough for sport divers to enjoy.

Among these sites is the Pfleuger Artificial Reef, east of 41st Street on Miami Beach, where 14 different ships have been placed in waters varying from 100 to 300 feet deep, over the past 15 years. Three of these ships are accessible to divers. Another site lies 4½ miles east of Key Biscayne, in water ranging from 85 to 350 feet. Of 15 vessels on the site, nine are in depths shallower than 135 feet. Of the most popular are the *Orion*, a 118-foot steel tug sunk in 95 feet of water on December 22, 1981; the *Lakeland*, a 200-foot steel freighter sunk in 135 feet of water on June 16, 1982; and the *Arida*, a 165-foot steel freighter lying at 90 feet. Even the recently sunk ships are already beginning to be painted by the sea with encrusting growth.

Several Miami area dive operations include these wrecks on their rosters of dive sites. For additional information about locating these and other artificial wreck sites off the Miami coast, send a self-addressed stamped envelope to the Artificial Reef Program, Environmental Resources Management, 909 S.E. 1st Avenue, Brickell Plaza Bldg., Miami, Florida 33131.

In addition, the Biscayne National Monument, directly off Key Biscayne, has numerous healthy patch reefs overgrown with colorful sponges and harboring a tremendous amount of marine life.

Many excited divers head for the Florida Keys where over 200 islands extend for 180 miles from the Florida peninsula into the sea. From Jewfish Creek to Key West, the chain is connected by the world's longest overseas highway. This 108-mile-long strip of asphalt links 31 islands with 40 bridges. The island chain separates the shallow flats of the Gulf of Mexico from the Florida Reef that lies at the edge of the Gulf Stream in the Atlantic. The reef, which parallels the entire length of the Keys, is the only living coral reef on the North American continent. Due to its accessibility and its beauty, the Keys still remain the most popular underwater recreational area in the world.

Pennekamp Coral Reef State Park's location, off Key Largo in the upper Keys, has traditionally been the diver's first stop. The Overseas Highway's allure and the longing to view other reef locations draws many divers further down US 1. They travel over large expanses of blue water, where each vista passed seems more beautiful than the last. Here, the ocean dominates—architecture, dress, life philosophy—everything is charmed by the omnipresent sea.

Florida's multifarious underwater realm will not only delight new divers with discovery, but, with its recently-found ocean and inland attractions, holds promise of adventure for the ol' divers as well.

Highway Mileage Chart for Popular Dive Locations and Major Cities in Florida

	Alexander Springs	Blue Grotto	Blue Spring—Orange City	Branford	Crystal River	Ft. Myers	Gainesville	Ginnie Spring	Ichetucknee Spring	Jacksonville	Key Largo	Little River Spring	Merrit's Mill Pond	Miami	Morrison Spring	Orlando	Peacock Springs	Panama City	Pensacola	Tallahassee	Tampa	Troy Spring	Vortex Spring	West Palm
Alexander Springs	—	66	35	127	90	203	77	97	105	98	320	132	288	282	329	50	150	305	406	213	111	134	334	216
Blue Grotto	66	—	89	61	45	232	23	42	54	102	366	66	288	328	230	102	84	237	338	141	100	68	246	266
Blue Spring—Orange City	35	89	—	145	113	183	100	131	158	106	300	150	311	262	352	30	168	204	328	236	115	152	357	196
Branford	127	61	145	—	87	234	47	35	8	84	420	5	161	382	200	156	23	259	429	94	110	7	201	317
Crystal River	90	45	113	87	—	187	47	83	88	133	405	52	211	145	272	90	110	448	549	356	124	238	463	254
Ft. Myers	203	232	183	234	187	—	231	263	275	285	173	239	335	125	269	161	209	560	661	346	195	389	575	106
Gainesville	77	23	100	47	47	231	—	32	44	70	373	40	196	405	208	134	13	239	337	144	128	54	252	270
Ginnie Spring	97	42	131	35	83	263	32	—	27	80	405	40	196	367	235	124	58	239	340	129	139	42	236	285
Ichetucknee Spring	105	54	158	8	88	275	44	27	—	80	432	13	169	379	208	134	31	212	313	102	151	15	209	309
Jacksonville	98	102	106	84	133	285	70	80	80	—	398	89	229	345	269	134	95	261	360	190	91	209	270	277
Key Largo	320	366	300	420	405	173	373	405	432	398	—	425	472	62	614	270	443	598	699	360	287	427	613	122
Little River Spring	132	66	150	5	52	239	40	40	13	89	425	—	166	387	125	161	15	209	340	87	115	12	209	322
Merrit's Mill Pond	288	288	311	161	211	335	196	196	169	229	472	166	—	534	40	309	154	54	131	67	306	156	49	469
Miami	282	328	262	382	145	125	405	367	379	345	62	387	534	—	575	232	560	661	89	106	249	389	575	68
Morrison Spring	329	230	352	200	272	269	208	235	208	269	614	125	40	575	—	348	232	52	89	106	346	195	10	508
Orlando	50	102	30	156	90	161	134	124	134	134	270	161	309	232	348	—	179	193	308	101	85	163	192	166
Peacock Springs	150	84	168	23	110	209	13	58	31	95	443	15	154	560	232	179	—	207	308	97	130	19	192	340
Panama City	305	237	204	259	448	560	239	239	212	261	598	209	54	661	52	193	207	—	101	198	332	199	61	494
Pensacola	406	338	328	429	549	661	337	340	313	360	699	340	131	89	89	308	308	101	—	198	433	300	91	595
Tallahassee	213	141	236	94	356	346	144	129	102	190	360	87	67	106	106	101	97	198	198	—	240	112	105	402
Tampa	111	100	115	110	124	195	128	139	151	91	287	115	306	249	346	85	130	332	433	240	—	112	347	195
Troy Spring	134	68	152	7	238	389	54	42	15	209	427	12	156	389	195	163	19	199	300	112	112	—	197	324
Vortex Spring	334	246	357	201	463	575	252	236	209	270	613	209	49	575	10	192	192	61	91	105	347	197	—	509
West Palm	216	266	196	317	254	106	270	285	309	277	122	322	469	68	508	166	340	494	595	402	195	324	509	—

Florida's Diving Laws

Seasons

Crawfish (lobster) .... July 26-March 31
Oysters .... September 1-June 1
Stone Crab Claws .... October 15-May 15
Sports Fishermen's Crawfish Season .... July 20 and 21

The sportfishermen's season lasts for two days. Fishermen may not possess more than 6 crawfish on July 20th, nor more than 12 crawfish cumulatively for July 20th and 21st.

Limits

Stone Crab Claws. 2¾-inch forearm. No trapping except under permit of the Department of Natural Resources. Legal claw or claws may be taken but live crab must be released.

Oyster. 3 inches long.

Crawfish. Carapace measurement of more than 3 inches or tail measurement of 5½ inches. Crawfish must remain in a whole condition at all times while being transferred on, above or below the waters of the state and the practice of wringing or separating the tail (segmented portion) from the body (carapace or head) section shall be prohibited on the waters of this state except by special permit issued by the Division of Marine Resources. Any tail so separated under the provision of a special permit shall measure no less than 5½ inches measured lengthwise from the point of separation along the center of the entire tail in a flat straight position with tip of the tail closed. No eggbearing females. No spearing. 24 per day per boat without permit. No trapping except under permit from Department of Natural Resources.

Grouper. Must be 12 inches long.

Queen Conch. 10 per day, 20 only in possession.

Coral. Unlawful to take, possess or destroy sea fans, or any corals, or sell any specimens described unless it can be shown by certified invoice that it was imported from a foreign country.

Spearfishing. Illegal to spearfish in Pennekamp Coral Reef State Park, Collier County, that part of Monroe County from Long Key north to the Dade County line and the immediate area of the following: (1) All public bathing beaches, (2) Commercial or public fishing piers, (3) Bridge catwalks and (4) Jetties.

Also illegal to spearfish in fresh water or for freshwater fish in brackish water except for rough fish in special areas designated by the Game and Fresh Water Fish Commission.

Explosives. Explosives or power heads cannot be used to take food fish.

Manatee or Sea Cow. No persons, firm or corporation shall kill, injure, annoy, molest or torture a manatee or sea cow. Boaters should reduce speed in areas where the manatee is known to congregate.

Report any harassment observed to the nearest Marine Patrol Office.

Marine Turtles. No person, firm or corporation shall take, kill, disturb, mutilate, molest, harass or destroy any marine turtle. Any marine turtle accidentally caught will be returned to the water alive immediately.

No person, firm or corporation may possess any marine turtle or parts thereof unless they are in possession of an invoice evidencing the fact that said marine turtle or parts thereof have been imported from a foreign country.

No person may take, possess, disturb, mutilate, destroy, cause to be destroyed, sell, offer for sale, transfer, molest or harass any marine turtle nest or eggs at any time.

Drugs–Poisons. Illegal to place drugs or poisons in the marine waters unless that person has first obtained a permit for such use from the Department of Natural Resources.

Divers Down Flag

WHITE   BLUE

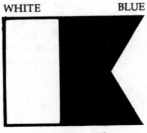

The Alpha Flag

While the recognized divers down flag has long been a rectangular flag with a white diagonal stripe running from the upper left to the lower right corner, upon publication of this book, a little-known federal law was brought to the attention of the diving community. The federal law states that, when diving from a boat, divers must display the international flag, Alpha, a blue and white flag. According to federal law, divers who fail to display the Alpha flag will be deprived of any legal rights or course of action against boaters in the event of an accident. Since federal law preempts state laws, it is almost certain that states with dive laws, such as Florida, will revise them to reflect these new specifications.

The newly recognized law has created a dilemma. The Alpha flag is necessary for legal protection, but its meaning is not yet widely known. The traditional flag is recognized, but provides no legal protection. Consequently, it is being recommended at the present time that divers fly both flags, until such time as the Alpha flag becomes effective in meaning. It should be noted that divers can be cited for failure to display the Alpha flag, and that the flag should not be flown unless diving operations are in progress.

The minimum size of flag(s) flown should be 12 by 12 inches. It should be positioned at a height of at least three feet above the surface. In open water, boaters should stay at least 300 feet from the flag. If you must approach the area of the flag, do so at a very slow speed and watch closely for diver's air bubbles.

Marine Patrol Offices

St. Andrews Marina/Panama City, FL	(904) 763-3080
South Marine St./Carrabelle, FL	(904) 697-3741
County Building/Crystal River, FL	(904) 795-3977
5110 Gandy Blvd./Tampa, FL	(813) 272-2516
1818 Jackson St./Ft. Myers, FL	(813) 334-8963
1275 NE 79 St./Miami, FL	(305) 325-3346
402 Causeway/Titusville, FL	(305) 267-4021
2510 Second Ave. N./Jacksonville, FL	(904) 241-7017
2835 Overseas Highway/Marathon, FL	(305) 743-6542
19100 S.E. Federal Hwy./Jupiter, FL	(305) 747-2033
1101 E. Gregory St./Pensacola, FL	(904) 438-4903
1845 20th St./Vero Beach, FL	(305) 567-7998
1313 N. Tampa St./Tampa, FL	(813) 272-3475

U.S. Coast Guard
Marine & Air Emergency

St. Petersburg	(813)-896-6187	Mayport	
Miami	(305)-350-4309	(Panhandle)	(904)-246-7341
Key West	(305)-350-5328	Charleston, S.C.	(803)-724-4382
		At Sea	VHF 16 or HF 2182

This is the Best Way to Learn to Dive...This is the Best Way to Teach Diving

This system makes learning to dive easy and fun. This system is used by more professional diving retailers and resort operators than any other. And regardless of your interest in diving, the PADI system can increase the enjoyment and personal satisfaction you get from being a diver.

Not yet a diver? This is the way to start! The *PADI Modular Scuba Course* lets you begin your diving education with a course that is convenient and enjoyable. The flexible, modular format is perfect for people with busy schedules — like you! PADI's unique training materials let you *learn more* in *less time*, compared to conventional methods and materials. Best of all, the PADI approach emphasizes practical open water experience — not boring academics or unrealistic drills. You'll spend the majority of your time in the PADI Modular Scuba Course — *under water...* enjoying the weightless freedom of scuba. Isn't that what you are looking for?

Already a diver? PADI's continuing diver education courses let you get more out of being an "under-water person."** PADI's advanced, Specialty, and leadership courses increase your knowledge and skills, while making diving easier and more enjoyable for you. These courses provide the opportunity to discover new activities and ways to increase the fun of diving. And, they give you the opportunity to make new friends with whom you can share the adventure of diving — together.

You can find the PADI system of diver education offered at more than 700 retail and resort facilities world wide. PADI is the choice of more diving professionals than all others com-

bined. Why? They know the PADI system will make their programs better for both new and existing divers. And, they know PADI's sophisticated training materials will make diving as easy to teach as it is for you to learn.

Find out how the PADI system can help you get more out of diving. Contact your local PADI Training Facility. For a list of PADI Training Facilities in your area, or for information on PADI Instructor training, write: PADI, 1243 East Warner Avenue, Santa Ana, CA 92705

PADI®

Building a Better World for Diving through Quality Education

© Copyright, (PADI) 1983

Chartering a Dive Boat

BILL CRAWFORD

The majority of divers who travel to Florida use one or several of the state's many diving charter boat services which are located conveniently for access to the better offshore diving areas. In most cases, these boats were specially designed by owners to provide safety and convenience for their diving customers. Their captains take great pride in their boats and expect divers to share their respect. Below is a list of things to consider when chartering a boat for diving.

1. Be sure the boat you plan to charter is used specifically for diving.
2. Double check the date, time and departure location of your charter.
3. Get information in advance about the area you plan to dive, such as depths, currents, expected visibility, type of bottom, etc.
4. Sign up only for trips that are within your proven diving ability level.
5. Let the captain know your diving ability level, and follow his advice in planning your dive.
6. Be sure you have all necessary equipment and that it is working properly *before* the trip.
7. Check to be sure that you have all the diving equipment that is required by the boat captain. Most boats now require buoyancy compensators and submersible pressure gauges.
8. If you plan to spearfish, ask the charter operator if spearguns are allowed on board. Never load your gun on the boat, and be sure your gun is unloaded after the dive.
9. Always find out the condition of currents before entering the water. If there is a current, start your dive against the flow.
10. Use the buddy system.
11. Use the anchor line when going to or leaving the bottom.
12. Don't take anything natural from the diving area, such as sea fans or corals. If you spot cans or other litter, bring it to the boat at the end of the dive.

DIVE ALL DAY WITH
SUPER SNORKEL

Enjoy a leisurely, relaxed tour of the underwater world without downtime limitations of air tank capacity. Stop, look closely at that nudibranch, tube-worm, octopus, lobster, fish or other curiosity. Take your time, inspect, study or just marvel in an unhurried way, at the underwater world and its inhabitants around you.

The Super Snorkel is easily stored in a small (19" x 19" x 13") space. Take it with you to your favorite out-of-the-way dive spot.

- Quick to set up, no tools required
- Won't scratch decks
- Quiet operation
- Crush resistant fittings
- Weighs less than 40 pounds
- Stores in less than 19" x 19" x 13"

Air Supply for 2 divers to 40 feet includes:
- —diaphragm compressor
- —3 h.p. 4-cycle engine
- —2 demand regulators
- —2 hoses (40' each)
- —diver's flag
- —float and inflator

INNOVATIVE DESIGNS INC.
1870 OAK CREEK DRIVE
DUNEDIN, FLORIDA 33528
(813) 784-5349

Florida Decompression Facilities

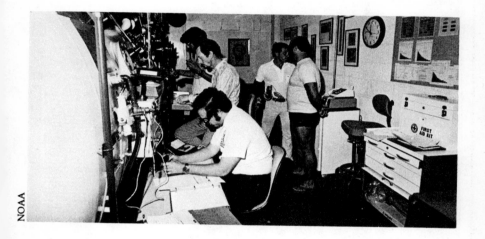

NOAA

It is important that every diver using SCUBA understand the possibility of contracting decompression sickness, more commonly known as "the bends." In addition, each diver should know the location of the nearest chamber for proper treatment. The phone numbers listed below are those of the facilities in Florida that provide the service of their decompression chambers to the general public.

Pensacola	(904) 452-2141
Panama City	(904) 234-2281 Ext. 370
Gainesville	(904) 392-3441
West Palm Beach	(305) 844-3515
Miami	(305) 350-7259 or 446-7071
	or 445-8926

From 7:30 a.m. to 4:15 p.m., a listing of all chamber locations in the United States may be obtained by calling (512) 536-3278.

In addition, the Diving Accident Network, headquartered at Duke University, is available 24 hours a day for emergency diving accident information, including chamber locations. Contact them in an emergency at (919) 684-8111.

SEVEN OUT OF TEN DIVERS PREFER OCEAN REALM

Far Right: Aruba's hotel row stretches along the powder white beaches of the west coast. Not far off the beach lies the wreck of the Antilla (right), harboring a variety of small animals within the cracks of its steel hull.

Destination:

The Dutch Antilles
The Caribbean's most spectacular trio of islands.

TEXT BY PATRICIA REILLY
PHOTOGRAPHY BY
RICHARD H. STEWART

Aruba The gleaming white ribbon of sand wrapped tidily around the 70-square-mile island of Aruba should be a sure giveaway that this is no ordinary Caribbean island. It's the stuff of which travel posters, and dreams, are made.

The fact that the island's only dive operator, Anton Segers, doesn't schedule the first dive of the day until 11 a.m. should tell you something else.

Aruba doesn't like to go to bed until many, many hours after the fiery red ball of sun has vaporized into the Caribbean deep. And Aruba is content to keep its eyes closed until the sun has come full circle and is high over head, and the crabs have crawled snugly into their sandy holes for shade, like little vampires.

Of the three islands—Aruba, Bonaire and Curaçao—that lie within 50 miles of the coast of Venezuela, and are known collectively as the Dutch Leewards, or ABCs, Aruba may be the real sleeper among them as diving destinations go. It's probably because no one can ever stop partying for long enough to get serious about the diving.

Yet, those who make a determined effort to resist life in the fast lane will be rewarded in daylight by a gala extravaganza of undersea life.

Aruba's most-talked-about dive site is the wreck of a German freighter, the Antilla. The 400-foot steel freighter was a casualty of World War II, and its final resting place is in 50 feet of water, off Malmok Beach. When the war broke out, the An-

tilla was docked in the Dutch port of Aruba. With no guns to protect his ship, the German captain decided to surrender, but prior to doing so, he opened the cocks of his ship and flooded her.

Since its submersion in May 1940, the wreck has attracted myriad macro marine life, and a lush assortment of corals and fish. Grey and red snapper, yellow grunts, soberjack, trumpetfish, filefish, and even rays, now patrol the ship's corridors. A wide assortment of crustaceans including arrow crabs, branded coral shrimp and hermit crabs, plus thousands of colorful cup corals, bring the wreck to life at night, offering delightful photographic possibilities for the photographer Segers' Sub-sea Safaris schedules a night dive to the Antilla once a week.

A shallow dive, popular with snorkelers as well as divers, is on the wreck of the Pedernalis, lying in 25 feet of water. The flat-bottomed oil tanker was ferrying crude oil from Venezuela to Aruba when it was attacked by a submarine during World War II. Later, the stern end was towed into shallow water, where it was subsequently used for target practice by locally stationed marines. The bow end is visible from shore, sticking up out of the water.

You can actually enter the bow of the wreck, where sunlight streams in, lending an eerie look to the hulk. Queen angels, parrotfish, rock beauties and yellow grunts parade about, while anemones and brittle worms festoon the bulkheads. At certain times of the year, huge schools of baitfish can make the wreck almost invisible, spreading apart as if choreographed to let determined divers through to see it.

[Continue page 28]

19

Because Ocean Realm Magazine takes them on a journey to the most exciting dive destinations with each turn of a page. Places such as Australia, the Red Sea, the Philippines and Caribbean islands like the Caymans, the Bahamas, Jamaica, the Dutch Antilles and the British and U.S. Virgin islands.

Spectacular color picture spreads and informative up-to-date editorial highlight the most interesting areas and their marine life. Each travel article features a special "destination information"

WINTER 1983 $2.50

Ocean Realm

Destination: Bay Islands / Florida   Profile: Richard Ellis
Photography: Copyrights / Maintenance   Portfolio: Carl Roessler
Marine Life: Manatees / Whales   Invertebrates: Gorgonians

page a source guide that includes pertinent names, addresses and phone numbers of airlines, hotels with dive packages, things to do, and special diver emergency information.

For domestic travel, Ocean Realm's "U.S.A." reviews a different area in every issue, ranging from Florida to California and Washington to Texas, covering cold water New England diving, the tropical diving of the Keys, and much more.

Send $11.80 today for four exciting issues of Ocean Realm.

OCEAN REALM, 2333 Brickell Avenue, Miami, FL 33129 (305) 285-0252

The Living Reef

The formation and preservation of our coral communities.

BY TOM AND WANDA ARTEAGA

One might compare the life cycle of the reef to the well-known story of ancient Troy where the remains of civilization after civilization accumulated on top of one another. When coral dies, its skeleton becomes the foundation for new coral growth, and life begins again.

In order to understand how a coral reef is formed, one must keep in mind that it is a living animal (*Coelentrata*) which reproduces both sexually and asexually, and that a single coral animal is called a polyp. Individual polyps vary in size from eight inches to those which can barely be seen by the naked eye. The most common, however, is about one-eighth of an inch long.

A coral reef begins to form when one or more polyps settle on a firm surface and attach to it. The polyps assimilate the calcium which is in the seawater and deposit it beneath and around their bodies. This process forms a "cup" of calcium carbonate, otherwise known as limestone. A particular type of coral is formed when polyps with the same hereditary characteristics come together to form colonies of varying sizes and innumerable shapes and colors. This phenomenon takes place mostly on the warmer western sides of oceans and in open tropical seas. Southern Florida is the only place in the continental United States with water warm enough for coral reefs to subsist.

Coral polyps feed mostly on planktonic forms of life which move with the tides and currents. The coral communities are most active during changing tides, since there is a better chance, then, for the polyps to catch food with the tentacles that surround their mouths. When there are sufficient ocean currents to furnish food and the water is warm, relatively shallow and clean, there is a good possibility of a reef evolving.

Living coral grows at the rate of 1.2 centimeters a year—less than one-half inch. Even this slow growth can be inhibited. The tiny polyps are easily clogged and killed by silty or polluted water. Improper sewage disposal and dredging are the two worst enemies of reefs.

As divers who know, understand and love the Florida reefs, much of the responsibility for protecting them should be ours. If we do not fight for them and support proper legislation to save them, these magnificent ecological systems called "living reefs" will become underwater deserts.

There are many things individual divers can do to protect the reefs on each visit. Start by seeing that the dive boat is anchored properly. The thousands of anchors used annually on reefs can cause tremendous damage. Always anchor on the edge of the reef in the sandy areas. Never throw the anchor, but lower it gently to the bottom. Grappling type anchors seem to cause less damage to the reef than heavier types.

It is common on shallow reefs to see snorkelers resting on coral heads.

Mystery Reef, a Miami coral garden.

This damages the tiny polyps. Rest in the boat or inflate your vest, but care enough to stay off the coral.

Fewer sights are more disheartening than a diver tearing through living coral to obtain a particular shell specimen or collector's item. The most caring, lasting and beautiful underwater souvenirs are taken on film.

Cans and other trash are no enhancement to the lovely corals. It takes only a few moments to collect litter and take it back to the dive boat. The most foresighted divers always show their care in this small but exceedingly important way.

A privilege, a responsibility and a-joy, our reefs are a living celebration of color and drama that lure and enchant us. May we continue to share and delight in them.

Ocean Realm Guide To

Reef Creatures
MARINE INVERTEBRATES

Text and Photography By Paul Humann

a revolutionary new book about reef creatures in readable, understandable language. Written specifically for divers, by diver/photographer Paul Humann, this book is a "plain English" guide to identification of marine invertebrates. Without unnecessary scientific jargon, the author clearly and comprehensibly points out observable features of animal groups that will enable divers to easily identify most animals they see underwater. Lavishly illustrated with over 125 full-color photographs from throughout the world, this book is not only a useful text, but also an outstanding and beautiful portfolio of undersea life. Available in both hard and soft cover, every diver will want to add this book to his library.

CLIP HERE

Please send me _____ copies of *Reef Creatures* ($9.95 per soft cover copy; $16.95 per hard cover copy). My check or money order for $ _____ is enclosed. Add $1.50 for postage and handling.

Name _____

Address _____

City_____ State_____ Zip _____

Ocean Realm Publishing Corporation
2333 Brickell Avenue, Miami, FL 33129 305/285-0252

Manatees
Florida's Gentle Giants

BY SHARELL HOLVERSON

In addition to Florida's many well-known attractions, each year hundreds of divers enjoy a special treat—swimming with the rare and endangered manatees. The King's Bay area of Crystal River is the most accessible spot for divers to encounter these animals in their natural habitat. The experience is especially unique in light of current estimates which indicate there are only 750 to 1,000 sea cows in Florida waters.

Manatees, like people, are mammals and need to maintain a constant body temperature. Though they live in water all their lives, they breathe air at the water's surface through nostril flaps. Females suckle their young, which are born alive. Births are usually single, but twin births are seen.

The huge grey mammals are lured to spring-fed fresh-water rivers by their constant 72-degree temperatures during the cold winter months. They are also seen near warm-water discharges of power plants along the coast when water temperatures fall.

The 'composite' animals have skins resembling that of elephants, greyish in color, varying from rough to smooth in texture, and with occasional sparse body hairs. Flippers, which appear to be attached backwards, have nails reminiscent of an elephant's toenails. Their noses are short, enhancing a 'puppy dog' appearance. Rubbery, bristle-covered jowls easily manipulate the manatees' favored food supply—hydrilla. Although relished by manatees, the frilly aquarium grass is considered a nuisance to boaters. Sea cows have only grinding teeth. No incisors or cutting teeth exist in the front of their mouths—only bony arches or 'gums' similar to those of a cow. They are incapable of attack, flight being their only defense.

Though shy by nature, the Crystal River manatees have become accustomed to snorkelers and divers over the years. Some individual animals actually seek out and enjoy the attention of non-aggressive divers.

As a snorkeler or diver quietly enters the water from his boat, he will often find a large grey shape within a few feet, observing him. A moment of mutual respect may set the stage for a memory of a lifetime. As a diver hangs motionless in the water or swims slowly, the curious animal may invite contact.

At times, the manatees enjoy gentle, open-handed stroking on their torpedo-shaped bodies and short necks, but rarely on their large, flat tails. Finger-jabbing is never welcomed! As they become familiar with a diver, face and flipper stroking seems to be a pleasure to them. A respectful diver

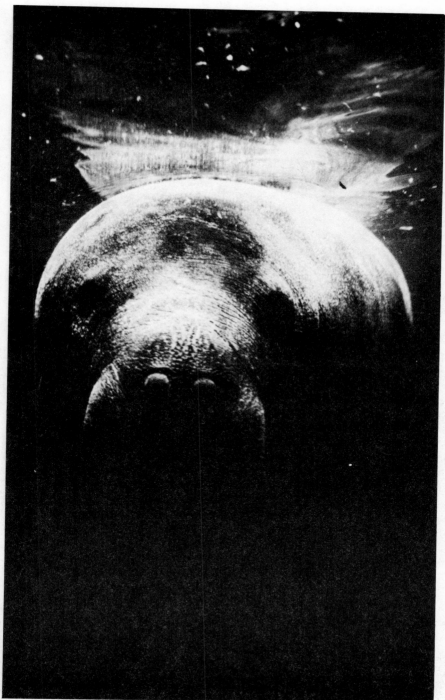

ALAN WILLIAMS

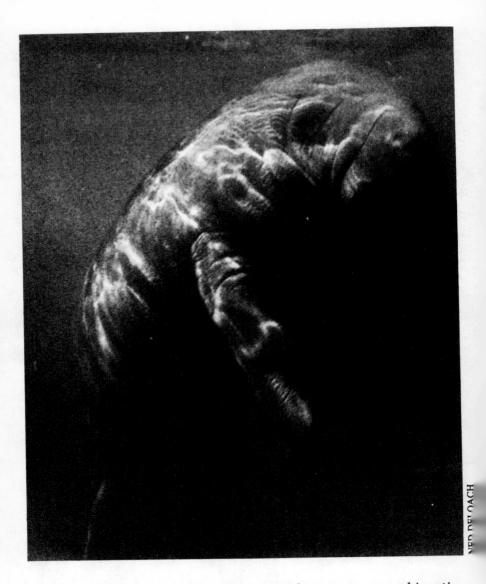

NED DELOACH

may soon have a huge sea cow rolling over in the water to expose his entire lighter-colored underside for petting and stroking. Some will even emit audible grunts of pleasure.

High-pitched squeaks and whistles are also heard in the water near manatees. Although not anatomically the same as the echo-location used by dolphins, manatee cows and calves keep track of each other in murky waters with their sounds. They also have been observed to whistle when confused or frightened by approaching boats or aggressive divers. Do not chase or pursue manatees! Try not to disturb a sleeping, eating or nursing sea cow. An animal resting on the bottom or hanging motionless near the surface may be sleeping. He will come up periodically for air even in his sleep and may be startled by a diver he didn't know was there.

In addition to hydrilla, manatees also eat water hyacinths and other river and sea grasses. They may consume as much as 100 pounds of weeds and grasses a day to maintain their impressive body weight of up to 1,500 pounds. Obviously, this much eating takes a lot of undisturbed time. Even in poor visibility, it is easy to detect when a manatee is eating. Loud crunching, grinding sounds travel for some distance underwater.

Nursing behavior is often seen. The mammary glands of a female are just under the flippers. A baby manatee at his mother's 'elbow' is a good "Do Not Disturb" sign.

Manatees are often deeply cut by boat propellers. It is important to recognize the signs of their presence from above the surface of the water. Periodically, they surface to breathe, sucking in air with a loud, rushing sigh. Alert ears will hear them easily, especially if boat motors are at idle speed (required by law in manatee waters from November 15 through March 31). Also, watchful eyes will note evenly spaced swirls in the water several feet apart made by a manatee's powerful tail as he swims near the surface.

Although considered 'ugly' by some standards, a manatee is truly graceful in motion underwater. His spatulate tail propels him in gentle body curves. His flippers provide smaller adjustments of direction and balance. Air exchange is very efficient, occurring, on the average, every four minutes.

In the past, manatees were used by man as a food source. They are now protected by law from hunting and harassment, but are still endangered by boat props, monofilament line and possibly by the spraying of their major food supply, the hydrilla. Cases of monofilament fishing line or polyester crab trap line gradually amputating flippers have occurred. Most sea cows now bear prop scars. It is very important that idle speed boating laws be observed and that synthetic lines not be left in the water. Many do not decay and are not only a hazard to manatees but also to wild birds.

Manatees are presumed to be long-lived. One has existed in captivity for more than 32 years. Longevity is offset by the fact that births are usually single and gestation is approximately 13 months. A mother manatee nurses and cares for her baby for two years. Each adult female can usually produce only one manatee every three years and only under the best conditions of food, protection, adequate warmth and nondisturbance. It is estimated that sexual maturity is reached in six to ten years.

The sea cows have proven to be their own most charming ambassadors. The joy of diving and playing with them creates the desire to promote their continued existence. Several active and established organizations and individuals have addressed themselves to their plight.

From those whose hearts have been won by the playful nature and docile grace of the huge underwater creatures: "Please enjoy, protect and care for them so that their years of unique evolution will not be lost, and others will also enjoy the priceless moments they so freely provide."

THE MANATEE NEEDS YOU.

Without your support, future generations will know these gentle marine mammals only through museums.

JOIN THE
SAVE THE MANATEE CLUB

I'd like to help save the manatee from extinction.

Name _ _ _ _ _ _ _ _ _ _ _ _ _

Address _ _ _ _ _ _ _ _ _ _ _ _ _ _
_ _ _ _ _ _ _ _ _ _ _ _

Telephone _ _ _ _ _ _ _ _ _

Please check one:

__ Individual Membership $15.00

__ Individual Student Membership $10.00

__ Family Membership $20.00

__ Donation

Please make checks payable to:
Save the Manatee Clubs
1101 Audubon Way
Maitland, Florida 32751

Sea Turtles
Fragile Knights of the Reef

BY SUSAN KUNTZ AND
SHARELL HOLVERSON

Modern sea turtles evolved into their present shelled and toothless form over 100 million years ago. No other air-breathing vertebrate group has lasted unchanged so long. But during the last 100 years, man has managed to alter their evolutionary course decisively. The body armor (or carapace) which has well-protected them for so long has done little to shield sea turtles from devastation by man. Once prolific in tropical waters, today, sadly, all varieties of marine turtles appear on the endangered species list. Those most valued for meat, eggs and shells closely brush the limits of extinction. The green turtle has been especially desired for its meat and eggs, while the hawksbill has been prized for tortoise shell, used in making ornaments. Sea turtles are further pressed by pollution and man's rapid encroachment onto once undisturbed beach areas, mandatory for successful egg-laying.

Sea turtles are not able to withdraw into their shells for protection as many land turtles do. They are dependent on their size and swimming abilities for defense. Impressive in terms of sheer body mass, some leatherbacks are estimated to have reached 1,500 pounds and eight feet in carapace length. But the most remarkable capability of the sea turtles is their graceful flight underwater. They do not paddle, but "fly" like shelled marine birds. Some are able to skim over 100 yards of reef in ten seconds.

In Florida's coastal waters, sea turtles mate in April, May and June. Nesting season is May through August. Females come on land only to lay their eggs. The mothers drag themselves above the high-water mark and dig a small hole with their hind flippers. After laying 100 or more eggs, they fill in the hole and then, using their front flippers, disturb a large area of sand so that the location of the nest is not apparent. Man, seldom fooled by this effort at camouflage, often decimates the nest, removing the eggs for food.

The babies, which measure only a little more than an inch, face a very difficult beginning in life. When they hatch at the end of the summer, they must make a precarious trek across open sand to their saltwater home. Lying in wait are sea birds, crabs, dogs, cats, racoons and other animals and insects which relentlessly pursue their vulnerable prey. During this difficult period, only one out of 100 baby turtles is destined to survive. Even when they reach the water, large fish and sharks continue the unremitting pursuit.

It is against the law to harass an endangered species, including all marine turtles! Even riding a turtle underwater is considered harassment. It is also illegal to bring any turtle product into the U.S., including captive-bred turtles. Products made from turtles, often purchased as souvenirs, are confiscated by U.S. Customs.

There are several things divers can do to help sea turtles, in addition to obeying the laws.

1) Be careful boating. Marine turtles spend much time basking at the surface. Every year turtles die from propeller injuries.

2) Learn to identify turtle tracks and nests. If you see a nest that looks like it will be inundated by high tide, report it to local authorities or turtle

SUE KUNTZ

A loggerhead lumbers in to nest on a Florida beach.

specialists. If you help in removing the eggs (with permission), be careful to move one egg at a time. Do not rotate it. Set it down in the new nest or bucket maintaining the same vertical axis.

3) If you see or suspect any egg poachers, report them immediately to the local police or the Florida Marine Patrol.

4) Do not disturb a mother turtle on her egg-laying mission. She may return to sea and abort her efforts altogether.

5) If you spot the tiny tracks of freshly hatched turtles, follow the trail to be sure the babies made it safely to the sea. Upon hatching, the young turtles are instinctively drawn toward the light of the horizon. However, they often become disoriented by city and traffic lights and head away from their intended destination. They may also become entangled in land vegetation or sargassum weed. Deep impressions in the sand and sea walls create other barriers.

Divers who have observed the grace and beauty of the armored knights of the reef will long carry the image of these unique beings. Unfortunately, their continued survival is at risk. Only concern and effort will halt their rapid course toward extinction.

Jewfish

Lords of the Gulf

One of Florida's natural phenomena are the large Jewfish colonies that inhabit the ledges and wrecks of her Gulf waters. Dropping down through 50 feet of haze onto a wreck is exciting, but to suddenly discover 15 to 20 living monoliths moving boldly through the broken rubble is awesome. Often weighing several hundred pounds (some reported to 700 pounds), the huge fish are lords and masters of their domain. Their formidable size deters all natural enemies and allows them to live unmolested for years.

Jewfish are bottom-dwellers, usually spending their lives in protected areas at shallow to moderate depths. Although cumbersome in appearance, the fish can cover short distances quite quickly with a stroke of their powerful tails. They draw fish and crustaceans into their voluminous gullets by the suction created when they open their cavernous mouths. Dinner is held tenaciously by thousands of small, rasp-like teeth that cover the jaws, tongue and palate. The prey is then swallowed whole.

There are few Gulf divers who do not have a favorite Jewfish story to relate. These tales most often involve the fish's gluttonous, assertive habits. Curious by nature and emboldened by size, they often approach visitors who enter their realm. Often, when irritated, they make a loud "booming" sound with their gills, warning those who approach of their pugnacious mood. Although seldom aggressive toward divers, they have been known to attack a spearfisherman's catch and, intent on stealing an easy lunch, to engulf a finned leg in the melee. Such encounters are never fatal, but the leg is seldom pulled free without a nasty set of lacerations.

A few divers choose to make pets of individual Jewfish. A friendship is nurtured by repeatedly taking cut bait on dives to a favorite underwater site. A voracious appetite generally proves more overpowering than caution. Patience and gentleness soon have the big fish coming up to greet divers as they descend toward its lair. This practice is rewarding to divers, but often detrimental to the longevity of the fish. The befriended giant becomes an innocent victim to men with spears.

Because of their large trophy-size and fearlessness, Jewfish have already become void from most readily accessible Gulf diving locations. This devastation has come about by a disregard for their uniqueness. Their stringy, usually wormy meat is seldom palatable. A spectacular sea creature that could thrill hundreds of underwater observers is destroyed simply to inflate a single hunter's ego.

Ocean Realm and Planet Ocean
Present

The International Oceans Recreational Show

with over 200 displays, island seafood festival, marine art and photography show, live island music, audio-visual programs and evening film festival.

Plan now to attend the world's largest consumer sport diving show at Miami's 100,000 square ft Coconut Grove Convention Center on the Dinner Key waterfront.

"April 20-22, 84"

For detailed information, write:

PLANET OCEAN

3979 Rickenbacker Causeway, Miami, Florida 33149   305/361-5786

Florida Lobster

*These clawless crustaceans are
nonetheless a delicious delicacy.*

BY ED DAVIDSON

The Florida lobster is actually the crawfish, *Langusta*. It lacks the pincer claws characteristic of the true northern lobster. Its taste, when broiled in butter, however, is just as delightful as that of the lobster. *Langusta* typically crawl out in the open in search of food just after sunset, and return to their homes under rocks, ledges and coral heads at pre-dawn light. They are basically scavengers which augment their diet with small fish and crustaceans. There are also periodic mass migrations, or crawls, which may involve thousands of lobster in weaving columns, miles long. Such migrations have occurred in the months of September, December and late March, under circumstances which are still not clearly understood.

Lobster season is open from August 1 to March 31. It is closed during June and July, the months when spawning and molting cycles reach their peak. Commercial lobstermen use slat traps baited with a variety of tasty tidbits, ranging from kerosene-soaked bricks, sardines and catfood to cowhide and chopped fish heads.

Without a commercial license, you can take lobster only by hand or with hand nets. They must never be gigged or speared. The minimum size crawfish that can be kept must measure three inches from the apex of the eyes between the supraorbital horns to the after edge of the thoracic shell or carapace. It is wise to purchase a gauge for measuring this dimension, as possession of a "short" can cost you a hefty chunk of vacation money and a visit to the local magistrate. The lobster laws are actively enforced by the Florida Marine Patrol, which maintains a constant presence with fast patrol boats and metes out substantial fines for violations such as possession of "shorts"; spearing and gigging; having more than the legal limit of 24 lobster in your boat; wringing off tails before you reach the dock; possessing egg-bearing females (easily identified by the yellow eggs covering their undersides); and robbing commercial traps.

Since the local lobstermen have been known to occasionally unlimber their blunderbusses in the direction of people poaching their traps, it is best to stick to grabbing the desired crawfish by hand with a good pair of gloves—then fire up the broiler!

Can You Protect Your Right To Dive In The 1980's?

UNDERWATER SOCIETY of AMERICA

THINK DEEP

Join the UNDERWATER SOCIETY OF AMERICA and help protect divers rights today.
Get involved — DIVE, READ, ACT!

THE U.S.A. HAS DONE IT SINCE 1959

$10.00 Annual Dues —
provides card, magazine
and insurance

Underwater Society of America
732 50th St., W. Palm Bch., FL 33407

Spearfishing

Challenge and Responsibility

Skindiving started with spearfishing. Selecting, stalking and subduing quarry in an unknown environment, without the ability to draw a second breath, was a challenge well-suited to man's instinct for adventure. Throughout the '50s and into the '60s, few ventured below without a spear in hand. Divers were known by the amount and size of fish they brought to the surface. Few of the enthusiastic hunters imagined that their newly discovered sport would have any negative impact on reefs that, then, overflowed with fish.

A new generation of divers appeared when SCUBA became available to the public. This group soon far outnumbered the handful of free divers who preceded it. Now able to spend long periods underwater, many divers became devoted observers of reef systems. Through their observations, one unequivocal reality became apparent—where reefs had been regularly hunted, few, if any, gamefish remained. Word of the depleted reefs was received by a world just awakening to its obligation to protect delicate environments from man's rapid encroachment. What followed came to be known as "the great spearfishing controversy."

For over three years, underwater ecologists and underwater hunters fenced in the arena of opinion. Never before or since has the generally composed diving community rippled with so much passion over a single issue. Ecologists, armed with fish-barren reefs and the trend of the time, forged an unrelenting attack on those who dared to carry a spear. Such august personalities as Dr. Hans Hass and Philipe Cousteau gave credence to the inspired lobby.

Two basic arguments were leveled: spearfishing had a negative impact on the ecosystem of the reef, and it wasn't equitable for a few hunters to deny many divers the right to observe the reefs complimented by nature's full array of inhabitants. Soon sanctions were being instituted against the hunters. The diving equipment manufacturers were discontinuing the sales of spearguns. Resort islands banned spearing; tournaments were cancelled; and charter boat operators ceased to allow guns on board their vessels.

The old guard of spearfishermen, who had so recently been favored with esteem, watched stunned as they were suddenly cast in the role of villains. They rallied with a salvo of their own. A primary contention was that commercial and line fishermen annually took many more fish than the spearfishermen and that neither group could be selective in what they took from the sea.

Another accusing finger was pointed at novice divers and meat hunters. Beginning hunters, in haste to prove their prowess, shot indiscriminately, killing everything from sea cucumbers to queen angels. To produce profits at the fish market, meat hunters systematically annihilated all gamefish from entire areas. It was stressed that true underwater hunters were not the culprits and should not be denied the right to procure fish for their tables.

Nearly a decade has passed since the controversy settled, but in its wake has come constructive change. As with most disputes, resolve tends to fall somewhere in between the ideologies of both camps. For a time, diving ecologists seemed a bit overzealous in their meritable attempts to protect the seas. A ban on spearfishing would have lamentably denied many sportsmen the right to savor one of hunting's most challenging and rewarding experiences. But, at the same time, veteran spearfishermen were well aware that many claims made against their sport were valid. They, too, had observed a marked decline in gamefish activity in repeatedly hunted areas.

One fact stood solidly: the voiding of gamefish on reef systems and wrecks frequented every year by hundreds of sport divers would no longer be tolerated. Changes had to be made in order to protect fish life on popular dive sites, and to preserve the rewards of underwater hunting.

The spearfishing contingent tacitly imposed a set of standards that has vastly improved spearfishing's image and also helped renew fish life at many prominent diving spots. Today, spearguns are seldom seen at shallow, close-in, clear water sites. Skilled hunters, instead, voyage further out to sea relentlessly searching for new bottom, often in deeper, darker, less placid waters. They limit the hunt to fresh meat for their dinner tables. Large fish, such as jewfish, once prized as trophies, are passed over for smaller fish that yield a higher quality meat. Tournament prizes are no longer awarded for mass poundage, but instead go to the largest in each class of gamefish indigenous to the waters hunted. Contest entries are now donated to local charities.

The education of new divers is paramount to preservation. First, they must be taught that the world's waters are not theirs to greedily plunder. Instead, they must learn to understand, respect and help sustain the seas' vulnerable creatures.

In many parts of Florida, spearfishing remains the premiere underwater activity. On the east coast from Jacksonville to Melbourne, and in the Gulf from Pensacola to Naples, underwater hunting thrives. Many of the world's best hunters choose these waters as stalking grounds, while most sport divers flock to the clear waters off the lower east coast and the Keys.

Successful underwater hunting requires skill, strategy, daring, knowledge, a contempt for hardships and a willingness to venture. Florida welcomes those divers with a penchant for spearfishing, especially those willing to respect and preserve her treasure—the life in her seas.

The Man Who Would Save The Ocean

Every polluted river eventually runs to the sea. We sink our garbage into offshore waters. We spill oil. Through development, we destroy coastal environments essential to the ocean ecosystem. We harvest marine animals to extinction. And the sea is showing signs of this mistreatment.

Captain Jacques-Yves Cousteau, the crew of *Calypso* and The Cousteau Society have embarked on an urgent mission. They are documenting the destruction of the ocean. And they hope to save the ocean through a campaign of public education. While the ocean is a boundless source of life and beauty, it is not the limitless resource we once thought. If we continue to damage the ocean, we risk our own future.

You can help support the work of Jacques Cousteau and the explorer/scientists of the *Calypso* through The Cousteau Society. For a $20 annual membership fee, you'll receive a monthly bulletin and a quarterly magazine, the *Calypso Log*. For $28, a family membership, you'll also receive *The Dolphin Log* for children. In addition, "Project Ocean Search" invites a limited number of divers to join the Society's scientists in a 12-day field study program conducted in the Caribbean. Write: The Cousteau Society, Inc., 930 West 21st St., Norfolk, VA 23517.

Florida Springs

Spewing forth crystal clear water, the state's springs offer the best freshwater diving in the world.

Florida alone accounts for 17 of the 75 "first magnitude" springs in the U.S. A "first magnitude" spring discharges 100 cubic feet of water a second. The state also has 49 springs of the second magnitude, with a flow of between ten and 100 second-feet. Silver Springs, located northeast of Ocala, is the world's largest spring, with an average flow of 500 million gallons a day (m.g.d.). Wakulla Spring, located south of Tallahassee, is the deepest, with a depth to 185 feet. Many of the spring's underwater caves have been penetrated to amazing depths, while others have been explored for hundreds of feet, their entire patterns running close to the surface. Many of the underground channels are interconnected, and divers have been able to follow patterns that lead to neighboring springs.

Their water temperature is cool, varying between 68 and 78 degrees in different springs. The flow from the springs varies with the amount of water held in their contributing underground basins. Since the basin depends mainly on rainfall for its supply, the discharge of the springs can be related to the amount of rainfall over the state.

Many of the springs near rivers (Troy, Little River, Otter and others) are subject to flooding several months of the year. In September and October, when the rivers rise, their dark waters invade the clear springs, making them unfit for diving. It is best to check with one of Florida's dive shops to learn the condition of the springs during late summer and early fall.

Activities

SCUBA DIVING. Scuba diving is a fast-growing and rewarding sport. The deeper springs offer hours of challenging diving, exploration and beauty. All persons using SCUBA should have the proper training and use the proper equipment. It is foolhardy to strap on a tank, or knowingly let someone else use gear, without being certified by a nationally recognized training school such as NASDS, PADI, YMCA, NAUI, PDIC or SSI. Your life is worth the best training. Sign up at your local diving school for proper instruction.

SNORKELING. People without the proper training for scuba diving can still enjoy the underwater beauty of springs by using only a mask, fins and snorkel. Simply snorkeling around the surface of a boil or down its run can be a great adventure. Snorkeling is the only way to explore some of the springs where scuba diving is not allowed.

UNDERWATER PHOTOGRAPHY. Because of the superb clarity of the water in the springs, usually 100 feet-plus, they are ideal for underwater photography. The limestone cliffs, crevices and cave entrances make spectacular settings for either color or black and white shots. Most of the fish are accustomed to divers and can be approached easily. In many springs, a handful of bread will bring out bream by the hundreds. The white sandy bottoms reflect the sunlight, so there is little need for flash outside the caves. Care should be taken by the photographer not to stir up the sand or silt, though, as this will detract greatly from the picture.

RELIC HUNTING. Throughout the ages, the white sands of the springs and limestone bottoms of the clear rivers they feed have become a treasure chest of relics dating from prehistoric times through the development of man.

Mammoth and bison bones, giant sharks' teeth, arrowheads, stone fish hooks, clay pipe bowls, old bottles and coins, and a vast assortment of other relics that trace Florida's development lie hidden, waiting to be uncovered by the patient collector.

CAMPING. Camping has become quite popular in the spring areas in recent years. Many of the commercially operated springs offer sites for truck campers and trailers with complete hookup facilities. Shower and toilet facilities can also be found. A few of the owners of springs located on private land allow camping, but only as long as their land and property are not abused. Several beautiful springs have been closed to the public during the past few years because of misuse by campers and divers. We have heard story after story from these spring owners about the problems they encounter when they leave their areas open. The grounds and spring bottoms are littered with trash. Livestock has been chased and even killed. Gamefish have been illegally speared, leaving few large fish. Remember, when you use an area, the owner is bending to keep it open for you. End a dive by bringing up cans and bottles from the springs. Help protect your privilege to dive.

LEDGE DIVING. Ledge diving offers those divers who are not properly trained in the advanced techniques of cave diving a safe underwater experience by allowing them to penetrate only short distances in water-filled caverns.

There are two classifications of ledge dives. In a *ledge dive* itself, the divers penetrate no more than 25 yards into an underwater cave and remain within sight of the natural light from the cave entrance at all times.

An *advanced ledge dive* takes place when divers penetrate a cave entrance no more than 25 yards, but lose sight of the natural light, or when divers penetrate the cave no more than 25 yards at night.

Underwater lights should be carried by every diver on all ledge dives. A safety line should always be used during advanced ledge dives.

TUBING AND CANOEING. Many of the large runs flow for miles throughout Florida's woodlands. Drifting in a slow current on crystal waters for miles and miles through green walls of vegetation is a peaceful experience, long remembered.

Florida is probably the only state where used tire tubes are at a premium. They are grabbed up on weekends and taken to some of the popular tubing runs in the state. They are cheap and easy to carry, and with a little practice you can get in and out of them with ease.

Canoes are used for longer trips. Florida canoeing is a popular activity and the state has several canoe trails. Divers have learned about the adventure of canoe trips down the Suwannee and Santa Fe Rivers. You can plan them for a few days or a few hours. While paddling down a river, you can easily locate a spring where its run empties into the river. Spend as long as you like exploring a spring—then continue downriver searching for new areas.

NATURE STUDY. A diver can spend many fascinating hours studying the underwater ecological systems of the springs. The clear water makes the springs one of the few places where freshwater habitats can be observed firsthand. The springs located near rivers have become the homes of many saltwater fish and mollusks as well as freshwater inhabitants, creating fascinating underwater communities. Many divers keep aquariums stocked with spring inhabitants. Lobsters, flounder, crabs, jumbo snails and small fish can be collected easily, and live quite hardily in clean home aquariums.

At Crystal River, it is common to see many varieties of salt and freshwater fish swimming around the boil area. In winter, large manatees come into the area and are a real attraction.

GLOSSARY OF SPRING TERMINOLOGY

Boil. Surface disturbance of the spring pool caused by the velocity of the spring's flow.

Chimney. A vertical tubular opening in the rock.

Crevice. A narrow crack or split in the rock.

M.G.D. Million gallons daily.

N.A.C.D. National Association for Cave Diving.

N.S.S. C.D.S. National Speleological Society Cave Diving Section.

Natural Bridge. Short section of ground covering surface of stream.

Permanent Line. Safety line permanently left in a cave.

Run. Water course flowing off from a spring.

Safety Line. White nylon line used to mark paths through caves.

Florida Cave Diving

BY SHECK EXLEY

Since National Speleological Society (N.S.S.) divers first took SCUBA into a cave at Blue Hole Spring along the Ichetucknee River in 1951, cave diving has been pursued in Florida by hundreds of thousands of divers. Some enter the springs and sinks for serious speleological purposes such as exploration and survey, archaeology and palaeontology, but most simply thrill to the warm, clear water—about 72 degrees year 'round—and the fascinating limestone formations. Unfortunately, cave diving is not without its hazards: more than 150 divers have drowned since 1960 while cave diving. While these victims represent only a very small percentage of persons entering caves, N.S.S. recovery teams have found that, invariably, the accidents could have been avoided.

Why have these divers drowned? N.S.S. studies have shown that in *every case*, one or more of three major safety procedures was violated. Many perished because they became lost, having failed to run a single, continuous guideline from the entrance throughout the dive. Another major cause has been running out of air. At least two-thirds of the diver's air should be reserved for the trip out of the cave. Finally, the small percentage of fatal accidents where the victims *did* use a continuous guideline and *had* apparently planned their air reserves properly, were all found to have involved diving to excessive depth. 130 feet has been well established as the maximum safe depth for sport divers, and this goes for cave divers as well.

In the past few years, most of the best cave diving spots have been closed to diving for various reasons. Some spots have been ruined by pollution caused by drainage wells, surface pollution, construction of canals and reservoirs, etc. Many springs that were clear a few years ago are now always muddy, and virtually all Florida springs are starting to get that way. In some cases, health authorities have been forced to close spots because of contaminated water. A much larger percentage of these closed spots, however, have been restricted because of the thoughtlessness of some divers, from cutting down trees, carving names on walls and littering to making too much noise and riding a farmer's livestock. However, the biggest problem remains cave diving fatalities. Fear of lawsuits, bad publicity, and concern about accidents have forced many landowners to post diving areas. Fortunately, the number of cave diving fatalities has declined sharply since 1974, despite a probable increase in the number of participants. This is due in large part to the educational efforts of the N.S.S. Cave Diving Section and other volunteer diver training agencies.

Equipment and Procedures

Tanks should not have "J" valves. These are easily knocked down and have been known to malfunction. A dual-valve manifold should be used in conjunction with two independent, single hose regulators so that if one regulator should malfunction, you can simply cut off the air to the bad regulator, then switch to the other one and make a safe exit from the cave. One of the regulators should be equipped with a longer hose to facilitate buddy-breathing, as well as a submersible air pressure gauge. This gauge is all-important: the entire dive revolves around the diver's air supply. Ever since it was founded in 1941, the N.S.S. has advocated the use of three independent sources of light for each caver, and this is just as important for cave divers. A buoyancy compensator, either front- or back-mounted, is necessary to provide the lift needed to stay off the silt on the bottom. Watches, depth gauges and submersible tables are needed to monitor decompression requirements. Finally, the cave diving team must have a good nylon safety line of at least 160 lbs. tensile strength on a good underwater reel. Of course, all open-water gear, such as tanks, wetsuits, masks, fins and knives are also used, with the exception of a snorkel.

A dive plan must be formulated before entering the water, including planned depth, penetration, bottom time and air turnaround point. The most important of these factors is the air turnaround. N.S.S. recommends the "third rule," where the cave diving team automatically turns around and starts out of the cave as soon as the first member exhausts one-third of his original air supply. The feeling is that two-thirds or more left would be ·sufficient to cope with any emergency situation. One diver is designated team leader. This diver will be the first one into the cave and the last one out. The team leader secures the line once just outside the cave entrance under water; then once just inside, before daylight is lost. As the leader deploys the safety line from his reel, his teammates follow him closely, maintaining contact with the line at all times. The divers also maintain contact with each other by glancing back, watching the reflection of each other's lights, hand signals, etc. If the desired turnaround is reached, or the dive is called by any member of the team, then the entire team starts out of the cave together. It is very important that any member of the team feel free to call the dive for any reason at any point. Not infrequently, experienced cave divers abort dives for no reason other than simply "feeling a little uptight." Throughout the entire dive, the team stays up near the ceiling to conserve air and to keep from stirring up the silt on the bottom.

Types of Caves

There are four general types of underwater caves in Florida—springs, sinks, spring-syphons and natural bridges. A spring flows out of the

PETE VELDE

A safety line guides cavers through an underwater passage.

49

ground, forming a run that goes to a nearby river, ocean, etc. A sink has no discernible flow and is generally enclosed by a sunken area known as a depression. A spring-syphon has two caves, one with water coming out, the other with water going into the ground. When the river rises in periods of heavy rainfall, causing dark water to "back up" over the springs, many springs reverse their flow to become syphons, draining the dirty river water. Natural bridges cover surface streams, such as that over the Santa Fe River at O'Leno State Park. Most of these surface streams have poor visibility. However, some springs have short, diveable natural bridges over their runs.

Hazards

Cave diving involves surmounting a number of natural hazards, the most important of which is the cave ceiling. Should any emergency occur while cave diving, the distressed diver cannot make a free ascent to the surface. He must rely on his own knowledge, skill, equipment and experience—and that of his partner as well. Other important hazards include currents, visibility, and various physical peculiarities of the cave. Current can lead to overexertion, and certainly makes buddy-breathing much more difficult. Syphons are to be avoided—the strong downward flow makes it necessary to use much more effort and air to swim out of the cave, which could possibly be critical should a problem arise. In periods of warm weather, many sinks and springs become cloudy with algae growth. Heaviest growth (and poorest visibility) are usually in the surface layers. Most caves also contain deposits of silt on walls, ledges, and, especially, the bottom. A careless movement, such as a flipper stroke, can cause the soft sediment to stir up instantly—reducing visibility from hundreds of feet to inches. Often, the diver is not aware of this problem until he glances behind himself. Many caves branch off into underground mazes, making a safety line mandatory to find one's way out. Restrictions (narrow areas in caves) are to be avoided. Deep caves should also be avoided because of potential problems with narcosis, decompression, etc. Perhaps the best rule to follow in deciding whether or not to penetrate a given cave is to ask one's self the following question: "If anything were to happen in the cave at the worst moment, could I still be certain that I could get my buddy out alive? Or he get me out?" If the answer is no, only a fool goes on.

Emergency situations are unlikely to arise for the well-prepared cave diving team. However, everyone entering a cave should be prepared to deal with them. A few of these emergency situations include air supply loss; lost diver; line entanglement; broken safety line; loss of visibility (light failure or "silt-out"); hurt diver; and unconscious diver. The procedures for coping with these situations should be mastered with your buddy under simulated conditions in open water at night before entering an underwater cave, and reviewed together frequently.

It is well to remember that a cave diving accident may not result in one diver's death alone. Many cave diving accidents are multiple drownings—

STEVE STRAATSMA

The N.S.S. Cave Diving Section emphasizes the importance of proper training.

the initial victim's partner may well die also. If he drowns in a hazardous area, he may jeopardize the lives of a body recovery team. His drowning may also result in not only the closing of that particular cave to all diving, but also other caves and, possibly, an entire county. However, worst of all—at least from the victim's standpoint—is the tragic effect of grief that the accident will have on his immediate family and friends. And for what? A foolish dive that could easily have been made safely if the diver had been willing to wait and learn cave diving the safe way.

The Safe Way

The minimal training received in a basic scuba course is simply not enough for cave diving. A majority of victims have been certified basic scuba divers, but, nevertheless, drowned before making their fifth cave dive. Fortunately, the Cave Diving Section of the N.S.S. now offers an inexpensive introduction to cave diving through its two-day "Cavern Diver" certification program. This qualifies divers to "ledge dives" in the shallow areas just inside large cave entrances where there is plenty of natural light. Persons interested in more serious cave diving may enroll in the more extensive N.S.S. "Cave Diver" certification course, which usually takes eight days or longer to complete. Other national agencies offering this training include NAUI, PADI and YMCA.

The N.S.S. Cave Diving Section also offers periodic cave diving workshops all over the country, where novices and experts alike can get together and exchange ideas on various aspects of cave diving. Such workshops usually include actual guided practice dives as well as lectures and discussions in an informal atmosphere. Typically, the workshops are held in Branford, Florida each year on Memorial Day weekend and New Year's weekend, as well as summers at the N.S.S.Convention.

Publications

In addition to cave diving courses and workshops, the N.S.S. Cave Diving Section has made available several current publications regarding cave diving. "Cave Diving Safety" is a free pamphlet published as a public service by the Section that briefly describes many of the basic procedures required for cave diving. Safety maps of the most popular springs in Florida are available in large blueprint format at $3.00 each, as is a 25¢ brochure explaining their use. *Basic Cave Diving: Blue Print for Survival* ($2.95) by Sheck Exley gives an introduction to the fundamentals of cave diving in Florida. The *N.S.S. Cave Diving Manual* ($11.95) is America's first complete authoritative text on the subject, with more than 300 pages covering virtually every aspect of cave diving. For information on any of these books, courses or workshops, write the N.S.S., CDS Publications, H.V. Grey, P.O. Box 575, Venice, Florida 34284-0575.

PETE VELDE

At Branford Springs, divers journey from Peacock to Olson Sink.

NED DELOACH

Equipped to cope with any emergency, cave divers make a safe penetration.

Conservation

You can choose whether or not you want to risk destruction by foolishly taking unnecessary risks while cave diving, but the cave has no such choice. It is there, and it is vulnerable to vandalism. Caves have unique scientific, recreational and scenic values that should be preserved for future generations to study and enjoy. N.S.S. members must pledge to do nothing that will deface, mar or otherwise spoil the natural beauty and life forms in caves. Be kind to the cave, and remember the N.S.S. motto:

"Take nothing but pictures… Leave nothing but footprints… Kill nothing but time."

The N.S.S. Cave Diving Section

The N.S.S. Cave Diving Section is by far the largest cave diving organization in the western hemisphere and its members, novice and expert alike, engage in an enormous amount of activities to encourage safe, productive and enjoyable cave and cavern diving.

Membership in the N.S.S. is open to all persons interested in caves. Applications may be obtained by writing to the National Speleological Society, Cave Avenue, Huntsville, Alabama 35810. Any N.S.S. member may join the Cave Diving Section by sending $5.00 to Sandy Fehring, 3508 Hollow Oak Place, Brandon, Florida. Non-members may subscribe to the bimonthly magazine of the Section, *Underwater Speleology,* by sending $8.00/year to Sandy Fehring.

Biographical Note

Sheck Exley is the most experienced cave diver in the world, with more than 2,500 cave dives logged in many countries on four continents. He is a charter member of the N.S.S. CDS and was its first Chairman. For his cave rescue work, he is the only diver ever to receive the Distinguished Service Award of the Florida Sheriffs Association. He has also received the Lew Bicking Award as America's top cave explorer in 1981, the Abe Davis Cave Diving Safety Award, and is a Fellow of the N.S.S. and the Explorers Club. He has written more than 100 articles and six books on the subject of cave diving safety.

"Available Early 1984"

NEW

Ocean Realm Guide To

Underwater Bahamas

Hundreds of dive locations
and resort information.

Before you make your plans, get your copy of
Underwater Bahamas, the only up-to-date
divers guide for the islands. $4.95
Available at your local dive store.

Ocean Realm Publishing Corporation, 2333 Brickell Ave., Miami, FL 33129

BRANFORD

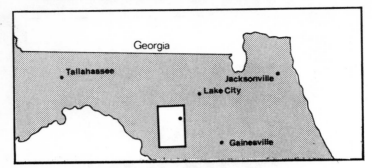

Spring Diving Locations

1. Charles Spring
2. Blue Spring-Lafayette Co. (Snake, Yana, Bob Cat & Stephens Sinks)
3. Spring Quarries
4. Telford Spring
4. Telford Sink
4. Terrapin Sink
5. Bonnet Spring
6. Peacock Springs
6. Pot Hole
7. Olson Sink
8. Challenge Sink
9. Orange Grove Sink
9. Cisteen Sink
10. Royal Spring

11. Troy Spring
12. Little River Spring
13. Branford Spring
14. Rock Bluff Spring
14. Rock Bluff Ferry River Dive
15. Sun Spring
16. Hart Spring
17. Otter Spring
18. Running Springs
18. Cow Spring
19. Fanning Spring
   Not on Map:
   Manatee Spring
   Blue Springs-Madison Co.
   Blue Sink-Madison Co.
   Suwannee Spring

Area Information

Branford, located on the east bank of the famous Suwannee River, has long been the center of spring diving in Florida. Dozens of springs are located both north and south of the town. The Peacock Slough area is one of the most popular groups of springs in the state. A diver can enjoy over 20 different springs and sinks, all within a one-and-a-half-mile radius. Troy Springs, located on the west bank of the Suwannee, has a large open basin with a depth to 80 feet. The interesting remains of an old paddle-wheeler lie in the middle of the run near the river. Motels, restaurants and a complete dive shop are located in Branford.

NO. 1. CHARLES SPRING
Location: From the bridge over the Suwannee River on S-51, travel east 5.5

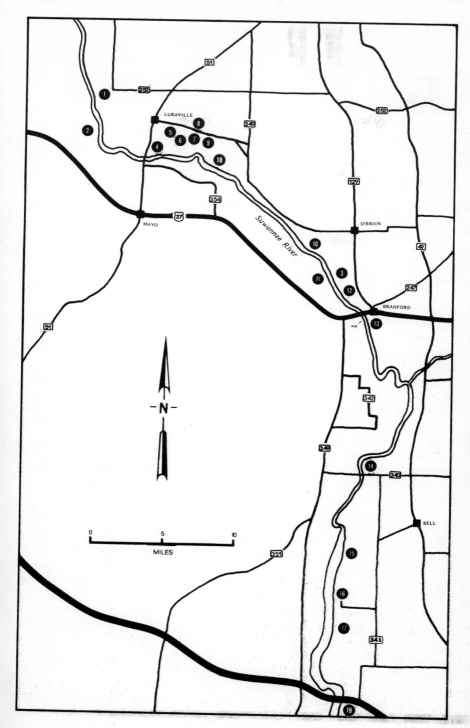

miles. Turn left on S-252 and go 3.1 miles to sharp right bend in road. Go straight at the bend on small dirt road 1.4 miles to the spring.

The head pool is about 50 feet in diameter, with a ten-foot depth to the cave entrance. There are two natural bridges in the run that can be free-dived. The cave is dangerous due to extreme silt and cave-ins. There is an open area near the spring for camping, with a boat ramp to the Suwannee.

NO. 2 BLUE SPRING-LAFAYETTE CO.
(SNAKE, YANA, BOB CAT AND STEPHENS SINKS)

Location: From Mayo travel northwest on US 27 for 5 miles to S-251-B. Turn right and go 2.2 miles. Turn right (east) onto a sand road just before a guard rail. In .8 mile, turn right to Yana Sink or continue .1 mile further to Blue Spring-Lafayette Co.

Blue Spring, situated on the west bank of the Suwannee River, is a 25-foot basin skirted by a high bluff. About halfway down the short run leading to the river is a large, natural bridge under which you can free-dive.

A large cave entrance opens into a wide room before narrowing again into a 300-foot tunnel that leads to Snake Sink at a depth of 47 feet. The water of the spring and connected sinks has a green tint and an average visibility of 50 feet. Snake pool is about 250 feet long and 30 feet wide. A cave entrance at the west end runs for 20 feet at a 45-foot depth to Yana Sink.

Yana's basin is 150 feet long and 70 feet wide, and has a maximum depth of 35 feet. The cave at the west end leads into the Dome Room. The larger room's most prominent features are two large solution domes. The first is 40 feet across and has an air pocket where divers can converse. Only those with *advanced cave diving training* should proceed beyond the Dome Room. Stop when depths drop to 60 feet. The system continues for over 20,000 feet back into the woods. Bob Cat, Stephens I, II and III, and Skiles Sinks all open the system to the surface at various points along the channel.

NO. 3 SPRING QUARRIES

Location: From the intersection of US 27 and S-129 in Branford, travel north 3.1 miles to a paved road. Continue past the paved road, turning left (west) on the first dirt road. After crossing railroad tracks, turn right (north) and continue parallel with tracks. Turn left on the first dirt road. Follow this road around a tricky left turn. Park in front of Spring Quarry.

There are five abandoned quarries in the vicinity. Only two are recommended for diving. You will park in front of the largest and best site. Spring Quarry is large—125 yards by 100 yards. Water depth is to 35 feet, and visibility to 50 feet can be expected most of the year. Visibility never drops below 20 feet. The basin is filled with bream, bass and catfish, as well as a variety of aquatic plant life. If you are lucky, you might catch sight of a gator. Because of the clear, open expanse of water, this is an excellent area for instruction and check-out dives.

Come to:
Branford Dive Center
in the

Owner: Gene Broome

Heart of SPRING Country!

The Ideal Location to Serve the
Suwannee, Santa Fe & Ichetucknee
Rivers
As well as a multitude of springs!

Great Diving Year-Round!

Complete Diving Facility • Sales & Service
Gear Rentals • Instruction • Pure Air Fills
Custom T-Shirts • Information • Rental Homes
Canoe & Boat Ramps • OPEN 7 DAYS A WEEK

ANNOUNCING the SECOND STAGE OYSTER BAR & TAVERN

BRANFORD'S NEW
OYSTER BAR & TAVERN
Serving a delicious menu of
Oysters, Shrimp, Deli Style Sandwiches,
Pizzas and a variety of Cold Beer.

(904) 935-1141
IN U.S. 800-874-0443
IN FL. 800-342-0442

P.O. BOX 822 • BRANFORD, FLORIDA 32008

The adjacent L-shaped quarry is called Crane Quarry. It has the same underwater environment and conditions as Spring. There are a few rock overhangs.

NO. 4 TELFORD SPRING
Location: Travel north on S-51 from Mayo toward Luraville. After crossing the bridge over the Suwannee, turn right on the first road (dirt road across from truck inspection station). Go a short distance to the stop sign and turn right. Continue .9 mile to spring.

Diver enters the small spring-siphon known as Cow Spring.

Telford Spring is located on the edge of the Suwannee River. Bare dirt banks slope gently down to the spring, which has a run about 40 yards long. A small crevice ends in a small cave.

NO. 4 TELFORD SINK
Location: Just north of dirt road before reaching Telford Spring, about 200 feet from the spring.

A small sink with three round holes forming limestone shafts which connect underwater in a room with depths to 33 feet make up Telford. Two small tunnels lead off from the room. Both are extremely silty.

NO. 4 TERRAPIN SINK
Location: In a shallow depression, just past Telford Spring, about 150 feet west of dirt road. A footpath leads to the sink.

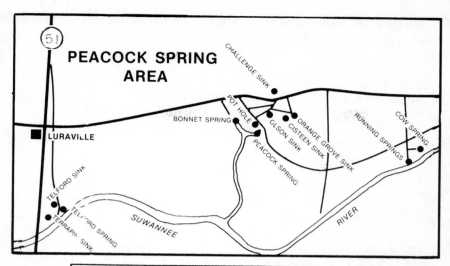

PEACOCK SPRING AREA

51

CHALLENGE SINK

POT HOLE

BONNET SPRING

ORANGE GROVE SINK

CISTEEN SINK

OLSON SINK

RUNNING SPRINGS

COW SPRING

LURAVILLE

PEACOCK SPRING

TELFORD SINK

TELFORD SPRING

TERRAPIN SINK

SUWANNEE

RIVER

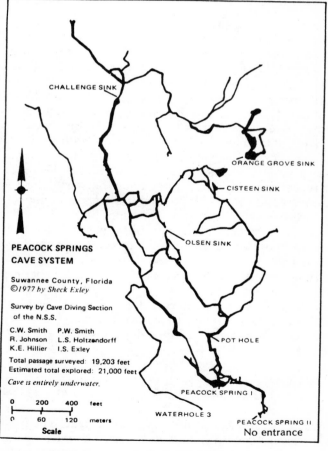

CHALLENGE SINK

ORANGE GROVE SINK

CISTEEN SINK

OLSEN SINK

PEACOCK SPRINGS CAVE SYSTEM

Suwannee County, Florida
©1977 by Sheck Exley

Survey by Cave Diving Section
of the N.S.S.

C.W. Smith   P.W. Smith
R. Johnson   L.S. Holtzendorff
K.E. Hillier   I.S. Exley

Total passage surveyed: 19,203 feet
Estimated total explored: 21,000 feet

Cave is entirely underwater.

POT HOLE

PEACOCK SPRING I

WATERHOLE 3

PEACOCK SPRING II

No entrance

| 0 | 200 | 400 | feet |
| 0 | 60 | 120 | meters |

Scale

This small sink is believed to be a spring-syphon and connects to Telford Sink. Depths are to 35 feet.

NO. 5 BONNET SPRING

Location: Go north on A-51 from Mayo. After crossing the bridge over the Suwannee River, go 1.7 miles. Turn right on paved road across from the Bay Service Station. Go 2 miles and turn right at the first dirt road past the fence line.

Bonnet Spring is a small spring in a beautiful setting. There is interesting snorkeling in rock crevices and through a large area of lily pads filled with many fish.

NO. 6 PEACOCK SPRINGS

Location: From Mayo going north on S-51, travel 1.7 miles from the middle of the bridge over the Suwannee. Turn right on paved road across the highway from the Bay Service Station. (This is the second road on the right after leaving the bridge.) Travel 2.2 miles and turn right on second dirt road past the fence line. Go .4 mile to the springs which are located on your right.

OR

From Branford travel north for 6 miles on US 129 to O'Brien. Turn left on S-349 and go 12 miles. Turn left on another paved road (Philadelphia Baptist Church sign) and go 1.5 miles and turn left again. Continue on for 3.5 miles. Turn left on small dirt road and go .4 mile to the spring.

A beautiful series of three springs flow 1.5 miles down the slough to the Suwannee. Snorkeling is excellent down the run through a large covering of lily pads. There is a large area for camping around the springs, but no facilities. The headspring offers a good cave dive, with a tunnel that winds its way to Pot Hole Sink, about 75 yards from Peacock.

The mouth of the cave system starts in about 18 feet of water and is about nine by five feet, making access to the first room easy. The Blue Room is large and runs east to west. At the mouth there is a permanent line that runs to the west end of the room, where it ends tied to the ceiling about 15 feet off the floor. At the north end of the Blue Room at a depth of 45 feet is a sign that warns those who are not trained cave divers to venture no farther. Those divers with proper training and experience may want to continue on to Pot Hole Sink. Below the sign, a three by ten foot slit drops through the floor where a permanent line starts at a depth of 65 feet. From there, you follow the line down a main corridor which is 60 feet by 100 feet in places. Following the line about 400 feet, you start an ascent to the surface in Pot Hole Sink. Surface light is difficult to spot. Proceed up the narrow shaft one at a time.

NO. 6 POT HOLE

Location: About 75 yards north of Peacock Slough. It is 20 feet to the side of the entrance road.

Pot Hole Sink is almost obscured by dense foliage. The basin drops 30 feet to water level. Caution should be exercised in entering the sink. The water at the surface is six feet by ten feet, but four feet under, it narrows to a small three-foot chimney. A submerged tree limb and loose sand increase the hazards of entry. The narrow passage spirals down to 15 feet, where its path becomes regular and begins widening gradually as you approach the entrance to the main corridor in Peacock.

From Pot Hole there is also a connecting tunnel that travels 1,200 feet at a depth of 50 to 70 feet to Olson Sink. These, as well as all other cave transverses, should be undertaken *only* by trained, experienced cave divers.

NO. 7 OLSON SINK
Location: Travel north on S-51 from Mayo toward Luraville. Go 1.7 miles past center of bridge and turn right on paved road across from Bay Service Station (same road to Peacock). Go 2.5 miles and turn right on small dirt road. Go .2 mile and park in the clearing on the right side of the road. A footpath on the left side of the road leads to sink.

Olson is a beautiful sink located deep within the woods. On the north side at a depth of 20 feet there is a tunnel that opens into a small room at a depth of 65 feet. On the right side of the room there is a small tunnel with a low ceiling. This is a very silty sink, and is for advanced cave divers only. The entrance to the south tunnel is partially hidden by fallen limbs. The tunnel runs to Peacock Spring at a depth of 70 feet.

National Speleogical Society

CAVE DIVING MANUAL

An encyclopedia detailing every facet of cave diving.
Over 300 pages • Photos • Charts • Illustrations
• Maps • Tablets.

$13.00 (Shipping & Postage Included)

ORDER FROM
N.S.S. Cave Diving Section Publications
P.O. Box 575
Venice, Florida
34284-0575

NO. 8 CHALLENGE SINK
Location: Directly across the paved road from turn-off to Olson Sink. Follow the footpath back 100 feet into the woods.

This is a small sink, ten feet deep, with a narrow entrance on the south side that opens up and drops to a depth of 70 feet, going to Olson Sink. It is considered a very advanced cave dive.

NO. 9 ORANGE GROVE SINK
Location: Travel north on S-51 from Mayo toward Luraville. Go 1.7 miles past center of the bridge over the Suwannee. Turn right on the paved road across the highway from Bay Service Station (same road to Peacock). Travel 2.6 miles and turn right on the fourth dirt road past the fence line. It is .2 mile to the sink.

This is a large sink located in a rugged setting. Massive limestone cliffs drop to the surface waters, which are covered through much of the year with a thin green layer of duckweed. Visibility is usually 100 feet. The bottom slopes to a depth of 60 feet, where it is covered with large tree trunks and limbs. The cave is located on the north wall of the sink at a depth of 53 feet. The entrance measures 15 by seven feet, and opens into an immense room named the Coliseum. The room is about 60 by 80 feet, with depths of 65 feet at the ceiling to 100 feet, where large boulders line the bottom.

For the experienced diver only, there is a five by eight foot entrance to a corridor at the 70-foot level. This corridor winds for 75 feet and enters the Throne Room. Conditions become very adverse due to a deep layer of fine black silt.

NO. 9 CISTEEN SINK
Location: A short distance west of Orange Grove Sink.

From the surface, this sink resembles nearby Orange Grove. The diameter is about 30 feet, depending on the height of the Suwannee. There is a cave entrance in ten feet of water that leads to a corridor which winds down 50 feet to a room called the Witches' Kettle. The room is named for its precarious entrance and extremely silty condition. From here, the corridor winds on and on.

NO. 10 ROYAL SPRING
Location: From Branford, travel north for 6 miles on US 129 to O'Brien. Turn left on S-349 and go 8.9 miles. Turn left on graded road and go .8 mile; then turn left on sand road that runs by brown house on a small hill. Continue .2 mile to the spring.

The spring is surrounded by steep banks. A concrete retaining wall is built on the east side with steps to the water. The basin is about 40 yards in diameter, with a shallow 60-yard run to the river. A large cave entrance is located about 50 feet down the side of the limestone cliff. There is not much flow, and the cave is very silty and dangerous. To the left of the run is a good boat ramp. No camping is allowed, and all persons should leave by 9 p.m.

NO. 11 TROY SPRING

Location: From the intersection of US 129 and US 27 in Branford, travel northwest on US 27 for 5.3 miles. Turn right on the paved road (across highway from white house) and go north 1.3 miles. As the paved road curves left, you will see a small green house trailer on the right. Turn onto the dirt road that runs between the trailer and a fence line for .6 mile to the spring.

Troy is a large spring located on the west bank of the Suwannee River. The large open area with depths to 80 feet provides one of the best dives in the state for large groups of divers.

There is a large run with depths from four to six feet. At the end of the run near the river lie the broken remains of the old Suwannee River steamboat *Madison*. She was scuttled in September 1863 by her captain, who abandoned her to lead a company of Confederate soldiers in Virginia.

NO. 12 LITTLE RIVER SPRING (Restricted to certified cave divers)

Location: From the intersection of US 27 and US 129 in Branford, travel north on US 129 for 3.1 miles. Turn left on paved road at large Camp O' the Suwannee sign. Go across the railroad tracks. After 1.8 miles, bear left at the second sign and go up the spring. This spring is closed from time to time.

Little River is rated among Florida's finest cave dives. The spring basin is large, with a bare limestone and sand bottom. There are few aquatic plants or fish. The entrance to the underground system begins with a small cave, ten feet in diameter, in about 15 feet of water. The cave slopes to

"I get more out of diving through my
Diving Ventures International
membership."

"My DVI membership gives me access to a wide variety of local diving activities and new educational experiences available from my participating PADI Training Facility. It also lets me save money at many of the world's top diving resorts. Best of all, my DVI membership is an excellent *value*. One low yearly fee provides all these opportunities *plus* a membership card, decals, *and* a year's subscription to *Diving Ventures* magazine.

"Why not enjoy all these benefits yourself? Contact your local PADI Training Facility or PADI Headquarters. You can save money, discover new activities, and make new friends — all through Diving Ventures International."

Diving Ventures International
The PADI Diving Society

1243 East Warner Avenue • Santa Ana, CA 92705
(714) 540-PADI (7234) • Telex 678400

NED DELOACH

Crystal clear water typifies Florida's spring country.

a level of 60 feet; then it makes a sharp left turn where all surface light disappears. At this point, all inexperienced cave divers should end their penetration. There is a permanent sign which serves as a reminder.

Continuing past the sign, the experienced cave diver enters a complex and silty maze area beyond which is a small room with a chimney that drops from 70 to 100 feet. At 100 feet, the cave levels off into a picturesque winding tunnel known as the "serpentine passage." The passage leads to a large section, 800 feet from the entrance, that has been named the "Florida Room." Past the big section, the cave begins branching, gradually becoming smaller and siltier.

NO. 13 BRANFORD SPRING
Location: 100 feet from the southeast corner of the bridge over the Suwannee in the town of Branford, adjacent to the Branford Dive Center.

This is a great place to cool off or check out your gear. The clear, blue spring is about 65 feet across, with depths to 15 feet. A wooden deck and ladder allow easy access to the water.

NO. 14 ROCK BLUFF SPRING

Location: From the intersection of US 27 and US 129, 4 miles east of Branford, turn right on US 129 and travel south for 14 miles. Turn right on C-340, traveling west to the white inspection station on the east side of the Suwannee. Turn off just past the station into a parking area next to a boat ramp. Launch your canoe or boat here, and go upstream (north) for about 150 yards. Watch for the clear spring run on the right side of the river.

A scenic, cypress-lined run winds inland for 40 yards to a large, shallow basin. There are many bream, mullet and turtles in the clear, inviting water. The main dive is into a rock fissure, 60 feet long and 20 feet wide. The edge is in ten feet of water and drops to a small cave entrance at 35 feet.

The cave system is extensive but narrow, difficult and dangerous. A strong flow issues from the small cave. All the surrounding land is privately owned. A home is next to the spring. Absolutely no trespassing is allowed. It is alright to explore the spring as long as you stay in the water. Anchor in the basin. Don't pull your boat ashore. Please be quiet and leave no litter.

NO. 14 ROCK BLUFF FERRY RIVER DIVE

Location: About 30 feet directly out from the boat ramp near C-340.

This is a naturally deep area of the Suwannee where a ferry used to cross. The water is clearest during low-water periods. Be careful of boat traffic, especially on weekends, and always use a diver's flag. There is good relic hunting on the rock and gravel bottom. Numerous fish inhabit the area.

NO. 15 SUN SPRING

Location: Leave Wilcox east on S-26. Turn north on S-341, and go 10 miles to Sun Spring Road (small sign). Turn west onto the dirt road and go 1.7 miles until the main road ends. Turn left and go .2 mile to spring on right.

Sun Spring is a small spring that forms a narrow run leading to the Suwannee. A circular rock cliff, ten feet below the surface, drops to a depth of 20 feet. It provides interesting snorkeling with many fish and turtles.

NO. 16 HART SPRING

Location: From Wilcox, go north on S-232 for 4.7 miles. Turn west on S-344 and travel 1.8 miles to the entrance of Gilchrist County Recreational Park.

Hart Spring is a pleasant family recreation park with picnic tables, refreshments and a large swimming area. Diving is not permitted in the boil area. A large run lined with cypress trees flows a short distance to the Suwannee.

NO. 17 OTTER SPRING

Location: From Wilcox, go north on S-232 for 1.8 miles to the Otter Spring sign. Turn onto the dirt road and travel 1.1 miles to the park entrance. Continue .6 mile through the campgrounds to the spring.

The headspring is located in a small basin with a long, narrow crevice which drops down about 25 feet to a small cave. The second crevice runs parallel to the first, with depths to 14 feet. A small, circular tunnel interconnects the two, and a small corridor runs from the cave. It is very silty and has a weak flow. Snorkeling is good over the basin and down the run. There are excellent camping facilities with trailer connections.

NO. 18 RUNNING SPRING
Location: Travel north on S-51 from Mayo toward Luraville. Go 1.7 miles past

Running Springs, on the banks of the Suwannee River.

center of the bridge over the Suwannee. Turn right on the paved road across the highway from Bay Service Station (same as the road to Peacock). Travel 3.8 miles. Turn right on the dirt road across from a small church and go .8 mile to where the main road bears to the left, but continue straight ahead on the small dirt road .6 mile to the springs.

These two beautiful springs are located on the banks of the Suwannee. The right spring is ten feet deep with a short run that syphons under the river bank to the Suwannee. The left spring has an underwater natural bridge with a three by five-foot opening that can easily be free-dived.

NO. 18 COW SPRING
Location: Follow the directions to Running Springs, but bear left on the small dirt road .2 mile before arriving at Running Springs.

Cow is a small spring-siphon filled with crystal clear water. The cave is beautiful to dive, but limited in size. There are two entrances leading into a small room that goes back about 25 feet. Maximum depth is 40 feet. There are two tunnels leading from the room. The tunnel on the left is the spring entrance. It is restricted in size. The siphon entrance, at the back of the room, is also narrow and a difficult dive.

NO. 19 FANNING SPRING

Location: In the small town of Fanning Spring on the east bank of the Suwannee River. Turn right off US 19-98 on the second road past the bridge.

A large, open basin on the east side of the Suwannee River, the spring pool is 30 yards across with a maximum depth of 20 feet. The water issues from a sand boil. There is no cave. The land is owned by a church group and there is a 50¢ admission charge. There is a dock, concession stand and bathhouse. No camping is permitted.

MANATEE SPRING (Not on map)

Location: Just north of Chiefland on US 19, turn west on S-320 and follow signs to Manatee State Park.

A large spring, Manatee discharges 96 m.g.d. into the Suwannee. A limestone cliff drops to a cave at a depth of 40 feet. The area is filled with aquatic plants and fish. There is good snorkeling in the run. Camping facilities are excellent. This large cave is quite silty despite extremely strong currents. The park has developed a set of rules to be followed by all divers. When entering the park, let the ranger know of your intent to dive. He will be happy to discuss the current rules with you.

BLUE SPRINGS-MADISON CO. (Not on map)

Location: From Madison, go east on US 90 for 2.5 miles. Turn left on S-6 and travel about 6 miles to the bridge over the Withlacoochee River. Turn right (south) on the west side of the bridge and go .1 mile to the spring.

Blue at Madison is a large spring, about 25 yards in diameter, and is situated in a basin with 30 feet of sand and rock cliffs. A near horizontal cavern opens to 20 feet by 30 feet at a depth of 30 feet. The strong flow is rated 94 m.g.d. The short run to the river is lined with large cypress trees. There is a large area for camping with no facilities.

BLUE SINK-MADISON CO. (Not on map)

Location: From S-6 over Withlacoochee River, go west on S-6 for .3 mile to graded dirt road on right. Go .5 mile to second sharp bend to the left; continue straight ahead onto another dirt road and go about 1 mile to the parking area 200 feet west of the sink.

This is a large sink, about 300 feet by 100 feet, on the edge of a swampy area. Visibility averages 50 feet, with depths to 45 feet on a rock crater near the middle. Some fish and turtles are present.

SUWANNEE SPRING (Not on map)

Location: From Live Oak, travel north on US 129 for 8 miles to the Suwannee River Bridge. Turn east on the south end of the bridge and go .1 mile to the spring.

An interesting rock formation in the spring issues about 20 m.g.d. of clear green sulfur water. The entire spring is surrounded by rock walls that look like an old Spanish fort.

FORT WHITE- HIGH SPRINGS

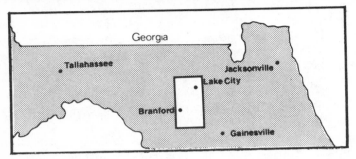

Spring Diving Locations

1. Ichetucknee Springs
2. Blue Hole Spring
3. Ginnie Springs
3. Devil's Eye Spring
3. Dogwood Spring
4. July Spring
5. Blue Springs-Santa Fe River
5. Naked Spring
6. Rum Island Spring
7. Lily Spring
8. Poe Spring
9. Magnolia Sink
10. Cliff Sink

Area Information

This area of north central Florida boasts the clearest diving waters to be found anywhere in the world. A beautiful series of springs line the picturesque Santa Fe River, offering the diver a variety of large deep-water basins. Both Blue Springs and Ginnie Springs are commercially operated. Not only do they provide interesting diving, but also have restrooms with showers and great camping facilities.

One of the best ways to visit these springs is to take a short canoe trip down the Santa Fe. The springs are easily spotted from the river. You can dive and then rest at each location for as long as you like before continuing downstream. The clear, captivating waters of the spring-fed Ichetucknee rate high for underwater fun. The headsprings, as well as three miles of the river, are operated and protected by the state. Be sure to plan for at least a full day's diving.

There are two dive shops with air systems in the area. Gainesville also offers complete diving supplies and air. Canoe and raft rentals are easily found. Motels are located in Branford, High Springs, Lake City and

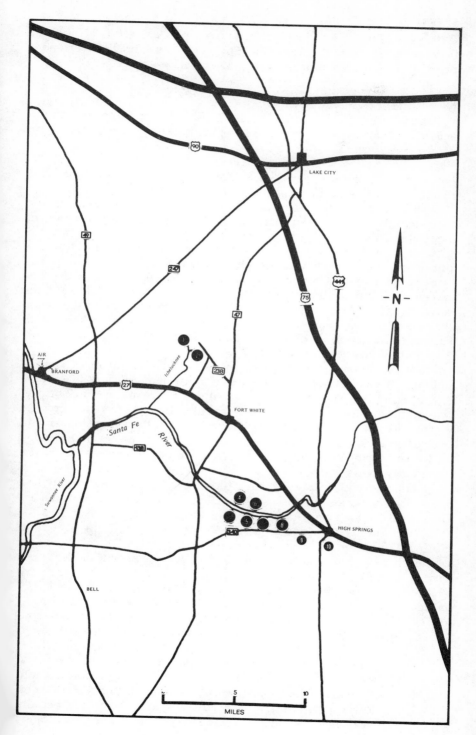

Gainesville. The Ichetucknee Park has no camping areas, but facilities can be found at Ginnie Springs and Blue Springs on the Santa Fe River, and in private campgrounds near the Ichetucknee park entrance.

NO. 1 ICHETUCKNEE SPRINGS
Location: From the intersection of US 129 and 27 in Branford, go east about 7 miles. Turn left onto C-137 and travel 1.3 miles. Turn right and go 3 miles to the north park entrance.

OR

From the intersection of I-75 and S-47, travel south on S-47 for 11.3 miles. Turn right on S-238 by sign. Go 4 miles to park area.

Several springs, located in a beautiful wooded area, form the Ichetucknee River, a recreation paradise for both divers and nature lovers. The state now owns and operates the springs and more than three miles of their run to the bridge on US 27. They have done a magnificent job of preserving the area's natural beauty. A three-hour float down the run remains unspoiled. There are no signs, houses, roads or concrete. The voyager will instead enjoy lush virgin woods filled with wildlife and the songs of birds. The headspring forms a circular pool of about 100 feet in diameter. The water emerging from a horizontal cavern beneath the north bank has a 13-foot depth to the cave floor. The rate of flow is approximately 20 m.g.d., with a temperature of 72 degrees.

The float down the run can be made on an assortment of items— anything from old tire tubes (the most popular item) to canoes. You drift slowly along in a two-knot current until you arrive at the US 27 bridge, two-and-a-half to three hours later. In the past, two cars were required for a group to make the trip. One car had to be left at the bridge to take you back to the headspring. Now, however, a bus service runs from the bridge to the headspring every hour (during summer only), thus eliminating the need for two cars.

Divers enjoy snorkeling the run, studying the underwater beauty and searching the sands for fossils and relics. A wetsuit is recommended because of the long exposure to the cool water.

In 1983, the park opened an access to the River just below Mill Pond Spring. The entrance leading to a parking area is off US 27, half a mile east of the Ichetucknee Bridge. Now divers have a choice of drifting the upper river section from the headspring to the northern section of the south park (1.4 miles), or from the northern section of the south park to the US 27 bridge (1.7 miles), or the entire stretch of 3.1 miles from the headspring to the US 27 bridge. When you start down the run, remember there are no other roads or paths to leave the river by, and you will become exhausted trying to return against the current.

The new extended section of the south park provides a tram route to carry park visitors and a 1.8 mile pedestrian path. The state enforces a limit of 3,000 visitors daily—1,500 floaters are allowed on the upper section and 1,500 on the lower part of the river. It is advisable to arrive early, especially on summer weekends, if you plan to make the river trip. The park rangers have been assigned the duty of checking containers (including purses) for items that may cause litter in the river. No food, drinks or pets are allowed. Please cooperate.

NO. 2 BLUE HOLE SPRING
Location: From the Ichetucknee headspring, follow on foot the small dirt path turning south through the woods.

This is a beautiful spring that feeds the Ichetucknee River. The entrance, 15 feet across, is located near the center of the basin in about 13 feet of water. A shaft drops almost straight down 37 feet to a sand floor that widens to about 40 feet across. Diving into the shaft is made difficult by a strong flow. On the south side of the room there is a cave, seven feet in diameter. Its corridor is filled with a constant flow which makes penetration very difficult and tiring.

Blue Hole has been temporarily closed to scuba divers due to the destruction of aquatic plants around the spring basin. The area should be reopened sometime in 1984. A fence across the run blocks access to the run from the main spring.

NO. 3 GINNIE SPRINGS
Location: Going south from High Springs on US 41, turn west on S-340 (Poe Springs Road) and travel 6.6 miles to a graded road running to your right (Ginnie

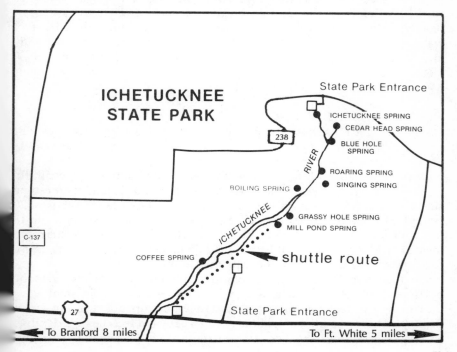

Springs Road). Go 1.2 miles to the entrance to Ginnie Springs. Travel straight on small dirt road and Ginnie Springs office will be ahead on your right.

OR

From Branford travel east on US 27 to Ft. White. Turn right (south) on S-47 and go 9.9 miles. You will see a Ginnie Springs sign at this turn. Turn left on graded road and go 1.4 miles to the end; turn right and travel .7 mile to the entrance to Ginnie Springs. Turn left onto the small dirt entrance road and Ginnie Springs office will be ahead on your right.

Ginnie Springs (formerly called Jenny), Devil's Eye Springs, Dogwood Spring and several smaller springs located along the banks of the beautiful Santa Fe River are now part of an outstanding camping and recreational facility. There is a charge to enter the area for diving or camping, but the improvements that have been made around the springs make it more than worth the price. The popular springs and their surroundings have been developed with much forethought and planning.

Every convenience is available to the diver here, including strong cypress decks around the springs, two large bathhouses with hot showers, a 5,000 psi air station, scuba shop and complete line of rental equipment. Private campsites, with or without hookups, are available. A country store is located on the premises. Combined, these all make Ginnie Springs one of America's best diving resorts.

Ginnie's basin is a four- to five-foot limestone shelf that suddenly drops 18 feet to a white sand floor. The entire area is bordered by waving eelgrass, creating a beautiful underwater setting. The cavern entrance runs horizontally to the sand floor, and is approximately four to six feet. Just inside the mouth, the first chamber widens to 30 feet, with a nine-foot ceiling. You next enter a large, sloping room, approximately 60 feet wide and 70 feet long. The room slopes downward from a depth of 35 feet to 60 feet, where it splits into two tunnels. The entrance into the narrow tunnels has been closed off with heavy grating.

NO. 3 DEVIL'S EYE SPRING

Location: Follow the same directions as given for Ginnie Springs. Turn right just before the bathhouse and follow the dirt road to the parking area. Cypress decks are located on both sides of the spring.

Devil's Eye is the middle of three boils and is one of the most beautiful combinations of springs in the state. A perfectly round shaft of limestone starts in six feet of water and drops straight down to a sand bottom at 20 feet. On the north side of the shaft, a cave entrance three feet high and 18 feet wide leads into a dark room called the "Devil's Dungeon." This room measures 30 feet long by 20 feet high. The limestone walls of the entire cave system are dark due to the mineral content of the water.

Certified cave divers with cave diving equipment can continue on to the north end of the room where they will find an extremely small cave measuring two feet by four feet. This dangerous corridor runs out under the river where a small room, about seven feet by ten feet, lies at a depth of 65 feet. Continuing a short distance farther, you'll see a shaft of sunlight.

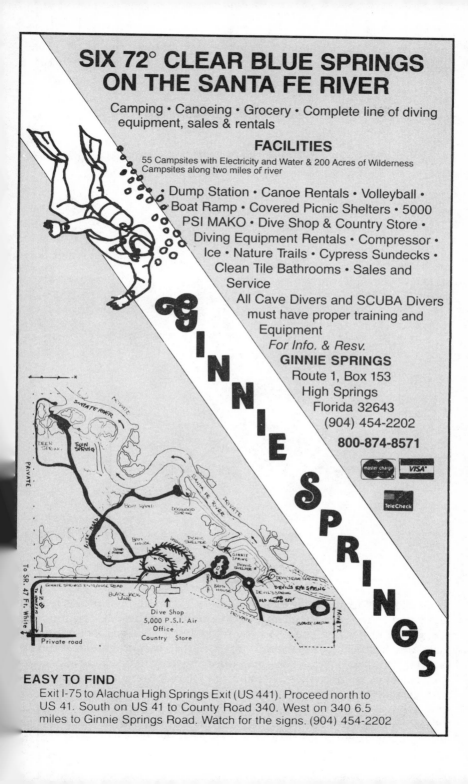

SIX 72° CLEAR BLUE SPRINGS ON THE SANTA FE RIVER

Camping • Canoeing • Grocery • Complete line of diving equipment, sales & rentals

FACILITIES

55 Campsites with Electricity and Water & 200 Acres of Wilderness Campsites along two miles of river

Dump Station • Canoe Rentals • Volleyball • Boat Ramp • Covered Picnic Shelters • 5000 PSI MAKO • Dive Shop & Country Store • Diving Equipment Rentals • Compressor • Ice • Nature Trails • Cypress Sundecks • Clean Tile Bathrooms • Sales and Service

All Cave Divers and SCUBA Divers must have proper training and Equipment

For Info. & Resv.

GINNIE SPRINGS
Route 1, Box 153
High Springs
Florida 32643
(904) 454-2202

800-874-8571

master charge   VISA

TeleCheck

EASY TO FIND
Exit I-75 to Alachua High Springs Exit (US 441). Proceed north to US 41. South on US 41 to County Road 340. West on 340 6.5 miles to Ginnie Springs Road. Watch for the signs. (904) 454-2202

Follow the light up a steep rising chimney, about three feet by seven feet, until you enter the mouth of a nearby spring located in the Santa Fe River.

NO. 3 DOGWOOD SPRING
Location: Follow the directions given for Ginnie Springs. The spring is 100 yards downriver (west) of Ginnie's Run.

Dogwood is a beautiful little spring with depths to 12 feet. There is good snorkeling in the spring and down the run. A deck has been constructed next to the spring for the convenience of divers.

NO. 4 JULY SPRING
Location: Directly across Santa Fe River from Devil's Eye Spring. Swim across the river and up a short run bordered by lily pads.

July Spring is a small spring with a depth of 15 feet. The water flows

Ginnie Springs offers caverns, camping and canoeing.

from a long, narrow crevice. Because there are numerous springs feeding the Santa Fe in this area, a large section of the river becomes clear during periods of low water levels. As you glide down the river, its underwater habitat will unfold to reveal large turtles, mullet, bass and bream hiding in a maze of sunken logs. The mud-filled crevices in the limestone floor conceal many relics and fossils. Slowly fan the silt from the cracks to reveal hidden objects.

NO. 5 BLUE SPRINGS-SANTA FE RIVER
Location: Going south from High Springs on US 41, turn west on S-340 (Po

Spring Road) and travel 4.5 miles to Blue Spring sign. Turn north and follow the dirt road to the gate.

Blue Springs is commercially operated and an entrance fee is required. Although SCUBA is not allowed, it isn't really needed. Free-diving in the spring is great. A large limestone cliff drops 25 feet to a small cave entrance.

This is a good spring for underwater photography, combining excellent visibility with bold cliffs and aquatic plant life. The bream are tame and come out of the shadows by the hundreds when bread is offered. A 1,500-foot boardwalk runs down the east side of the boil and follows its crystal run to the Santa Fe River. A small spring called Little Blue is located about 25 yards west of Blue.

A sand beach borders Blue Spring on its south bank, and a swimming dock is located over the cliff drop-off. There are picnic tables and grills provided. Concessions are sold at the office. Good camping facilities are provided, and include a clean bathhouse. (This is a good place to stay while diving the other springs in the area.)

NO. 5 NAKED SPRING
Location: About 150 yards east of Blue Spring.

Naked Spring is 25 yards in diameter, with three small crevices lying about 12 feet below the surface. The water flows through thick woods and

BEAUTIFUL BLUE SPRINGS
A YEAR 'ROUND SPRING PARADISE,
OFFERING SWIMMING, SNORKELING, CAMPGROUNDS, PICNICKING, REFRESHMENTS

AN IDEAL SETTING FOR THE PHOTOGRAPHER

———————— ● ————————

SURROUND YOURSELF WITH UNSPOILED NATURAL BEAUTY ON A WALK DOWN OUR 1500' BOARDWALK THAT FOLLOWS THE CRYSTAL CLEAR RUN TO THE HISTORIC SANTA FE RIVER

———————— ● ————————

TAKE ALACHUA-HIGH SPRINGS EXIT OFF INTERSTATE 75
5 MILES WEST OFF 340 FROM 441 AND 27
AT HIGH SPRINGS, FLORIDA

TELEPHONE FOR RATES 904/454-1369
P. O. BOX 331   HIGH SPRINGS, FLA. 32643

connects with Blue Spring's run before it reaches the Santa Fe.

In the olden days, the people who had swimming suits swam in Blue Spring, while those who couldn't afford trunks went back into the woods to swim at "Naked" Spring.

NO. 6 RUM ISLAND SPRING

Location: From Branford travel east on US 27 to Fort White. Turn south on S-47 and go 4.2 miles. Turn left (east) on S-138. After 4.5 miles, turn right onto dirt road. Stay on primary dirt road for 1.4 miles until you reach the river. Continue on the road along the river for .2 mile to the spring.

Floating down the Ichetucknee: three hours of solitude in lush, virgin woods.

A small spring located on the north bank of the Santa Fe River, Rum Island spring fills a basin 40 feet in diameter with extremely clean water. Depths are to 12 feet. The spring is filled with a beautiful variety of aquatic plant life.

NO. 7 LILY SPRING

Location: Go south from High Springs on US 41; turn west on S-340 (Poe Spring Road). Travel 3.4 miles and turn north onto dirt road. (Dirt road is located where the paved road changes texture.) Go .5 mile to a fork and bear left. Go .2 mile t the spring.

This small, picturesque spring area, located on the south bank of th Santa Fe River, is no longer open to the public. Plans for the area includ the building of private homes around the spring basin.

NO. 8 POE SPRING

Location: From US 27-41 in High Springs, go west on S-340 (Poe Spring Road) for 2.4 miles to a limestone road. Follow this road .7 mile to the spring.

This spring is fed by three small springs flowing down a 40-yard run to the Santa Fe River. It is ideal for family recreation, swimming and snorkeling. A crude boat ramp is available for launching fishing boats. The spring's temperature is 73 degrees and its flow is 45 m.g.d.

NO. 9 MAGNOLIA SINK

Location: Go about 1 mile west on S-340 (Poe Spring) from US 41 in High Springs. Turn right onto a dirt road just past a small hill and just before the gated asphalt road, also on the right. The sink is next to the dirt road, 50 yards from the highway.

A steep 50-foot-deep depression makes access to the water difficult. The cavern at the west end of the surface pool, which is 30 feet in diameter, extends to a depth of 120 feet. There are several large logs in the sink. As with most Florida sinks, algae growth lessens visibility considerably in the shallow pools during summer.

NO. 10 CLIFF SINK

Location: From the junction of US 41 and S-340, just south of High Springs, continue south on US 41 for about .2 mile to the first bend in the road. The sink is in a wooded depression, just 50 feet from the east side of the highway. Enter the sink via the ravine on the side away from the highway.

An interesting sink with a small pool of 20 feet in diameter, Cliff is named for its location at the base of a scenic cliff that rises 30 feet high. There are interesting lighting patterns in the well-lit shafts which interconnect with the cliffs. A large but silty cavern extends under the highway to a depth of 55 feet. There are reports that you can hear large trucks passing overhead. Visibility to 80 feet can be expected during winter droughts. In summer, however, algae clouds the upper 25 feet.

ICHETUCKNEE SPRINGS
Family Campsites & Grocery

- Full hook-ups • Large tent area
- Tube, raft and canoe rentals
- Bath house and laundry
- Game room

Your Hosts: Bob & Joan Taft

"At the head of the springs & just west of the park entrance"
Rt. 1 Box 127 • O'Brien, Florida 32071 • (904) 497-2150

CENTRAL FLORIDA

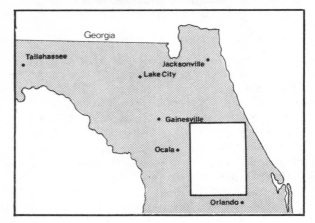

Spring Diving Locations

1. Devil's Sink
2. Orange Spring
3. Croaker Hole
4. Beecher Spring
5. Salt Springs
6. Silver Glen Springs
7. Juniper Springs
8. Alexander Springs
9. Ponce de Leon Springs
10. Blue Springs-Orange City
11. Wekiwa Springs
12. Rock Springs
13. Apopka Spring
    Not on Map
    Kingsley Lake Spring

Area Information

Some of the state's most beautiful and accessible inland diving areas a found in and around the Ocala National Forest in central Florida. T most popular diving locations are commercially operated and have var ing requirements for scuba diving. Juniper Springs, Alexander Sprin and Blue Springs at Orange City are operated by the state park syste SCUBA is allowed in Alexander Springs and Blue Springs for certifi divers. Canoeing is popular, and canoe rentals are available at S: Springs, Silver Glen Springs, Juniper Springs and Alexander Springs. / and divers' supplies are available in Gainesville, Orlando and Dayto Beach.

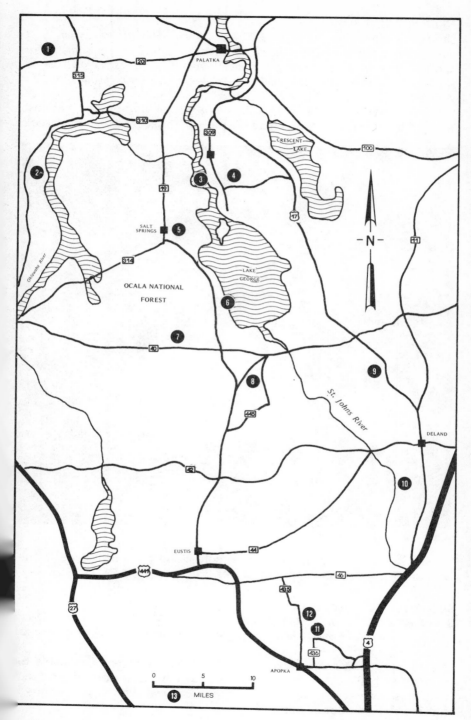

PALATKA

CRESCENT LAKE

SALT SPRINGS

Ocklawaha River

OCALA NATIONAL FOREST

LAKE GEORGE

St. Johns River

DELAND

EUSTIS

APOPKA

-N-

20
315
310
309
100
17
11
19
314
40
445
42
44
46
435
12
11
436
44
27
4

0   5   10

MILES

13

1
2
3
4
5
6
7
8
9
10
11
12
13

NO. 1 DEVIL'S SINK

Location: From Gainesville, take S-20 east through Hawthorne. Where S-21 turns south to Johnson go straight for 1.9 miles on S-20. Turn left on the paved road that runs up the side of the hill (road is across from the lake). Go about 100 yards and take one of the two small sand roads running through the woods on your left. Follow the road back to the sink.

Devil's Sink is a spectacular sight, with a 75-foot bluff plunging almost straight down to water level. There is a path on the south side which leads

A new frontier beckons divers to Florida's cave country.

down. The sink widens into a large room a short distance beneath the surface, and drops to a depth of 80 feet.

NO. 2 ORANGE SPRING

Location: In the town of Orange Springs. From S-21 south of Orange Creek bridge go east on dirt road. Then turn north on next intersecting dirt road and go .2 mile to spring.

Orange Spring contains some of the largest sand boils available to divers. The boil issues 6 m.g.d. from a sandy bowl near the middle of the pool. It is always clear and reaches a depth of 25 feet. The water contains a considerable amount of sulfur.

NO. 3 CROAKER HOLE

Location: From Palatka, go south on US 17 for 10 miles to S-309. Turn right on S-309 and continue for 10 miles to Gateway Fish Camp (4 miles south of Welaka). You can rent or launch a boat from there and go 1.5 miles downstream (north) to Little Lake George. Croaker Hole is near the southwest corner of the lake, about .2 mile north of Norwalk Point. The spring is easily located in calm weather because of a "slick" formed on the surface. Fishermen have sunk poles into the bottom around the spring to tie their boats up.

Dive directly into the boil after tying your safety line to one of the poles and you'll emerge from the terrible visibility of the lake into clear spring water at a depth of 20 feet. At 40 feet there is a horizontal cave entrance, 25 feet by 12 feet. By pulling your way in against the strong current, you can swim into an exceptionally picturesque tunnel for about 100 feet before it ends in a tumble of boulders. The flow enters from several narrow crevices around the boulders which are too small for entry. One of the crevices issues salt water, creating eerie lighting effects.

There is absolutely no surface light coming through the dirty water over the spring. Lights and line must be used.

NO. 4 BEECHER SPRING

Location: From the town of Welaka, follow S-309 south for 5 miles to the fish hatchery. Turn left onto first dirt road past hatchery. Follow this road for about 1 mile to the spring.

FLORIDA STATE DIVE & SKI
YOUR COMPLETE DIVING CENTER

Learn the right way to dive from skilled professionals. Train on quality Scubapro equipment. Join exciting trips to the hottest dive spots. Get involved with advanced diving techniques through experienced instructors. See your Scubapro Dealer for all your diving needs. Look for the Scubapro "S" Symbol of the serious diver.

TRUST
THE BEST

Professional Instruction • Equipment • Repairs
Travel • Charters • Air • On Premise Heated Pool

OPEN 7 DAYS

380 E. Hwy. 436 Casselberry 305-831-3200

Beecher Spring provides interesting snorkeling in a clear sulfur spring surrounded by beautiful woods. The depth is about 15 feet at the spring boil. This is a good place to clean up after a dive at Croaker Hole.

NO. 5 SALT SPRINGS
Location: Just north of the intersection of S-19 and S-314 in the Ocala National Forest.

Salt Springs is a commercial spring that offers excellent family recreation. Three boils issue 53 m.g.d. which feed a five-mile run. Snorkeling is

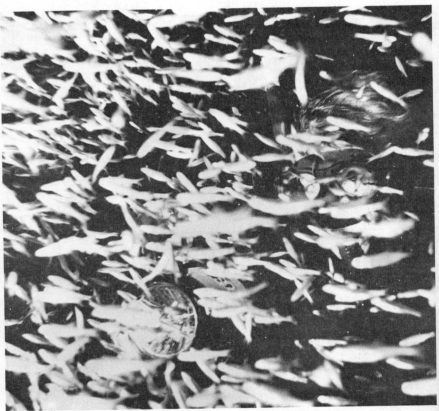

Diving at night in a Florida spring, explorers are engulfed by fish.

good around the small caves and crevices in the basin and down the run. There are many blue crabs and mullet in the area, as well as pleasant swimming in 75-degree water. The camping area near the spring has well-stocked concessions, with masks, fins, snorkels and Sea Scope belly boards for rent.

NO. 6 SILVER GLEN SPRINGS
Location: From the intersection of S-19 and S-40 in the Ocala National Forest.

travel 6.4 miles north on S-19. Turn east on a dirt road that runs under a large wooden archway (sign by the road).

This is a large spring area with two boils issuing a flow of 72 m.g.d. The cave on the north side of the spring drops to 39 feet, but it is closed to divers and swimmers. The main boil, located at the end of a wooden dock, drops 28 feet to a small cave. No SCUBA is allowed.

Silver Glen is a wonderland for the snorkeler. Hours can be spent exploring its grass beds and white sand floor. Fish are plentiful and easily approached. Relics have been found in the half-mile run to Lake George. It is a good area for family recreation, with a white sandy beach and a section roped off for swimmers. A boat and canoe rental service is provided at the office. The area also boasts four-and-a-half miles of wilderness camping along the lake, with several Indian shell mounds dating back 400 years. Sixteen small sand boils, called the Laughing Sands, are located along a small path which runs north from the spring. Cabins are available for rent, and there are many trailer and tent camping sites around the grounds.

NO. 7 JUNIPER SPRINGS
Location: From the intersection of S-19 and S-40 in the Ocala National Forest, travel west on S-40 for 4.7 miles to a sign at the entrance.

This is one of the oldest National Forest Recreation Areas in the east. Surrounded by beautiful semi-tropical scenery, the area offers excellent camping facilities. No SCUBA is allowed, but there is good snorkeling in the spring run. Canoes and concessions are available.

NO. 8 ALEXANDER SPRINGS
Location: From the intersection of S-19 and S-40 in the Ocala National Forest, travel east on S-40 for about 5 miles. Turn right at Alexander Springs sign, and go a short distance; turn right at the stop sign. After .5 mile, turn left on S-445 and go about 6 miles to the sign at the entrance.

JIM HOLLIS
SCUBA WORLD

SALES
SERVICE • RENTALS

One of Central Florida's largest facilities for group & individual training. 14 years of teaching at local YMCAs.

(305) 273-3373

Discounts to Disney, Sea World & Navy personnel. Major credit cards accepted.

5107 E. Colonial Dr., Orlando, FL 32807

Alexander Springs is a National Forest Recreation Area. There is an entrance fee, and all persons using SCUBA are checked for certification. The huge spring basin is fed 96 m.g.d. of clear water from a single cave located at a depth of 27 feet. The area surrounding the boil provides good snorkeling. A large covering of lily pads hide hundreds of bream, mullet and bass. A beautiful 15-mile run flows to the St. John's River, and provides good relic hunting. It is an excellent camping area with complete trailer connections and numerous tent sites.

NO. 9 PONCE DE LEON SPRINGS
Location: Just east of the town of de Leon Springs, which is 9 miles north of DeLand on US 17.

Once closed to diving, the spring has been reopened for open-water diving, but absolutely no cave diving is allowed. The 20-foot-deep basin is well-known for its wealth of Indian artifacts, fossils and legendary Spanish treasure.

NO. 10 BLUE SPRINGS-ORANGE CITY
Location: From Orange City, travel south on US 17. Turn west at the first caution light after crossing a railroad bridge. The paved road will turn south, but continue straight onto the dirt road for .2 mile to the spring.

Blue Springs is now a state park with strict diving regulations. This large spring issues 121 m.g.d. Its shaft starts at 15 feet and drops 50 feet, where it narrows and continues down at a steep angle to 125 feet. An exceptionally high velocity of water makes it impossible to go deeper.

Fossil shells, shark teeth and plenty of fish are found in the .5 mile run to the St. John's River. In winter, Blue Springs is one of the few places sea cows can be observed by divers.

NO. 11 WEKIWA SPRINGS
Location: From the town of Apopka, travel east on US 441 for 1 mile. Turn left on S-436 and go 1.5 miles. Then turn left on the paved road, and go 2.9 miles to sign on left of road.

The spring is now part of a state park. No SCUBA is allowed. There are two springs in a kidney-shaped pool which measures 120 feet in diameter and attains a depth of 20 feet. The flow is measured at 44 m.g.d., and the water temperature is 75 degrees. The run is one of the headwaters of the Wekiwa River, a tributary of the St. John's.

NO. 12 ROCK SPRINGS
Location: From Apopka, go north on S-436 for 5.8 miles to the dead end at Bay Ridge-Rock Springs Road. Turn right (east) and travel .4 mile to Kelly Park entrance and the springs.

This spectacular spring emerges from the partially air-filled cave at the base of a high limestone cliff. Unfortunately, a grating prevents access into the spring cave. The long 1.5-mile run is picturesque, and has many plants and fish which provides hours of interesting snorkeling.

NO. 13 APOPKA SPRING

Location: In the southwest section of Lake Apopka, near a narrow arm of land called "Gourd Neck." From the small town of Oakland (about 10 miles west of Orlando), go west for 3.7 miles on S-438. Turn right onto sand road that runs through an orange grove. Continue for .5 mile until the road ends. The spring is 150 yards north of road's end. It might be best to go by boat from the Gourd Neck Fish Camp. Murky surface water nearly always covers the spring area, so watch for the boil.

The soft, debris-strewn lake bottom slopes gradually like a bowl to the spring vent at a depth of 35 feet. Since the water may not be clear until you reach the cave, it is best to tie a line to a float in the center of the boil and descend straight down into the spring. The narrow (two feet by three feet) spring vent opens into a beautiful sloping cavern, 25 feet wide and 50 feet long, and goes to a depth of 80 feet. This must be considered an advanced cave dive because of the complete absence of light, the debris covering the surface, and the large amount of lost monofilament line and hooks.

KINGSLEY LAKE SPRING (Not on map)

Location: In Kingsley Lake in Clay County, just out from Strickland's Landing.

This spring contains very clear water and reaches a depth of about 45 feet. The spring opening is too narrow to enter. The lake itself is reasonably clear, with visibility of about 20 feet and a depth falling off evenly to 85 feet in the middle.

- Open 6 Days
- Only Legal Access to 40 Fathom Sink
- Air • Rental
- Professional Guide Service
- Scuba Schools International
- Trainers of Four Deep Diving World Record Holders Listed in the Guinness Book of World Records
- Instructor Training Center.

WANT TO BE AN ADVANCED OPEN WATER INSTRUCTOR?

Contact Hal Watts,

Instructor Trainer for Scuba Schools International (SSI)

2219 E. Colonial Dr., Orlando, FL (305) 896-4541

WEST COAST

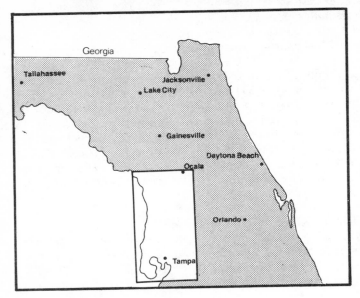

Spring Diving Locations

1. Rainbow River
2. Nichols Spring
3. Crystal River
4. Chassahowitzka River Springs
5. Joe's Sink
6. Weeki Wachi Run
6. Hospital Hole
7. Saw Grass Spring
8. Palm Sink
9. Blue Sink-Pinellas Co.
10. Blue Sink Syphon
11. Sulfur Spring
12. Crystal Springs
13. Lithia Spring

Area Information

Large springs, sinks and spring-fed rivers are common along Florida's west coast. Good diving conditions generally remain constant throughout the year. However, a few sinkholes sometimes become problematic due to algae growth during the summer months. Crystal River, located just off US 19, is one of the world's most popular freshwater dives. Water visibility remains superb throughout the year, providing exciting diving for both novice and experienced divers. Air and divers' supplies are available in Crystal River, Tampa, St. Petersburg, Clearwater, Ocala, Zephyrhills and Lakeland. Rainbow River and Chassahowitzka River must also be considered as two of Florida's best freshwater diving attractions.

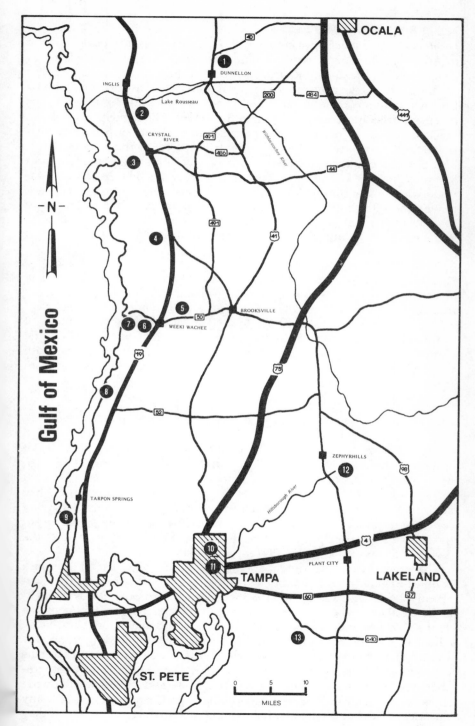

Gulf of Mexico

OCALA

DUNNELLON

INGLIS

Lake Rousseau

CRYSTAL RIVER

Withlacoochee River

BROOKSVILLE

WEEKI WACHEE

ZEPHYRHILLS

TARPON SPRINGS

Hillsborough River

PLANT CITY

TAMPA

LAKELAND

ST. PETE

0 5 10

MILES

NO. 1 RAINBOW RIVER

Location: From Dunnelon, go north on US 41 4.5 miles past overpass. Turn east (right) on paved road and travel 1.2 miles (past railroad tracks). Turn left and go .7 mile to K.P. Hole County Recreation Area.

This is a large, clear river that runs for five and a half miles from Rainbow Springs to the Withlacoochee River. The area around the headsprings (once a tourist attraction) is closed to the public. The headsprings can be reached by boat, which can be launched from the boat ramp at the recreational area. It is a two-and-a-half-mile trip upriver to the springs. Rainbow Springs is a large basin fed by many sand boils. Depths range from seven to 30 feet. The water is crystal clear, making this a good area for underwater photography. After diving the headsprings, you can drift back downriver with your boat, and either snorkel or use SCUBA. There are several smaller boils located along the river bottom. Relic hunting is good and fish are abundant. Depths range from 10 to 20 feet.

NO. 2 NICHOLS SPRING

Location: From US 19 south of Inglis, turn east on the first paved road south of the large group of power lines which are found just south of barge canal. The road angles sharply back north. Follow signs to boat ramp at the power dam.

There are actually two springs located in the river between the boat ramp and the dam. Their boils can be spotted easily from the shore. The closest spring is Nichols; the other is called Fire Hydrant Spring. Both provide interesting diving. Numerous fossils have been recovered from around the spring area and down the river.

NO. 3 CRYSTAL RIVER

Location: In the town of Crystal River along US 19, which runs down Florida's west coast.

Crystal River is truly one of the finest freshwater dives in the world. Although there are 30 known springs and sinks in the King's Bay area, only eight areas are of consequence to the diver. The springs are all located in King's Bay and connecting canals. A boat is needed to dive in the bay and canals, and they can be rented from one of four fully-equipped diving concessions on the bay. It is only a short boat trip to the springs from any of the shops. As the springs are little-affected by the wind, rain or tides, the diving is always good, with 100-foot plus visibility common.

The largest and most popular spring is King's Spring, just off the south bank of Banana Island. Anchor your boat in four feet of water that surrounds the spring. The spring is 75 feet across, dropping almost straight down to 30 feet, where you will find two entrances to a cave that goes to a depth of 60 feet and back about 50 feet. Inside the cave, your eyes quickly adjust to the dimness, and you'll have no problem finding your way around. The sunlight cuts its way through the clear water and streams inside the cave, creating a breathtaking sight. The underwater photographer will be in paradise among the bold cliffs and crevices. Silhouette shots are spectacular. Fish are always on hand and easy to approach. Many varieties of fresh and saltwater fish are common to the river. In winter they are attracted by the warm 72-degree water. In addition to bass and bream, the spring is filled with mullet, trout, redfish, sheepshead, gar, snook, tarpon and snapper. Spearfishing is illegal.

Just west of King's Spring is Grand Canyon Spring. It is a 35-foot-long crack in the rock at a depth of 25 feet. A strong flow issues from a three-foot hole at the west end of the canyon.

Mullet's Gullet, located 100 feet east of King's Spring, is a series of several small springs in 20 feet of water. The flow comes from crevices in the smooth rock bottom. The clear water of the area and shallow depths make this an ideal locale for the underwater photographer to get some great shots.

Shark Sink is located on the west side of the bay, about 100 feet out from a dock running off a land point. Two holes angle down to 45 feet. A strong flow comes from the bottom of the springs. There are no caves. The area around the holes is shallow and thick with aquatic plants.

Idiot's Delight is a group of three vertical shafts located in a canal system on the east side of the bay. They start in eight feet of water and drop straight down 20 feet. The largest shaft is about four feet in diameter. The water is unusually clear around the springs, and fish are plentiful. The land surrounding the springs is private, so stay with your boat.

Three Sisters Springs is a group of five springs situated a few hundred feet north of Idiot's Delight. Depths range from 18 to 25 feet.

Gator Hole is located in the canal system on the east side of the bay. Go under the bridge and to the second canal on the left, just out from a concrete dock. Gator

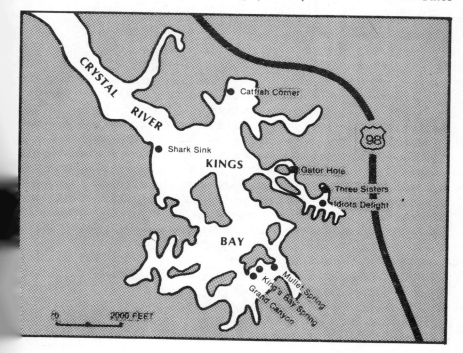

Hole is the entrance to an extensive cave system that reportedly collapsed in 1963, shutting off the passage. You can still dive into the entrance room to a depth of 35 feet. This is a good place to spot manatees in the winter, and there is always an abundance of fish around.

Catfish Corner is near the shore on the north side of the bay, just out from a wooden dock. A hole, four feet in diameter, starts in 15 feet of water and opens into a ten by 20 foot room. It is home to hundreds of catfish of various sizes. An underwater light is not necessary, but the dive will be more enjoyable if you bring one along.

There are other types of diving activities in King's Bay outside the spring areas. Underwater relic hunting is found a good three miles down-river from King's Spring on the north side of the river, just out from the 30-foot high Indian mounds at the archaeological zone. Arrowheads, bone tools and bits of broken pottery are commonly found along the rock bottom. Four miles farther downriver is a shell island with two Indian mounds. This is a good spot to camp for those who want to get away from it all. The water is still clear this far downriver. From May to November, scallops may be taken by divers in the estuary and Gulf. Oysters may also be taken in months that have "R" in them.

Crystal River is famous for its herds of sea cows (manatees) that come upriver in December and stay around the springs throughout the winter. One winter, there were more than 40 of the huge, warm-blooded mammals counted. The average cow measures eight to ten feet in length and is perfectly harmless. A sea cow is very timid, especially when several divers are in an area. Because they are scared of SCUBA, approach them only while snorkeling. Swim slowly over the animal and wait for him to come up to you. Be gentle: if the manatee doesn't come to you, be satisfied to view him from a distance.

The manatee was officially designated an endangered species in 1967. Laws against harassment of the animals are strictly enforced by the state's Department of Natural Resources in the King's Bay area between November 15 and March 31 of each year. Harassment is defined in the Endangered Species Act as "An intentional or negligent act or omission which creates the likelihood of injury to wildlife by annoying it to such an extent as to significantly disrupt normal behavioral patterns which include, but are not limited to, feeding or sheltering." Aggressive pursuit of the manatee by a boat or diver affects the normal behavior of the animals and may cause injury to them by exposing them to cold water temperatures if they are forced to flee. This would be considered a violation of the Endangered Species Act. It is most important to travel slowly and keep a sharp lookout for manatees. They like to rest just under the water's surface, so look carefully when operating a motorboat.

NO. 4 CHASSAHOWITZKA RIVER SPRINGS
Location: 14 miles south of Crystal River, or 7 miles south of Homosassa Springs. On US 19, turn west on S-480. Follow the road for 1.9 miles as it curves through the small town of Chassahowitzka and ends at a fish camp.

Experience Crystal River

(Winter home of the Manatee)

THROUGH THE

Plantation Inn **& Golf Resort**

• a Total Sports facility •

Phone: 904-795-4211 (Dive Shop 795-5797)

- COMPLETE PRO DIVE SHOP
- RENTAL BOATS/DIVE SYSTEMS
- COMPRESSED AIR
- 5 DAY BASIC CERTIFICATION COURSE
- OPEN WATER CHECK-OUT DIVES
- 5 MINUTES AWAY FROM BANANA ISLAND

ASK ABOUT OUR SCUBA SAFARI PACKAGE

A "4 STAR MOBIL AWARD" HOTEL.

Tennis • Fishing • Fine Dining • Golf

The clear Chassahowitzka (Chassa-witz-ka) River, fed by more than a dozen freshwater springs, is one of Florida's most beautiful and unspoiled wildlife refuges. The shallow-water stream meanders through a primitive cypress and hardwood forest on its way to the Gulf. Numerous spring-fed creeks branch off into forgotten woodlands. Divers, canoeists, nature lovers, and adventurers will be spellbound by its majesty. Bass, bream, mullet, catfish, turtles, eels, crab, egrets, herons, pelicans, ospreys, hawks, cormorants and wild ducks live here in profusion.

At Crystal River, fish are always on hand and easy to approach.

The main spring, Devil's Punch Bowl, is located about 50 yards from the fish camp. It has depths to 30 feet and a constant 74-degree temperature.

From the main spring, continue downstream for 200 yards until you spot the large Crab Creek run on the right. Continue up the run 300 yards to Crab Creek Springs, a series of three saline boils in scenic limestone shafts. The flow emerges from openings too narrow for entry. Depths are to 20 feet with visibility about 40 feet most of the year. There's great crabbing for large blue crabs in the eel grass along the run.

Two hundred yards downriver from Crab Creek is Houseboat Springs. A series of crystal clear boiling springs is found in a 200-foot-diameter bay adjoining the river on the left (south) bank. There is picturesque diving with large schools of fish in the underwater hydrilla forest surrounding the springs. Maximum depth is 20 feet.

Blue Springs is at the head of half-mile-long Blue Creek. The mouth of Blue Creek enters the river 200 yards downstream from Houseboat Springs. The

DIVE CRYSTAL RIVER
WITH PALMETTO SCUBA
PORT PARADISE
DIVE SHOP
P. O. BOX 2532, CRYSTAL RIVER, FLA.

*BOAT AND CANOE RENTALS AVAILABLE FOR DIVING IN
THE CLEAR, WARM AND CALM SPRINGS OF CRYSTAL RIVER*

 Complete Dive Shop Facilities
Sales, Service and Rentals
5000 PSI Electric Compressor
5 Day Learn to Dive Week
6 Day Open Water Certification

DIVE WITH THE MANATEE OR OBSERVE THEM
FROM OUR GLASS BOTTOM BOAT—TOURS DAILY
(MANATEE SEASON—NOV. thru APRIL)

To Accommodate You
PORT PARADISE HOTEL
P. O. BOX 2532, CRYSTAL RIVER, FLA. 32629
Restaurant and Lounge
(904) 795-3111

A free diver enjoys clear Rainbow Springs.

narrow, fast-moving run winds its way through a subtropical jungle tee
ing with sights and sounds of wildlife. The large Blue Springs basin is
feet in depth. Water flow issues from numerous tiny cracks in the bedro
floor. Visibility is limited to 30 feet. The cloudiness of the blue water is d
to a form of brown algae. Nevertheless, the spring is quite an interesti
dive. There is a large sunken boat to explore. The good people at the f
camp take canoeists to Blue Springs for the start of an easy, scenic, fo
hour trip back to the main spring area. What a way to spend a lazy summ
afternoon in Florida!

Uncle Paul's Sink *was discovered by divers in 1982. It is found in a small bay*
the west side of the run, 300 yards below Blue Spring. It is a dramatic fissu

25 feet long by ten feet wide, that makes a sheer drop from five to 60 feet. The side walls spread slightly as the diver descends. Visibility is about 40 feet in the saltwater below the upper ten feet of cloudy fresh water.

Three Sister Springs is made up of three beautiful, freshwater boils in a clear run 100 yards upstream from the main spring. Depths are to 20 feet in the well-lit shafts. The springs are about 50 feet apart.

The clean, modern fish camp provides many services, including a boat ramp, boat dockage, canoe and shallow-draft boat rentals, gas, bait, ice, groceries and more. They also operate a campground and canoe trail service.

NO. 5 JOE'S SINK

Location: From US 19 at Weeki Wachee, turn east on S-50 and travel 2 miles. There are two sinks located 30 yards off the side of the highway and about 50 yards past the power lines. They are in an open area and can be seen easily from the highway.

The waters of Joe's Sink offer the coldest freshwater dive in the state. The temperature drops from the 70s on the surface to the low 60s as you descend to the bottom.

The sink has a peanut-shaped appearance on the surface, with the non-connecting sinks resting at each end. The west sink has a neck about ten feet in diameter which widens to 30 feet at the bottom, in 45 feet of water. The walls have a crater-like surface. Natural light vanishes at 30 feet in both sinks.

at Crystal Lodge Motel

Open 7 days a week
Boat and Scuba Rental

Post Office Box 456
U.S. 19 and 98 North
Crystal River, Florida 32629
Phone (904) 795-6798

"A Sportsman's and Diver's Paradise"
On the Beautiful Crystal River

CRYSTAL LODGE MOTEL

&

Swiss Inn Restaurant

All Major Credits Cards
and Personal Checks accepted

Luxurious units
and kitchenettes available.

Located on U.S. Hwy 19 North on the banks of the "Sparkling Crystal River." Dining room, cocktail lounge, color TV with H.B.O., air conditioning, and room phones.

Enjoy our own private dock, launching ramp, boats, guides, skin diving, water skiing, shuffleboard and fresh water pool.

U.S. 19 & 98 NORTH, CRYSTAL RIVER, FLORIDA 32629
TEL. (904) 795-3171

The east sink is similar in shape, but drops to a depth of 75 feet and is larger in diameter at the floor.

NO. 6 WEEKI WACHEE RUN
Location: Turn west off US 19 onto S-50 at Weeki Wachee. Go 3.6 miles to S-595. Turn south and go 1.5 miles to the bridge (Rogers Park).

At the park, there is a white sand beach and boat ramp. There are no boats for rent, so you must bring your own or catch a ride on one going upstream. Go to the private property line near Weeki Wachee and snorkel or tube back down the run. This very clear water runs for ten miles to the Gulf.

NO. 6 HOSPITAL HOLE
Location: From Rogers Park on Weeki Wachee run, swim or take a boat upstream about 300 yards.

A large crevice of bone white limestone opens on the south side of the run in about eight feet of water and drops to depths of 155 feet. From the 90-foot level on, there is a tea-colored layer of hydrogen sulfide gas which has an unpleasant odor and taste. Because of the depths and hydrogen sulfide layer, this must be considered an advanced cave dive.

NO. 7 SAW GRASS SPRING
Location: From the junction of US 19 and S-50 in Weeki Wachee, go west on S-50 about 5 miles to an inn on the left. 150 yards past the inn, turn left onto a dirt road and travel .1 mile. Turn right on small dirt road and continue for 100 yards to the spring.

This is a beautiful little spring filled with waving sawgrass. Depths are to 20 feet. There is saltwater in the spring, and visibility is usually 40 feet.

NO. 8 PALM SINK
Location: From the junction of US 19 and S-52 south of Hudson, travel north on US 19 for 1 mile. Pull off to the left side of the road (west) just before the highway bears to the right. The sink is located just behind a highway guard rail.

Palm Sink has depths to 45 feet. An overhang on the south side can be penetrated only a short distance. Due to the depths involved, this must be considered an advanced cave dive.

NO. 9 BLUE SINK-PINELLAS CO.
Location: Travel .8 mile north of the town of Palm Harbor on Alt. US 19. Turn right on a small dirt road just before the Palm Gardens Motel. Go up a small hill and take the first dirt road on the right and park.

The surface pond is just over 100 feet in diameter. The sink depths start at 15 feet and drop vertically to 150 feet. A small tunnel is located at 95 feet. The tunnel is extremely narrow and silty.

Blue Sink is known for its strata of water with different chemical contents. The first 100 feet is freshwater. From 100 to 125 feet, there is a layer containing hydrogen sulfide. The bottom is saltwater.

NO. 10 BLUE SINK SYPHON

Location: In Tampa, turn west off Interstate 75 onto Fowler Avenue. Travel 1 mile. Just before reaching the culvert you will see a vacant lot off to the left. Park and follow trail to the sink.

A large syphon has formed an oval pool measuring 150 by 80 feet, with depths to 100 feet. Visibility is usually very good. Neither cave can be penetrated because of the large amount of old tires that long ago filled the openings.

NO. 11 SULFUR SPRING

Location: In north Tampa, in the suburb of Sulfur Springs. Turn off Nebraska Avenue (US 41) just north of Hillsborough River.

The spring is enclosed by a concrete wall. Depths range from 20 to 30 feet, with average visibility 20 to 30 feet.

NO. 12 CRYSTAL SPRINGS

Location: Follow S-39 5 miles south of Zephyrhills to the town of Crystal Springs. The spring is located just west of town.

Several springs that form the headwaters of the Hillsborough River have been dammed to form a clear pool with depths from ten to 15 feet. 65 m.g.d. issue from the group of springs. The year-'round temperature is 74 degrees. The combination of clear water, aquatic plant life and numerous fish provides a great setting for the underwater photographer. A nice picnic area is located near the springs.

NO. 13 LITHIA SPRING

Location: From Brandon, located 8 miles west of Tampa on S-60, turn south on S-674. In 6 miles, cross the Alafia River and continue .5 mile to springs.

Lithia is a very clear spring with shallow depths that offer excellent snorkeling around the boil area and down the clear run to the Alafia River. A nice picnic area is adjacent to the springs.

SCUBA INSTRUCTION

AIR STATION

THE DIVER'S LOCKER, INC.
3088 N.W. Blitchton Road
Hwy. 27 • Ocala, Florida 32675

SCUBA
Sales • Service • Rental
Search & Recovery • Commercial Diving

DIVE TRIPS
(904) 622-4550
"WE SELL FUN"

SOUTH TALLAHASSEE

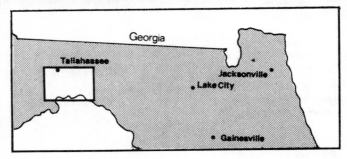

Spring Diving Locations

1. Gopher Hole Sink
2. Little Dismal Sink
3. Big Dismal Sink
4. Upper River Sinks
5. Fish Sink
6. Promise and Go-Between Sinks
7. West Hole Sink
8. Wakulla Spring
9. Cherokee Sink
10. Wakulla River
11. Osgood Sink
12. Wacissa River Springs

Area Information

A series of large, deep sinkholes surrounded by high steep walls typif[ ] the diving locations found south of Tallahassee. Underwater exploration o[ ] these sinks is both interesting and exciting. Poor visibility and bad siltin[ ] conditions are common, requiring extreme caution from all divers.

Located 14 miles south of Tallahassee is Wakulla Springs, one of th[ ] world's largest and deepest springs. It is commercially operated, wit[ ] glass-bottom boat trips offered. Scuba diving is not allowed. The diver wi[ ] have to be satisfied to view the spectacle from a boat or to snorkel over th[ ] huge basin.

Unfortunately, Natural Bridge Spring is now closed off to divers.

Located east of Tallahassee is the beautiful spring-fed Wacissa Rive[ ] This is a popular area for combining a canoeing-diving-camping trip. Th[ ] 14-mile canoe trail winds through some of Florida's most beautif[ ] countryside.

Divers will find three excellent locations to buy air in Tallahasse[ ] Motels, restaurants and camping facilities are plentiful.

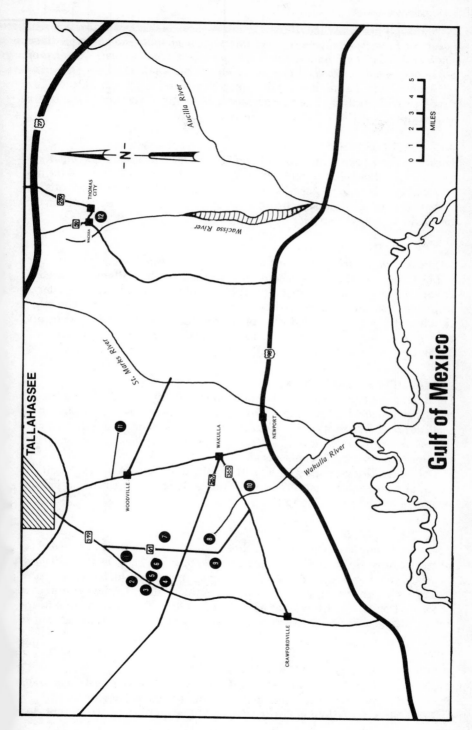

TALLAHASSEE

Gulf of Mexico

Aucilla River

Wacissa River

St. Marks River

Wakulla River

THOMAS CITY

WACISSA

WOODVILLE

WAKULLA

NEWPORT

CRAWFORDVILLE

0 1 2 3 4 5

MILES

N

NO. 1 GOPHER HOLE SINK

Location: From Four Points (a main intersection in south Tallahassee), travel south on US 319 for 6.6 miles (or .6 mile past C-260 intersection). Turn left off S-319 onto small dirt road. Bear right .1 mile to the sink.

Gopher Hole is a small sink with steep banks and depths to 100 feet. Two caves provide only a short penetration in either direction. This site is known locally as Oak Ridge Blue Sink.

NO. 2 LITTLE DISMAL SINK

Location: From Four Points, go south on US 319 for 7.3 miles (or 1.3 miles past C-260 intersection). Turn right (west) onto dirt road. Wind to the right at the first fork and bear left at the second fork. The sink is .6 mile from the highway.

A large cave is located on the northwest wall. A 400-foot penetration can be made at a maximum depth of 60 feet.

NO. 3 BIG DISMAL SINK

Location: Follow dirt road .2 mile west from Little Dismal Sink.

Big Dismal is the most recent sink formed in the Tallahassee area. It collapsed into the aquifer just after the turn of the century. The very large, impressive sink is surrounded by steep walls. There is no easy way to get down to the water. Most divers bring rope ladders for the descent and ascent. An overhang is located 85 feet below the surface on the north wall. It can be penetrated for about 100 feet.

NO. 4 UPPER RIVER SINKS

Location: From Four Points, go southwest on US 319 for 10 miles. Turn left (east) on first graded dirt road past River Sink Grocery. Go .4 mile before turning left on small dirt road (bad road, watch for deep ruts and loose sand). Go another .4 mile before turning left once again. Continue for .8 mile, turning right at small dirt crossroad. Sinks are 100 yards ahead.

This is a kidney-shaped sink with depths to 40 feet. A spring is on the north end and a syphon on the south. Lower River Sink is now on private property and inaccessible to the public.

NO. 5 FISH SINK

Location: Follow directions to Upper River Sinks, except bear left instead of right at the last turn. Go .5 mile. Sink basin can be seen as a depression about 30 yards to the left (west). Look for a rope swing hanging from a limb high over the water.

This is another spring-syphon with depths to 50 feet. The syphon cave is located on the south wall at a depth of 30 feet. The spring runs to the north. Because of the cave's depth, this must be considered an advanced cave dive.

NO. 6 PROMISE AND GO-BETWEEN SINKS

Location: Follow directions to Fish Sink but look for depression to your right (east) of dirt road. You can drive up to Promise, but the going gets rough.

Promise is a shallow sink (depths to 30 feet) with a short 35-foot dive under a natural bridge to Go-Between Sink.

Go-Between is even more shallow than Promise (depths from five feet to 25 feet). The cave leads to a big room that starts 150 feet back. A foot trail running east leads to about 12 other small sinks. Nearly everyone snorkels these areas rather than lug tanks through the woods.

NO. 7 WEST HOLE SINK

Location: From Four Points in Tallahassee, go south on US 319 to S-61. Two miles south of Wakulla Co. line, turn left on sand road (.1 mile past white fence on right side of S-61). Bear left for 300 yards to the sink. Enter water about midway on west side of sink.

The sink depths vary from 45 to 80 feet. A 150-foot ledge with a 110-foot penetration is located on the sink's south side. The bottom is very silty and the limestone walls are much softer than they appear. Please do not disturb the many saltwater fossils in the limestone walls.

NO. 8 WAKULLA SPRING

Location: 14 miles south of Tallahassee on S-61, turn left on Wakulla Spring Road.

This is one of the largest and deepest springs in the world. It is commercially operated with glass-bottomed boat trips going over the tremendous boil and down the river. A huge cave opening, over 100 feet wide, begins at a depth of 125 feet and drops to 185 feet, discharging 183 m.g.d. and feeding the beautiful Wakulla River. As no SCUBA is allowed, the diver

THE
SCUBA
DISCOVERY

TALLAHASSEE'S PROFESSIONAL DIVE STORE

TALLAHASSEE'S ONLY PADI TRAINING FACILITY

- *Knives, lights, gloves, mesh bags, etc.*
- *Complete lines of name brand diving gear*
- *Local and Caribbean dive trips and charters*
- *Open-water & advanced open-water dive courses*
- *Professional repairs • Spearfishing equipment*
- *Friendly, professional services • Specialty courses*

220-F W. THARPE ST. (next to Burger King)
TALLAHASSEE, FLORIDA 32303   PHONE (904) 386-PADI (7234)

will have to be satisfied to view the spectacle from a boat. It is a sight that he will long remember. There is a swimming area with a picnic table, and a large hotel with snack bar and dining room.

NO. 9 CHEROKEE SINK
Location: Directly across S-61 from entrance to Wakulla Spring, follow the dirt road for .1 mile; then bear left for 1 mile to a small trail running off to the sink on the right.

Troy Springs paddle-wheeler wreck.

Cherokee Sink is a large sink with thick woods surrounding the area. Depths go to 80 feet. There is little of interest, with visibility generally medium to poor, and a lot of trash in the water.

NO. 10 WAKULLA RIVER

Location: This is a clear river fed by Wakulla Spring. Enter at the US 219 bridge.

There is wonderful snorkeling through eel grass and over the white sand bottom here. There is also good canoeing, with relics and fossils hidden under the sands.

NO. 11 OSGOOD SINK

Location: Travel south from south Tallahassee's S-319 Truck Rt. on S-363 for 4½ miles. Turn left (east) onto Rhodes Cemetery Road and continue for 3 miles. The sink is about 20 feet to the right of the road.

Osgood provides an exciting dive with depths to 100 feet. A large ledge entrance is located on the east side of the sink. Maximum penetration is about 100 feet. Many fossils can be seen in the limestone walls, including concentric rings of prehistoric trees. This is usually the first sink to clear after periods of high water.

NO. 12 WACISSA RIVER SPRINGS

Location: From Tallahassee, travel east on US 27 about 20 miles. Turn right on S-59, continuing south for 4 miles to the S-259 intersection. Stay on S-59 for 1.7 miles to the headspring. When S-59 makes a sharp right turn, continue straight for .5 mile to the river.

A beautiful, primitive river fed by many springs flows south to its junction with the Aucilla River and forms the path for a 14-mile canoe trail. Big Spring, Garner Spring, Blue Spring, Buzzard Log Spring, Minnow Spring, Cassidy Spring and others form the head of the river. All these areas can be explored using a small boat or canoe. There are five camping areas along the river, and the bottom provides excellent relic hunting. There is a sand boat ramp and swimming area at the headspring.

COMPLETE RETAIL, RENTAL, REPAIR & HYDRO SERVICE
Scuba Instruction

DIXIE
DIVIN' SHOPPE

2015 N. Monroe St.
Tallahassee, Fla. 32303
904-385-1640

 SCUBAPRO

 SEAPRO

 NASDS

We Specialize in Underwater Photography.

—DIVE TRIP SERVICES—

PANHANDLE

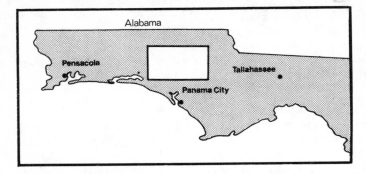

Spring Diving Locations

1. Merrit's Mill Pond/Blue Springs
1. Twin Caves
1. Shangri La Spring
1. Indian Washtub
1. Gator Spring
2. Blue Hole
3. Bozell Springs

4. Gadsden Spring
5. Cypress Spring
6. Becton Spring
7. Blue Spring-Holmes Creek
8. Vortex Blue Spring
9. Ponce de Leon Spring
10. Morrison Spring

Area Information

Because of their close proximity, the springs located in the Florida Panhandle have long been popular dives for the many sport divers in the surrounding southern states. Morrison Spring, Vortex Blue Spring and Merrit's Mill Pond are easily located and generally provide excellent diving conditions. A few of the other locations may be difficult to reach by car during the summer months because of poor roads and frequent rains. Underwater relic hunting is at its best in the spring-fed Chipola River and Holmes Creek. Large, prehistoric shark teeth and arrowheads are common discoveries for patient collectors. Air and divers' supplies can be found in Pensacola, Fort Walton Beach, Panama City, Vortex Blue Spring, Morrison Spring and Dotham, Alabama.

NO. 1 MERRIT'S MILL POND/BLUE SPRINGS
Location: From the courthouse square in Marianna, travel east on US 90 for 1.
miles. Turn left on S-71 and go 1.1 miles and turn right onto S-164. After 3.
miles, turn right at Blue Springs sign.

The pond is a large body of clear spring water that starts at Blue Spring

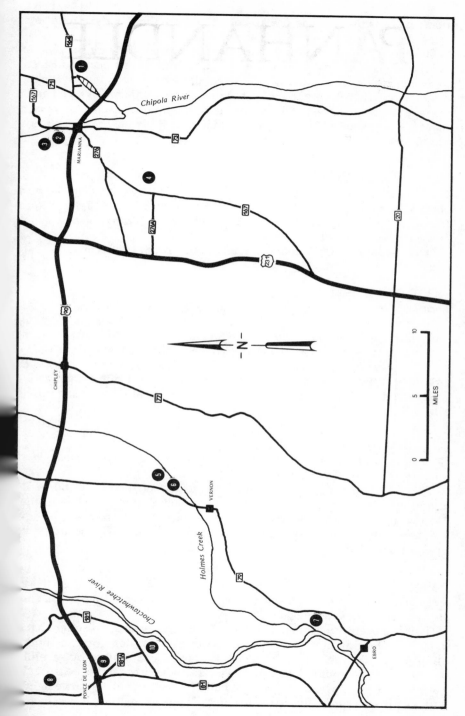

PANHANDLE

Chipola River

Chipola River
Choctawhatchee River
Holmes Creek

MARIANNA
CHIPLEY
VERNON
EBRO
PONCE DE LEON

N

MILES
0   5   10

1
2
3
4
5
6
7
8
9
10

pool and runs five miles to US 90. Both banks are lined with large cypress trees, making this a very picturesque locale.

Blue Springs is commercially operated from May through September. Admission is 25¢. Picnic tables and a large bathhouse are located adjacent to the spring. No scuba diving is allowed in the head pool, but snorkeling is permitted. SCUBA is allowed in the rest of the pond area, which has an average depth of 15 feet. The bottom is covered with patches of aquatic plants, and fish are plentiful. Areas of Merrit's Mill Pond worth exploring are as follows:

NO. 1 TWIN CAVES

Location: .5 mile downstream from Blue. You can get to the caves by boat from Hasty's Fish Camp, located .7 mile west on S-164 from Blue Springs Road (watch for the sign), or by snorkeling 250 yards east of Baptizing Landing, which is .5 mile west of the Blue Springs Road.

Two openings, 20 feet apart, connect with a room at 30 feet.

NO. 1 SHANGRI LA SPRING

Location: Shangri La is located on the northwest side of the pond about 400 yards below Blue Spring, at the base of a 15-foot limestone cliff. Anchor in the pond, away from the private property adjacent to the area.

Very clear water boils from a shaft two feet in diameter at a depth of five feet. The cave opens into a room 15 by 20 feet that slopes down to a depth of 25 feet. Water issues from a small slit at the deepest point. Shangri La offers good photographic possibilities if you are careful not to stir up the silt.

NO. 1 INDIAN WASHTUB

Location: On the northwest side of the pond, directly across from Twin Caves and just above Baptizing Landing.

This is an interesting area with depths to 20 feet. The water normally drains into tiny cracks in the bedrock and presumably exits at Hole-in-the-Wall Spring, nearly a mile away. During periods of heavy rainfall, the flow reverses, causing milky water to stream into the pond. This is a favorite spot for large black bass.

NO. 1 GATOR SPRING

Location: Found on the southeast side of the pond, 3 miles below Washtub and directly across from the public boat ramp.

This is a beautiful, unusual and fun dive. The cave itself is somewhat a rarity in Florida in that it is partially out of the water. You can snorkel more than 100 yards into the crystal clear cavern waters by careful running a line through the air pockets. Be sure to bring lights because the cave makes a sharp bend to the right halfway back and all entrance light lost. Depths vary from five to ten feet in the cavern stream. It is best to sta away from the floor because of its deep layer of silt. Large turtles are commonly sighted at the cave's entrance and, if you're lucky, you might spot an alligator.

The pond is dammed at US 90, forming a beautiful clear spring run that flows for about one mile to the Chipola River.

NO. 2 BLUE HOLE
Location: Florida Caverns State Park, 3 miles north of Marianna on S-167.

Blue Hole is a large spring area with a run to the Chipola River. Skin and scuba diving are allowed. A bathhouse and picnic area, as well as camping areas, are located near the spring. Be sure to take time to see the beautiful topside caverns while visiting the park.

Photo opportunities abound in Florida's clear springs.

NO. 3 BOZELL SPRINGS
Location: Bozell actually consists of four separate clear springs in a line bisecting the Chipola River. To reach the springs, launch a boat at the ramp in Florida Caverns State Park and go about 1 mile upstream until you see the run from the main spring coming into the river on the right.

Spring I is a vertical fissure in a small bay on the west side of the river. It has a strong flow and depths are from ten to 15 feet. Spring II is located at the bottom of the river and also has a strong outflow. Spring III, found in a bay on the east side, is more moderate in flow and is normally covered with duckweed (tiny green surface plants).

Spring IV is, by far, the most interesting. It is located at the head of a 200-yard run where a very small, silty cave opens at a depth of 15 feet. Avoid tying your boat up to private property surrounding the springs.

NO. 4 GADSDEN SPRING

Location: From Marianna, travel 4 miles southwest on S-275. Turn south (left) on S-167 and go 2 miles to a Standard Station. Turn left on dirt road across from the station and go .4 mile and turn right on first dirt road. Stay on this road for .9 mile to fork. Bear left at fork and continue .5 mile to spring.

The spring pool is 25 yards in diameter. The surface water is not very clear due to the lack of flow, but visibility improves with descent. A large limestone cliff drops 50 feet to a large cave entrance.

NO. 5 CYPRESS SPRING

Location: From Vernon, travel north on S-79 for 3 miles. Turn right on sand road just before the concrete bridge and go 4 miles to sharp left turn in the road. Park at turn and follow footpath 200 yards through a swamp to the spring.

A large series of boils fill a crystal clear pool which is about 175 feet wide. Cypress Springs provides some of the world's clearest water, which holds many logs, and a great variety of plants and fish. Depths are to 25 feet in boils. The run goes .3 mile to Holmes Creek, but is generally too shallow for snorkeling.

NO. 6 BECTON SPRING

Location: From Vernon, go north on S-79 for 1.9 miles. Turn east on sand road and travel .5 mile to spring.

Becton is a large spring, about 100 feet in diameter, with a flow of 32 m.g.d. and depths to 35 feet. The flow issues from crevices between giant boulders. This long, shallow run holds many plants and fish.

NO. 7 BLUE SPRING-HOLMES CREEK

Location: From Vernon, travel south on S-79 for 13.8 miles. Turn right on the dirt road (next to telephone pole with a large white box at the base) and continue .5 mile to spring.

This is a small spring surrounded by a growth of cypress knees. A small scenic run winds its way to nearby Holmes Creek. The maximum depth is 35 feet at a small cave entrance.

NO. 8 VORTEX BLUE SPRING

Location: From the junction of S-81 and US 90 in the town of Ponce de Leon, go 3.4 miles north on S-81. Turn right on the dirt road (by Vortex Blue Spring sign and go about 1 mile. Turn left at the second sign. Continue on a short distance to the spring.

Vortex Blue Spring is a large, commercially operated diving area. The head pool is 200 feet across and has a maximum depth of 50 feet. The cave can be penetrated 700 feet, with depths running as much as 125 feet. This is a nice run for snorkelers. Dorms are available for overnight visitors. A new staged platform has been installed for instruction.

NO. 9 PONCE DE LEON SPRING
Location: From the town of Ponce de Leon, travel south .3 mile on S-181A to spring entrance.

Ponce de Leon Spring is operated by the state. A bathhouse and picnic area are provided. The spring itself consists of a small head pool with depths to 15 feet. No scuba diving is allowed, but it is not needed to enjoy the shallow depths. An underwater natural bridge is formed by two cave entrances at 15 feet.

NO. 10 MORRISON SPRING
Location: Travel south from the town of Ponce de Leon for 4.8 miles on S-181-A. Turn left on the dirt road and continue 1 mile to the spring.

Morrison Spring is one of the finest freshwater dives in Florida. The huge spring basin and .5 mile run to the Choctawhatchee River are bordered by moss-covered cypress trees. The spring now has a diving concession with air, rentals and a snack bar. There is an entrance charge of $5.00 per day for divers. On-site camping is also available for $2.50 per night.

The spring pool slopes to a large limestone cliff that drops off suddenly to 50 feet. There are two caves that offer excellent ledge diving. Neither can be penetrated beyond the glow of natural light. The first cave entrance is large and begins at a depth of 30 feet. The second cave entrance is much smaller and lies at a depth of 50 feet. It soon opens into a large room with depths to 90 feet.

VORTEX SPRING

Always Clean Water
Deep Basin
Cavern & Cave
with permanent Line
Good Snorkel Run
Certified Air and Rentals
Camping year round
Barracks Lodging
for diving groups
Trip connections
for Gulf diving

Compressor Sales and Repair

VORTEX SPRING

4 miles N. of Ponce DeLeon, Fla.
on Hwy. 81 N.—5 miles from I-10 exit
Rt. 2 Box 18 A   32455
A/C 904-836-4979

PENSACOLA

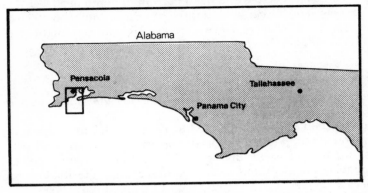

Offshore Diving Locations

1. USS *Massachusetts*
2. Three Coal Barges
3. Casino Rubble
4. Liberty Ship
5. Air Transport
6. Bridge Rubble
7. Russian Freighter—
   San Pablo

Area Information

The Pensacola area offers one of Florida's best-planned programs of activities for the sport diver. The Department of Commerce, the U.S. Navy, and local diving groups have established several exciting diving locations. You can choose from large ships, planes and building rubble. All these areas are fish havens containing grouper, snapper, barracuda, flounder, amberjacks and many beautiful tropicals.

All of the good diving must be done from boats. Beach diving consists of little more than large, flat expanses of white silica sand with an occasional sand dollar or starfish to be found. Excellent diving charters are available out of Pensacola throughout the year. It is best to make advance reservations, however, for charters during the popular summer holidays.

Summer is the in-season for diving in the Gulf. Calm seas are common during the months of April through October, during which water temperatures stay around 80 degrees. Underwater visibility averages 60 feet with days of 100-foot visibility common. Spearfishermen will find the underwater hunting good. Grouper, snapper, amberjacks and large Warsaw grouper are the most plentiful game fish. Larger fish move into the area during the winter. Underwater photography, tropical fish collecting and shell collecting are good in all dive locations and, of course, the wreck diver will be in paradise.

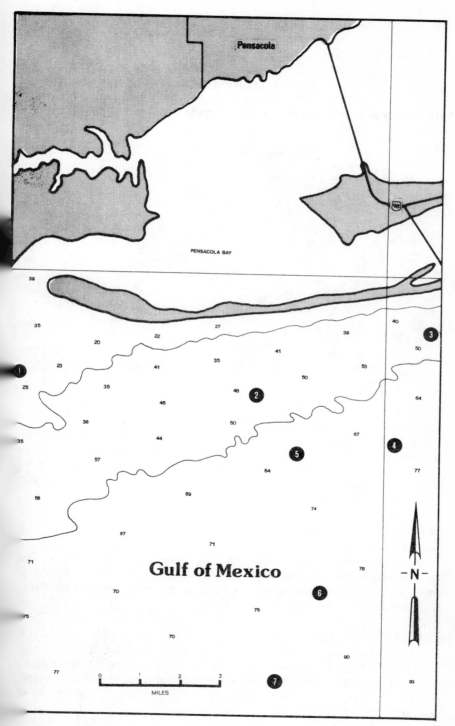

Pensacola

PENSACOLA BAY

Gulf of Mexico

–N–

0   1   2   3
MILES

NO. 1 USS *MASSACHUSETTS*
Location: A little over a mile off the rock jetties, this wreck is found easily.

This is one of the best small boat dives in the Pensacola area. The 500-foot battleship of WWI vintage was sunk by the Navy in 1927. Lying in 25 feet of water, part of the ship is still exposed. Though it is mainly intact, some sections of the USS *Massachusetts* are covered by sand. In winter, diving can be hampered by rough surge.

Diver on a Gulf wreck.

NO. 2 THREE COAL BARGES
Location: 1.8 miles off the beach, in 50 feet of water.

These three barges rest end to end on a white sand bottom, and form wonderful area for safe, easy diving. The top decks of the 200-foot barge are 15 feet off the bottom. The area has developed into an outstanding fis habitat. The clean sand surrounding the ships is covered with large sar dollars and other shells.

NO. 3 CASINO RUBBLE
Location: 1 mile off Pensacola Beach.

The rubble from an old casino (the first building constructed on Per sacola Beach) was dumped in 60 feet of water to form an artificial ree Large concrete bricks and other construction materials provide habitat f flounder and red snapper.

NO. 4 LIBERTY SHIP
Location: 7 miles west-southwest of the pass leading to Pensacola Bay.

The intact hull of a 480-foot Liberty Ship was sunk by the Departmen Commerce in November 1976 for their program to form areas for sp divers. She rests in 80 feet of water, her sides rising 20 feet off the bottom.

NO. 5 AIR TRANSPORT
Location: 5 miles off Pensacola Beach in 75 feet of water.

The remains of a large 128-foot air transport were sunk five miles off Pensacola Beach. Its tail section rises 28 feet off the sand bottom. The sunken plane is just one more example of Pensacola's outstanding program to provide interesting diving for the public.

NO. 6 BRIDGE RUBBLE
Location: 7 miles from Pensacola Beach.

Twelve barge loads of rubble from the old Pensacola toll bridge were dumped in 75 feet of water to form an artificial reef. The large, complete bridge spans an area nearly 300 feet in diameter, forming an exceptional fish haven. Snapper, grouper and flounder are common at the site. Excellent tropical fish collecting and shell hunting are also found. The remains of the 100-foot barge lie at the western end of the area.

NO. 7 RUSSIAN FREIGHTER *SAN PABLO*
Location: 9 miles off Pensacola Beach.

The *San Pablo* was torpedoed in the Florida Straits during WWII. She went down nine miles off Pensacola Beach while being towed to Mobile for repairs. She was later dynamited to clear shipping lanes. Her stern section and boilers remain intact in 75 feet of water. Her remains form an excellent fish habitat with many barracuda, grouper and snapper.

DIVE PENSACOLA'S WRECKS
1-904-433-4319

- USS MASSACHUSETTES—LIBERTY SHIP
- RUSSIAN FREIGHTER • 3 COAL BARGES
- REEF AND SPECIAL SPOTS

719 S. PALAFOX ST. PENSACOLA, FL 32501

OUR CHARTER BOAT IS RIGHT BEHIND THE SHOP WITH TRIPS AVAILABLE 7 DAYS A WEEK. AIR FILLS—RENTAL EQUIPMENT—REPAIRS—FISHING TRIPS—NASDS CLASSES

FORT WALTON BEACH-DESTIN

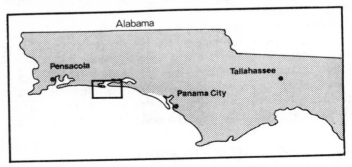

Offshore Diving Locations

1. Amberjack Rocks
2. Franciscan Reef
3. White Hill Reef
4. Airplane Rocks
5. Liberty Ship-Fort Walton Beach
6. Liberty Ship-Destin

Area Information

Fort Walton Beach is located in the heart of one of America's mo popular beach areas. Miles of beautiful white sand beaches extend bot east and west. The area has been developed into a playground for tourist with entertainment facilities everywhere along the beachfront. The wat is clear and calm during the summer months, with underwater visibili ranging from 40 to 100 feet. Years of active Air Force operations ha caused many planes and missile parts to end up at the bottom of the Gu creating excellent artificial reefs and exciting underwater exploratio Spearfishing is popular and is allowed everywhere except near bridge jetties and piers.

1. AMBERJACK ROCKS
Location: 3 miles south of Destin.

This is the largest and most popular reef in the area. Depths vary from to 85 feet. The crescent-shaped rock and coral reef is about 200 feet l with ledges ten to 12 feet off the bottom. Several of the ledges are unde with small caves. Large cuts divide the reef into sections. Large ba sponges are one of this reef's trademarks.

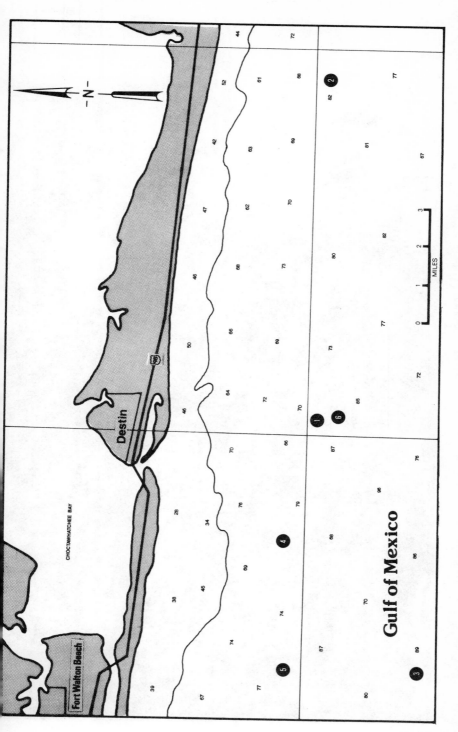

NO. 2 FRANCISCAN REEF
Location: 10 miles east of Choctawhatchee Bay entrance.

This reef area consists of a long expanse of five-foot-high ledges at a depth of 80 feet.

NO. 3 WHITE HILL REEF
Location: 8 miles offshore.

This is a deep, rocky reef with a depth range of 95 to 100 feet. It is excellent for spearfishing and shell collecting, and sometimes lobster can be found.

NO. 4 AIRPLANE ROCKS
Location: 4 miles offshore.

This is a typical rocky reef of the Gulf area, with a depth of about 70 feet. Spearfishing is popular.

NO. 5 LIBERTY SHIP—FORT WALTON BEACH

The Department of Commerce has plans to sink a 500-foot Liberty Ship on this location.

NO. 6 LIBERTY SHIP—DESTIN

The Department of Commerce has plans to sink a 500-foot Liberty Ship on this location.

DIVE DESTIN'S BEAUTIFUL REEFS ABOARD THE

Fantasea

Sightseeing
Shell Collecting
Photography
Spearfishing

U.S.C.G. Approved for 17 Passengers
Daily Trips
to natural and artificial reefs and wrecks
45′ Custom Dive Boat

FANTASEA SCUBA HEADQUARTERS AT THE FOOT OF THE DESTIN BRIDGE
P.O. BOX 63 # HWY. 98 DESTIN, FLORIDA 32541
(904) 837-6943 or (904) 837-0732   *For information call or come by*

PANAMA CITY

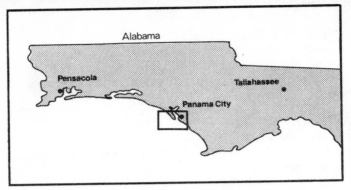

Offshore Diving Locations

1. Life Boats
2. Spanish Shanty Barge
3. *Simpson*
4. Navy Trash Pile
5. LOSS Pontoon
6. Warsaw Hole
7. *Tarpon*
8. Phillips Inlet

9. PC Barge/Long Beach Barge
10. *Sealab I*
11. Airplane
12. Liberty Ship
13. Stage 1-Stage II
14. Quonset Hut
   Not on Map
   Grey Ghost
   Empire Mica

Area Information

Panama City is virtually a sleeping giant for the underwater enthusiast. The last few years have seen the number of dive sites double, and with the increased interest in diving, local captains are continually working to locate even more varied spots. No matter what your diving interests are, Panama City has something to offer. The reefs have some of the rarest shells in Florida, and the many different types of wrecks never cease to entertain the underwater photographer. Spearfishing subjects are readily available for competent sportsmen, and this activity probably reaches its best during the winter months.

Panama City has numerous barges, varying in size from 46 feet to almost 100 feet. Their depths range from 48 to 90 feet. Although sizes and depths are assorted, they all have one thing in common: they offer the diver a kaleidoscope of underwater life, from the common and aggressive trigger-fish to the elusive and tasty red snapper. These artificial habitats have it all. Shelling, photography and spearfishing all are popular on these various structures, which include Davis, Twin, Smith, Holland, Blown-up and the Panama City Beach Barge.

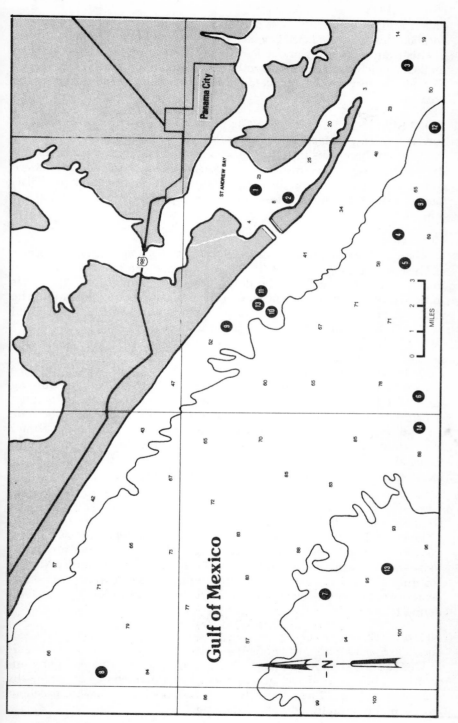

121

NO. 1 LIFE BOATS
Location: Inside St. Andrews Bay, about 1 mile north of Shell Island.

This is an interesting and safe dive site, consisting of five steel-hulled lifeboats which were chained together and sunk in 25 feet of water. Five-to 15-foot visibility can be expected. Scattered marine life hover about the area.

NO. 2 SPANISH SHANTY BARGE
Location: Inside St. Andrews Bay, near the Spanish Shanty cove.

An old tar barge lies in 18 feet of water and is often used for check-out dives. Visibility ranges from five to 15 feet. Sheepshead and mullet are commonly sighted around the barge. Many shells can be found, as well as various interesting subjects for close-up photography. The barge is 150 feet long.

NO. 3 *SIMPSON*
Location: Just outside the old pass in 20 feet of water, about ½ mile offshore.

The tug, *E.E. Simpson*, sank in 1936 in 25 feet of water. She is completely intact, and rests directly in the flow of the old channel. Visibility varies from 16 to 30 feet, but to see her under the best conditions, tides should be checked. The tug offers pleasant surprises for spearfishermen and should be seriously considered by the beginning diver.

NO. 4 NAVY TRASH PILE
Location: 3 miles off Shell Island.

This large area has been used for several years by the Navy as a dumping ground. Chains, metal containers and old airplane parts are among the debris that can be found scattered about the bottom. The area has become a fish haven, and offers good spearfishing, especially during the winter months when larger fish come into the area. Numerous flounder are also found at this spot. The Navy Trash Pile also is considered an ideal spot by local captains for practicing underwater navigation.

NO. 5 LOSS PONTOON
Location: 3 miles off Shell Island.

The LOSS Pontoon is a large metal object that was once used as a lifting pontoon by the Navy during large object salvage. Weighing almost 80 tons, she was sunk in September of 1978 as part of Panama City Marine Institute's Artificial Reef Program. Sitting in 60 feet of water, this site is destined to become a favorite site of instructors for introducing open Gulf diving to students.

NO. 6 WARSAW HOLE
Location: 9 miles southwest of St. Andrews jetties.

This is a good spot for spearfishing, with grouper and snapper common. The hole is in 85 feet of water, and has a diameter of 25 feet. Walls drop down about 12 feet. Sandstone and coral ledges allow for excellent close-up photography, as well as shelling.

Scuba Panama City

Exclusive Booking Agent for Charter Boats
"DUKE"   "AFTERNOON DELIGHT"
"DUCHESS"   "SUMMER WIND"

Empire Mica Trips • Air • Rentals
• Daily Wreck and Reef Dives

Write or call for the 40 page book *Scuba Panama City* for detailed information about diving in our waters. Send $3.95 plus $1.00 postage.

**Begin all your diving adventures
in the Panama City waters at**

Hydrospace Dive Shop
3605 Thomas Dr. Panama City, FL 32407
Call 1-800-874-DIVE (3483)

NO. 7 TARPON

Location: 9½ miles west of the St. Andrews jetties.

An old coastal freighter went down in 1937 with a load of beer bottles. Her broken remains rest on a flat sandy bottom in 90 feet of water. The boilers are still intact. The wreckage rises about eight feet off the bottom. Relic hunting is good. Divers are still bringing up brass pulleys and cleats and, of course, beer bottles are everywhere.

NO. 8 PHILLIPS INLET

Location: 13 miles west of Panama City.

This area is virtually covered with reefs, ranging in depth from 60 to 110 feet. Sandstone and coral formations provide excellent spearfishing opportunities, as well as photographic subjects. This site also offers countless specimens for avid collectors. Phillips Inlet is the stopping ground for transient Florida spiny lobster in the six- to 12-pound category.

These reefs vary in size from two to four feet, and range in lengths up to a half mile. Though mostly uncharted, these reefs have nonetheless been given names by local dive boat skippers. Sites include Grouper City, Hammerhead Reef, Anchor Reef and the Pyramids, and are identified by Panama City divers as readily as Molasses Reef is by South Florida captains.

NO. 9 P.C. BARGE/LONG BEACH BARGE

Location: Just off the Long Beach area of Panama City, just west of the jetties in 50 feet of water.

This is one of the oldest diving sites in the Panama City area, having been explored since the early '50s. Because of the shallow depths, it is a popular area for scuba classes.

NO. 10 SEALAB I

Location: 1½ miles west of the St. Andrews jetties, a few hundred yards east of Stage II.

The U.S. Navy's first manned saturation habitat is sitting upright in 50 feet of water. Easily accessible, this structure is a diveable museum for our Navy's underwater programs.

NO. 11 AIRPLANE

Location: Just south of Stage II.

As part of a special project, a small trainer jet T-33 was put down by the Navy and has become a welcome addition to the local diving. In 50 feet of water, this is an excellent dive for the beginner, but it also does a super job of attracting and holding the interests of more experienced divers because of its wide variety of marine life.

NO. 12 LIBERTY SHIP

Location: 7½ miles offshore, in 70 feet of water.

In October of 1977, Panama City received her long-awaited Liberty ship. The 360-foot ship was sunk by the Department of Natural Resources to serve as an artificial reef. Down for six years now, this wreck has become a local favorite, continually attracting new marine life. The towering bulkheads and intact stairways are an awesome introduction to wreck diving. The 70-foot depth puts this wreck far enough offshore to maintain a variety of fish, but is still shallow enough to allow plenty of time for exploration.

NO. 13 STAGE I-STAGE II
Location: Stage I is 13 miles offshore, in 107 feet of water. Stage II is 1 ½ miles west of St. Andrews jetties, in 50 feet of water.

There are two Navy-owned structures off the coast of Panama City. These towers are similar to the oil rigs seen off the Louisiana coast. They attract a wide assortment of marine life and visibility ranges from 20 to 100 feet.

Stage II is in 55 feet of water, and is in constant demand as a site for check-out dives. All types of fish frequent the area, and visibility ranges from ten to 60 feet.

Because the towers are Navy-owned, they are off-limits to civilians. Special arrangements are required for diving these structures.

NO. 14 QUONSET HUT
Location: About 10 miles due west of the St. Andrews jetties.

This large metal cylinder resting in 87 feet of water has been nicknamed Quonset Hut by local divers because of its similarity to that type of structure. Once used by the Navy for training exercises, it has since been abandoned and become a hot spearfishing spot. The amberjack and barracuda of the summertime give way to the winter's visitors: snapper and grouper. Visibility is generally around 25 feet, but can be as good as 80 feet.

NO. 15 *GREY GHOST* (Not on map)
Location: 22 miles from the St. Andrews jetties.

July 12, 1978 was the official start-up for Panama City Marine Institute's Artificial Reef Program. The project started with the sinking of a 105-foot steel-hull tugboat. Lying on her side in 96 feet of water, the *Grey Ghost,* in just a few short months, catapulted into being one of the most talked about dives in Panama City. She is virtually intact and on the edge of a reef, giving her possibly the widest range of animal life in the entire area.

NO. 16 *EMPIRE MICA* (Not on map)
Location: 20 miles south of Cape San Blas.

The *Empire Mica* is one of the most exciting wreck dives in Florida. The 480-foot British tanker was torpedoed by a U-boat in 1942. She sank almost immediately in 110 feet of water. Her bow section is intact and rises 60 feet off the sand. Visibility is usually excellent, providing the underwater photographer with dramatic settings. Spearfishing is great, with an abundance of amberjack, snapper, barracuda and grouper to be found. Although this wreck lies 52 miles from Panama City, there are several boats which run regular trips for either one or two days.

ST. PETERSBURG CLEARWATER TAMPA

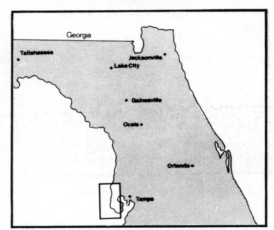

Offshore Diving Locations

1. Big Jack Hole
2. *Gunsmoke*
3. South Jack Wreck
4. Doc's Barge
5. South Jack Hole
6. St. Petersburg Reef
7. Twelve-Foot Ledge
8. Ten Fathom Wreck
9. *Mexican Pride*
10. Treasure Island Reef
11. Mecco's Barge/*Betsy Ross*
12. Indian Shores Reef
13. Pinellas County I
14. *Blackthorn*
15. Table Top
16. The Caves
17. Clearwater Wreck
18. 'G' Marker
19. Clearwater Reef
20. Dunedin Reef
21. Bomber
22. Masthead Ledge
23. Tarpon Springs Reef
24. Tugboat and Barge
25. Hellcat
26. Pasco County Artificial Reef 'PS'
27. Pasco County Artificial Reef 'CO'

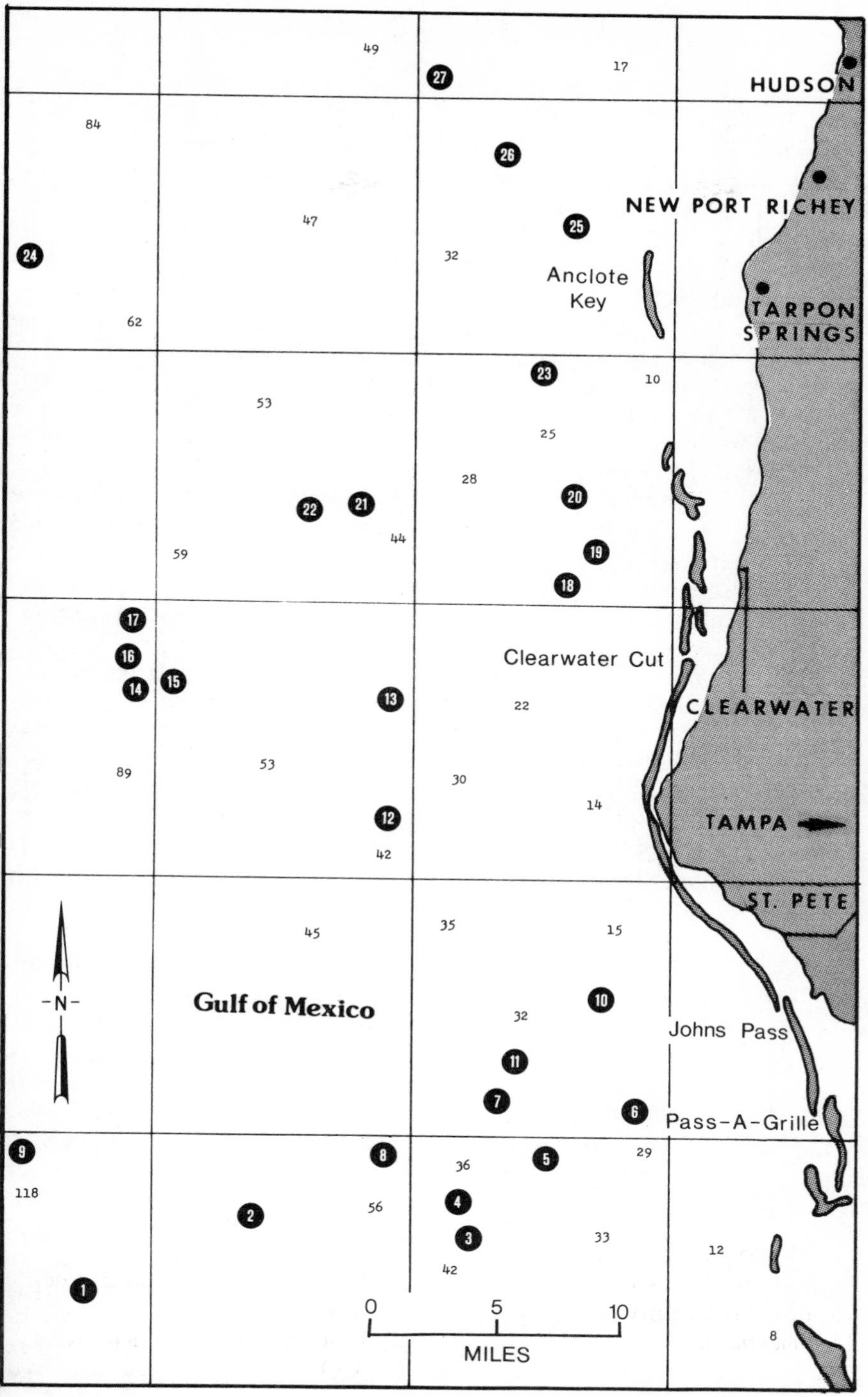

49
27
17
HUDSON

84
26
NEW PORT RICHEY
47
25
32
Anclote
Key
TARPON
SPRINGS
24
62

23
10
53
25
28
20
22 21
44
59
19
18

17
Clearwater Cut
16
14 15
13
22
CLEARWATER
89
53
30
14
12
TAMPA
42

45
35
15
ST. PETE
10
Gulf of Mexico
32
Johns Pass
-N-
11
7
6
Pass-A-Grille
9
8
5
29
118
36
2
56
4
12
3
33
42
8

0   5   10
MILES

Area Information

Florida's west coast divers can't boast of tropical coral gardens and crystalline seas in their surrounding waters, but they can boast of some things that will set the spirits of underwater explorers racing: game fish—large, bold and abundant; the most extensive and best-maintained artificial reef system available to sport divers; and great wrecks, great spearing, great shelling, and always great adventure.

There are four categories of diving sites in the Gulf: Ledges, "drowned" sink-holes, artificial reefs and wrecks. The presence of each breaks the monotony of an otherwise flat, sandy, ocean floor. All attract and house complex marine ecosystems with promise of security.

The ledges mark forgotten shorelines, long ago lost to the rising sea. These north-south rock reefs vary in height from one to 12 feet, some extending for miles. The most prominent lines are at depths of 36, 42, 50 and 60 feet. Many are undercut with deep pockets.

"Drowned" sinkholes break the flat submarine plain with limestone shafts that drop vertically to great depths, creating natural fishbowls teeming with sea life.

Artificial reef construction projects were inaugurated to better the marine environment and improve recreation as early as 1961. Close cooperation between county and city governments greatly expanded the scope of the vast undertaking throughout the '70s. Today, their efforts have resulted in a boon for fishermen and divers alike. Sites, carefully chosen with concern for ecology and accessibility, have been built up over the years using solid wastes that stand up to the rigors of the sea. Concrete culverts, building and bridge rubble, steel-hulled ships and barges, and "ganged" tires comprise the bulwark of reef construction materials. Today, however, the marked success of the project is threatened by dredging operations that dump their fill on developed reefs. These reefs, inundated with sludge, cease to exist. The fate of many prolific areas now rests with concerned divers and fishermen.

Wreck diving in the Gulf has always been spectacular, but the additions of the Coast Guard cutter *Blackthorn* and shrimper *Gunsmoke* make the Bay area's list of sunken vessels quite impressive. Both are magnificent dives.

Although spring and fall months are considered best for water activities, diving charters make runs during periods of good weather year 'round. Trips are always planned carefully around meteorological reports. Water temperatures vary from the mid-50s in winter to the low 80s in summer months. Water visibility ranges from only a few feet to over 60 feet during periods of calm seas.

Florida spearfishing is at its best in the Gulf. Florida's west coast divers have earned the reputation of being among America's best underwater hunters. National and state spearing competitions are regular occurrences in the region's bountiful waters. Cobia, snapper, bonito, kingfish, mackerel and red and black grouper are their game. Those who gather without spears dive for scallops, oysters, stone crabs and lobster. Here, the shovelnose and slipper lobster are more abundant than the spinies of the east coast and the Keys. Divers should always be ready for adventure when they enter the unpredictably wonderful world of Gulf diving.

NO. 1 BIG JACK HOLE
Location: 32 miles from John's Pass on a 225° course.

This is one of many "drowned" sink holes (freshwater sinks that were inundated by saltwater thousands of years ago when the ocean slowly spread its domain across the low, flat Gulf region) that dot the sandy floor of the Gulf.

The entrance (25 feet in diameter) is in 110 feet of water. It plunges straight down to an unknown depth. The limited visibility is totally lost 100 feet down into the shaft. Of course, the depth just at the rim of the hole requires the skills of an experienced open-water diver with advanced training for the depths. Lots of big fish inhabit the area.

NO. 2 *GUNSMOKE*
Location: 24 miles from John's Pass on a 240° course.

Great wreck dive! On her final voyage, the 65-foot shrimper lived up to her name. She was scuttled by her crew while the Coast Guard was in hot pursuit. Floating bales of marijuana were all that marked her grave when the cutter arrived. Government divers found only one crew member. He was located below, with a bullet hole through his head. Modern pirates still live by their creed-of-old: "Dead men tell no tales."

DIVE THE FAMOUS BLACKTHORN

40' CUSTOM DIVE BOAT – 22 DIVERS
DAILY REEF & WRECK TRIPS
• Spearfishing • Photography • Collecting

• Instruction
  Scuba-Ski-Boardsailing

• Equipment & Apparel

• Rentals

• Full Service Repair Center

  Indoor Heated Pool
  Revolving Alpine Ski Deck

2126 drew st., clearwater, fl 33515
(813) 461-7160, (813) 442-9931

ONE OF THE WORLD'S LARGEST DIVE STORES

The wreck is a beauty. She rests in 80 feet of water, listing slightly to starboard. Shrimp nets remain draped across her rigging.

NO. 3 SOUTH JACK WRECK
Location: 16 miles from John's Pass on a 220° course.

The broken remains of an old steel wreck are scattered in 60 feet of water. The intact portion of the wreck, consisting mainly of a large boiler, rests in an upright position on the sand.

NO. 4 DOC'S BARGE
Location: 16 miles from John's Pass on a 225° course.

The 75-foot-long barge rests in 60 feet of water. She is mostly intact, but split in half.

NO. 5 SOUTH JACK HOLE
Location: 16 miles out of John's pass on a course of 220°.

A nice section of ledge, seven to eight feet high, in 50 feet of water. Numerous crevices and undercuts hide large fish.

NO. 6 ST. PETERSBURG REEF
Location: 5.2 miles from hotel on St. Pete Beach on a 248° course.

This area is about 300 feet long with depths of 26 to 28 feet. The first drop was on March 18, 1976; currently, there are 151 sections of concrete culvert from the old Cory Avenue bridge on the bottom.

NO. 7 TWELVE-FOOT LEDGE
Location: 12 miles from John's Pass on a 240° course.

This is the largest ledge in Tampa waters. The 12-foot-high ridge runs for almost one-half mile. Depths are in the 60-foot range.

NO. 8 TEN FATHOM WRECK/TRAMP STEAMER
Location: 16 miles from Pass-a-Grille on a 260° course.

The broken remains of a 150-foot tramp steamer lie in 60 feet of water. There is good spearing, with plenty of hogfish and barracuda. Big lobster are found in the summer months.

NO. 9 *MEXICAN PRIDE*
Location: 37 miles west of Pass-a-Grille.

This is a large wreck resting in an upright position in 120 feet of water. I is 80 feet to her top deck. There is good spearing with plenty of red snapper, grouper, large jewfish, cobia, jacks and barracuda.

NO. 10 TREASURE ISLAND REEF

Location: 6.4 miles from tank on Treasure Island on a 262° course.

The reef is marked on each end by buoys. Depths range from 29 to 33 feet. The first drop was on January 23, 1976; currently in place are 40,000 car tires, 1,032 truck tires, and 561 sections of concrete culvert. This is a great area for tropical fish collecting.

NO. 11 MECCO'S BARGE/*BETSY ROSS*

Location: 10 miles from John's Pass on a 245° course.

A 75-foot barge, completely intact, rests in an upright position in 45 feet of water.

NO. 12 INDIAN SHORES REEF

Location: 24.4 miles from the tank on Sand Key on a 284° course.

125 pillboxes were the first placed on this site in 1962. A 235-foot naval landing craft was sunk in January 1976. Its depth is around 50 feet.

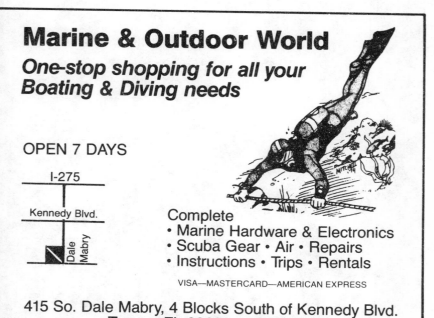

Marine & Outdoor World

One-stop shopping for all your Boating & Diving needs

OPEN 7 DAYS

I-275

Kennedy Blvd.

Dale Mabry

Complete
• Marine Hardware & Electronics
• Scuba Gear • Air • Repairs
• Instructions • Trips • Rentals

VISA—MASTERCARD—AMERICAN EXPRESS

415 So. Dale Mabry, 4 Blocks South of Kennedy Blvd.
Tampa, FL 33609   875-2376

A fine Gulf dive: the wreck of the **Blackthorn**.

NO. 13 PINELLAS COUNTY I

Location: 13 miles from the 153-foot penthouse on Clearwater Beach Island on a 247.7° course.

Depths vary from 37 to 44 feet. A large barge was sunk on August 11, 1976. Visibility averages 25 feet in the summer. The area is rapidly becoming a popular dive site.

NO. 14 *BLACKTHORN*

Location: 30 miles from John's Pass on a 292° course. Marked by an orange buoy.

The intact wreck of the 110-foot U.S. Coast Guard cutter *Blackthorn* is one of the Gulf's newest and most popular dives. The *Blackthorn*'s fate was international news in late '81, when the cutter was broadsided by a freighter in one of the channels of Tampa Bay. Twenty-two of her crew members lost their lives in the collision. Her hull, damaged far beyond repair, was towed to a site known as Pinellas County Artificial Reef #2 and scuttled.

The huge mass of steel is fast-attracting sea life as well as hundreds of divers each year. The rather shallow depths of the large wreck (30 feet to her upper decks; 80 feet to the ocean floor) afford an opportunity for less experienced divers to visit a magnificent wreck. Penetration of her inner chambers is not recommended because of the inherent dangers of all intact wrecks (lack of light; sharp, broken fittings; mazes of passages that easily disorient the diver; and silt). The broken remains of a barge and other debris lie nearby.

Terrace Watersports

"SOUTH FLORIDA'S DIVING HEADQUARTERS"

SALES • SERVICE • INSTRUCTION
RENTALS • TRIPS

—OPEN—
7 DAYS

- NEW & USED EQUIPMENT
- INTERNATIONAL CERTIFICATION PROGRAM

988-0642

9228 N. 56th STREET
5 MINUTES FROM BUSCH GARDENS

NO. 15 TABLE TOP

Location: ½ mile east of the Blackthorn.

The Table Top is a plateau over 200 feet in diameter that rises seven to eight feet from the sand. Large undercuts filled with sea life are interesting to explore.

NO. 16 THE CAVES

Location: ¼ mile northwest of the Blackthorn.

The caves are actually deep undercuts in an eight-foot-high ledge. This is a good area for underwater hunting. Depths go to about 80 feet.

NO. 17 CLEARWATER WRECK

Location: 23 miles from entrance bell marker #1 in Clearwater Pass on a 267° course.

The wreckage of a large steamer lies in 60 feet of water. Her hull is split in half and rises only 20 feet off the flat sea floor.

NO. 18 'G' MARKER

Location: 4½ miles from bell marker #1 in Clearwater Pass on a 295° course.

This is a nice close-in area, best dived on calm, clear-water days. The broken rock ledges run for nearly half a mile, rising about five feet off the bottom. This is a good spot to see larger marine life close to shore. Many jewfish, nurse sharks and turtles have been spotted. The depth averages 25 feet.

NO. 19 CLEARWATER REEF

Location: 3.8 miles from the 153-foot penthouse on Clearwater Beach Island on a 283° course.

A large area marked by several nun buoys, Clearwater Reef is one of the largest and most popular artificial reef sites in the area. Depths range from 23 to 25 feet. The reef was started on June 2, 1965, with an initial drop of 75 specially constructed concrete pillboxes; additional drops provided at least 45,000 tires. Although this is the oldest reef, the marine population was killed during a red tide outbreak in August 1974. The reef cycle began to regrow after the kill. A large variety of tropicals make their home among the rubble. Game fish such as snapper and hogfish are common, as well as some lobster. Spearfishing is popular.

NO. 20 DUNEDIN REEF

Location: 7.2 miles from the entrance bell marker #1 in Clearwater Pass on a 326° course.

The reef area is marked by buoys on its northern and southern ends. The northern buoy is near a natural rock ledge. Concrete culverts are scattered to the south for 300 feet. There are plenty of game fish and snook are often seen in the summer months. Depths range from 25 to 30 feet.

NO. 21 BOMBER

Location: 14 miles from Tarpon Springs on a 295° course.

The broken wreckage of what was probably a WWII transport lies in 50 feet of water. Only the fuselage remains intact.

NO. 22 MASTHEAD LEDGE
Location: 16 miles from bell marker #1 in Clearwater Pass on a 285° course.

A tall, long ledge section that rises eight feet from the bottom and runs for over a mile and a half, this is a popular dive because of the formation's size and the extensive marine growth of the rock outcropping. There are many deep crevices and undercuts offering plenty of hiding places for marine life. Shelling is good along the ledge. Helmet shells and large horse conch are commonly found.

NO. 23 TARPON SPRINGS REEF
Location: 12 miles from the entrance bell marker #1 in Clearwater Pass on a 338° course.

The south buoy marks the beginning of the artificial reef. The north buoy is over natural rock ledges. Depths range from 26 to 28 feet.

NO. 24 TUGBOAT AND BARGE
Location: 30 miles west of Tarpon Springs.

A large 105-foot tug and the 80-foot barge she was towing went down in 85 feet of water during high seas. The tug, mostly intact, rests upside-down on her superstructure. A jeep lies nearby. The barge came to rest less than a mile to the north.

NO. 25 HELLCAT
Location: Between 3 and 4 miles from the north end of Anclote Key on a 270° course.

A WWII Hellcat rests in 25 feet of water. She remains pretty much intact with wings and fuselage in place. There are no ledges in the area.

NO. 26 PASCO COUNTY ARTIFICIAL REEF 'PS'
Location: 11 miles west of Gulf Harbor in New Port Richey on a 270° course.

Four 200-foot barges were sunk in 25 feet of water. One barge is at buoy 'P'; another, 1,500 feet directly north at buoy 'S'. Cement culverts are scattered between the middle barges. There is a lot of fish activity around the wrecks. Jewfish, cobia, sheepshead and snapper frequent the area. Flounder are common in flat sand areas surrounding the reef. There is good spearfishing here.

NO. 27 PASCO COUNTY ARTIFICIAL REEF 'CO'
Location: 15 miles from Gulf Harbor in New Port Richey on a 284° course.

The broken remains of a barge lie near buoy 'C' in 30 feet of water. Several two-foot-high rock ledges run near buoy 'C'. The area is alive with fish life. Lobsters are often pulled from the ledges. Sea whips, sponges and fire coral are common.

BRADENTON
SARASOTA
VENICE

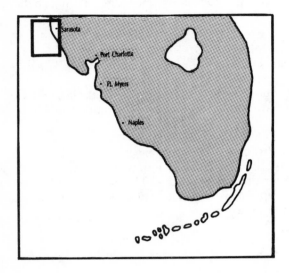

Offshore Diving Locations

1. Sugar (Molasses) Barge
2. Third Pier
3. Barracuda Hole
4. Gully's
5. Barge and Hopper

6. Venice Ledges
7. Venice Public Beach
8. The Rocks
   Not on map
   Bay Ronto
   Peace River

Area Information

Although huge jewfish are commonly sighted at many dive sites in the Gulf, Florida's southwestern coastal zone is called "Jewfish Country" because of their proliferation on the local ledges and wrecks. Few dives are made without spotting one or more. Often, over 20 of the gigantic fish are sighted on a single descent. The view of such a massive creature casually gliding through its sovereign domain is long remembered.

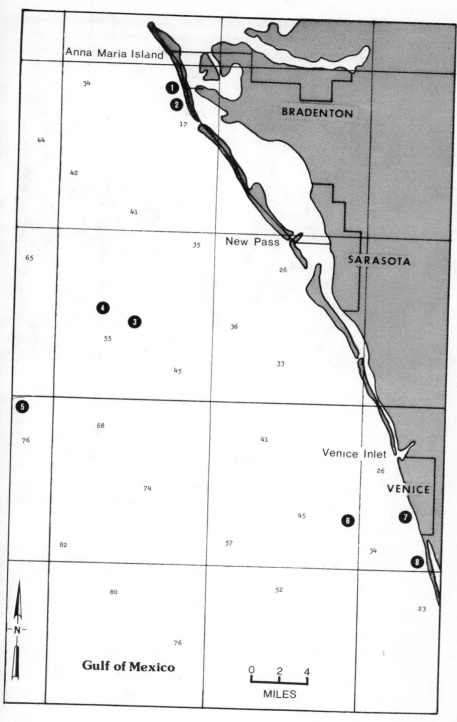

Anna Maria Island

BRADENTON

34

44

42

41

35

New Pass

SARASOTA

26

65

4

3

55

36

33

45

5

76

68

41

Venice Inlet

26

VENICE

74

45

6

7

82

57

34

8

80

52

23

76

Gulf of Mexico

N

0 2 4
MILES

137

Spearfishing is generally the activity of the day. Snapper and grouper are the prime game. Another popular pastime is searching for large, prehistoric shark teeth just off the Venice public beach or on the muddy bottom of the Peace River. The abundance and quality of the teeth rival those found in the Cooper River in South Carolina.

Diver explores a Gulf airplane wreck.

NO. 1 SUGAR (MOLASSES) BARGE (Beach Dive)
Location: About 100 yards straight out from Trader Jack's Restaurant on Bradenton Beach. A metal post on the barge's bow protrudes from the water, marking the exact location.

This old, 75-foot barge has long been a popular dive because of its close proximity to shore and its shallow depths (15 to 20 feet). If you catch a day with good visibility, you'll be delighted with the variety of sea creatures that make the wreck their home. Colorful soft corals and sponges are common.

NO. 2 THIRD PIER (Beach Dive)
Location: About 200 yards off Bradenton Beach. The entry site is adjacent to the intersection of Gulf Drive and 33rd Street. While swimming out, bear slightly south.

This is the best close-in ledge area on the Gulf coast. Depths vary from 20 to 30 feet. The broken reef line runs all along the coast to Trader Jack's Restaurant. Best diving conditions exist when the wind is out of the east. Westerly winds can reduce water visibility to zero.

NO. 3 BARRACUDA HOLE
Location: 9.5 miles from the New Pass sea buoy on a 240° course.

This area is known for its many rocky outcroppings and ledges up to six feet high. The bottom is in 50 feet of water. A large variety of fish are present, including snapper, amberjack, grouper and jewfish. Sponges and soft corals adorn the ledges.

NO. 4 GULLY'S

Location: 11 miles from the New Pass sea buoy on a 250° course. The area is just northwest of Barracuda Hole.

This is a ledge area pocketed with undercuts where depths range from 54 to 56 feet. The bottom is generally rocky, with a few hard coral formations. Spiny lobster are occasionally pulled from the rocks. Shovelnose lobster are more common and can be taken year 'round. A lot of tropical and game fish inhabit the ledges. Grouper, mangrove snapper and hogfish are the usual catch-of-the-day for spearfishermen.

NO. 5 BARGE AND HOPPER

Location: 19 miles southwest of the New Pass sea buoy on a 238° course.

This is a 100-foot barge resting upside-down in 80 feet of water. It has large breaks in the hull which lead inside. It is dangerous, however, to venture inside due to the weak structure of the collapsed sections. Large mangrove snapper can be found in and around the northern end of the barge. Jewfish, barracuda and amberjack are common.

The hopper is half a mile south of the barge. It is draped with nets and lines, and would be wise to stay clear of due to the possibility of entanglement. This is a good spot to grab a lobster. It has been reported that the hull and one wing of a large airplane are located near the hopper.

NO. 6 VENICE LEDGES

Location: A large area extending from 1 to 5 miles offshore. Located out from the Venice jetties on a 210° course, or directly west of the Venice fishing pier.

Depths range from 20 feet in the area close to shore to 50 feet on the outer fringes. The rocky bottom terrain and small ledges are popular spearfishing grounds. Visibility is moderate, but extends to 30 feet on good days.

FULL SERVICE DIVE SHOP

Full day trips to wrecks and reefs in 30' to 60' depths.

• **Sales • Rentals • Air • Photography • Boat Dives • Advance and Specialty Instruction • Diving Vacations • Charters**

OCEAN PRO DIVE SHOP 2259 Bee Ridge Rd. Sarasota, Fla.
(813) 924-DIVE

Large black grouper and jewfish are spotted on every dive. Large turtles frequent the area most of the year.

NO. 7 VENICE PUBLIC BEACH (Beach Dive)
Location: 30 to 40 yards off the Venice Public Beach, in 18 feet of water.

The area off this section of beach contains one of the largest deposits of prehistoric sharks' teeth ever found. Specimens of up to six inches across have been discovered, while smaller ones are quite common. They can be spotted on the bottom and uncovered by gently fanning the sand with your hand. Visibility of three to four feet can be expected on calm days. The best spots seem to be at the exact depth of 18 feet. Conditions are best during periods of easterly winds.

NO. 8 THE ROCKS (Beach Dive)
Location: From Route 775 in south Venice, take the Manasota Beach Road to the public beach area. It is a 1 ½ mile walk south to the site, which is located halfway between Manasota and Middle Road. Unfortunately, there are no closer access roads because the adjacent property is all privately owned.

A large, flat, rocky area that runs for about one mile and extends 75 yards offshore gives this site its name. Depths range from one to 18 feet. Visibility averages two to five feet, but reaches over 20 feet a couple of times a month. Large, flat, moss-covered rocks are closer to shore. The bigger rocks are in deeper water. Snook, snapper and grouper are frequently sighted.

NO. 9 BAY RONTO (Not on map)
Location: 30 miles from the Venice jetties on a 224° heading.

The *Bay Ronto* is a super dive, but should be limited to highly experienced open-water divers because of its depth of 110 feet. In 1919, the 400-foot German freighter went down in stormy seas when her cargo of grain shifted. She rests upside-down on a sandy floor. Her superstructure is not with the wreck. There are many areas through which the broken hull of this gigantic wreck can be entered. The site is rated excellent for the experienced spearfisherman and for underwater photographers. Recently, her huge bronze propeller was removed, lessening the photogenic aspect of the hull. Visibility is usually excellent, due to the water depth and distance from shore. Large amberjack and barracuda linger above the wreckage, while several large jewfish have taken up permanent residence inside the hull.

NO. 10 PEACE RIVER (Not on map)
Location: Travel west for 41 miles from Sarasota to Arcadia on S-72 (Bee Ridge Road). Go four miles on US 17 to the small town of Nocatee; then go east on C-760 to the river.

NED DELOACH

'lorida's clawless crustacean, the spiny lobster.

The Peace River has long been South Florida's most popular river ecreational area. Canoeing and camping are excellent. This shallow, lark-water river is dived for only one reason—large prehistoric sharks' eeth. Use only small boats to get about because the river is shallow, sually three to four feet deep. Canoes can be rented at the Canoe Outpost Arcadia.

One of the best spots for hunting is found at the river's double bend, ne-quarter to half a mile south of the Nocatee Bridge. Diving conditions e best during the winter, when the water level is low and the gator are t so active. Water visibility is non-existent. The hunter must carefully el around in soft mud. Be sure to wear gloves. Thousands of large, well-eserved shark teeth and arrowheads have been found using this ethod.

PORT CHARLOTTE, PUNTA GORDA AND FORT MYERS

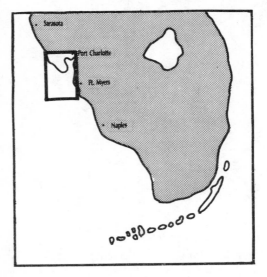

Offshore Diving Locations

1. Boca Grande Causeway
   Bridge & Railroad Trestle
2. Seventeenth Street Reefs
3. Boca Grande Jetties
4. Dock Wreck
5. *Cathy II*

6. The Gardens
7. Mud Hole
8. The "W"
9. Pinnacles
10. Mine Sweeper Wreck

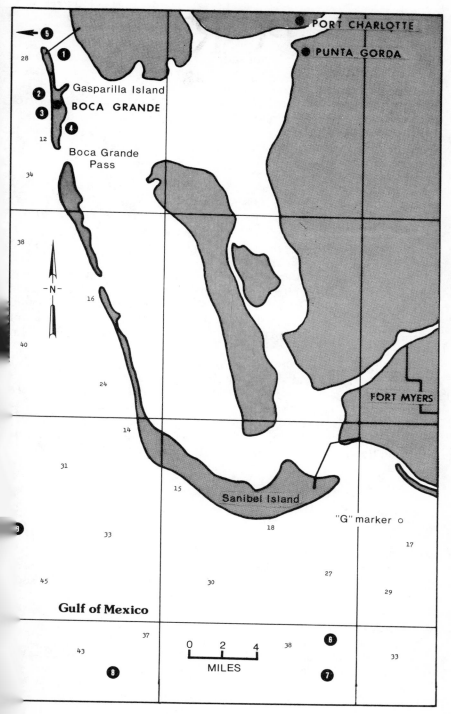

PORT CHARLOTTE

PUNTA GORDA

Gasparilla Island
BOCA GRANDE

Boca Grande
Pass

-N-

FORT MYERS

Sanibel Island

"G" marker o

Gulf of Mexico

0 2 4
MILES

143

Area Information

This area has long been famous for the prime shelling grounds found along the beaches of the coastal islands of Sanibel and Captiva. Unfortunately, the visibility in the surrounding waters is very poor due to the muddy runoff from the Peace River. Gasparilla Island, located just north of Charlotte Harbor, is an exception. Here, visibility varies from three to 15 feet. Spearfishing and gathering stone crab claws are popular activities. It is extremely dangerous to dive in the cuts between any of the islands due to strong tidal currents.

NO. 1 BOCA GRANDE CAUSEWAY BRIDGE
AND RAILROAD TRESTLE (Beach Dive)

Location: Travel 4 miles on US 41 from Port Charlotte. Turn west on SR 771. Go about 15 miles to the toll bridge over the Intracoastal Waterway. The bridge will take you to the small town of Boca Grande on Gasparilla Island. Tolls are $3.00 for trucks or vans; $1.50 for cars.

Good spearing and stone crabbing can be found around the support structures of the toll bridge and adjacent railroad trestle. Depths range from 20 to 25 feet. It is best to dive the area one-and-a-half hours before high tide. You can expect three-to-five-foot visibility. There are a lot of grouper and a few snapper in the area. Tide charts can be picked up at local dive shops.

NO. 2 SEVENTEENTH STREET REEFS (Beach Dive)

Location: Off the west end of 17th Street in Boca Grande. Bear slightly to the right as you swim out from shore.

The first group of rock ledges is in five to eight feet of water. These ledges are about a foot high. One hundred yards out, in 15 to 20 feet of water, the ledges are three- to four-feet high.

NO. 3 BOCA GRANDE JETTIES (Beach Dive)

Location: On the west (ocean) side of the island, about 1 mile from the south end

Three rock jetties extend out into the Gulf. Depths range from ten to 1 feet. There are few fish but plenty of stone crabs.

NO. 4 DOCK WRECK (Beach Dive)

Location: In the Intracoastal Waterway, just north of the large phosphate dock

The broken remains of an old shrimper lie scattered over the sar bottom.

NO. 5 *CATHY II*

Location: 5 miles west of the north end of Boca Grande.

The twisted hull of a 65-foot shrimper rests in 42 feet of water. The g tanks and engine are still intact. Visibility varies from 20 to 40 feet.

NO. 6 THE GARDENS

Location: About 7 miles from FL G "1" buoy off Ft. Myers Beach on a 210° course.

The Gardens is a large, scenic area with a lot of soft coral and fish life, including plenty of tropicals. Visibility ranges from 30 to 40 feet; depth averages 25 feet.

NO. 7 MUD HOLE
Location: About 9 miles from FL G "1" buoy, off Ft. Myers Beach on a heading of 197°.

Mud Hole is a poor choice of name for this live freshwater spring. The water issues from a fissure two-feet wide. On a calm day, the spring can be spotted by the change of water color and boil on the surface. The depth is 40 feet. Visibility averages 20 feet. Very large jewfish and sharks inhabit the area.

NO. 8 THE "W"
Location: About 16 miles from FL G "1" buoy off Ft. Myers Beach on a 240° course.

"W" stands for the shape of the rock reef that is the favorite hunting ground of local spearfishermen. Depths vary over the large bottom area from 45 to 48 feet. Good sponge and gorgonian growth is found on the rocks. Visibility averages 25 feet.

NO. 9 PINNACLES
Location: 22 miles due west of FL G "1" buoy off Ft. Myers Beach.

The Pinnacles consists of five or six very interesting rock formations which resemble steeples, rising 15 feet from the ocean floor. Depth averages 55 feet around the spires. Visibility averages 30 feet.

NO. 10 MINE SWEEPER WRECK
Location: 25 miles from FL G "1" buoy off Ft. Myers Beach on a 200° course.

This 60-foot wreck rests in 70 feet of water. Snapper and grouper hole up in the broken hull, making the Mine Sweeper wreck popular among spearfishermen.

CHARLOTTE DIVER

4549 F Tamiami Trail
Charlotte Harbor, FL
(813) 629-2722

Instruction • Sales • Service
Repairs • AIR • Rentals

NAPLES

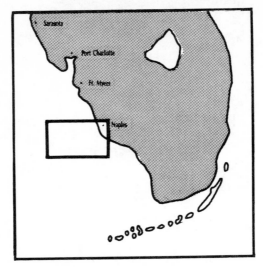

Offshore Diving Locations

1. Black Hole
2. House Boat Wreck
3. Mine Sweeper
4. Naples Ledges
5. Crater

Area Information

If you have a penchant for adventure when you dive, head for Naples. Here the Gulf sea covers an abundance of exciting bottom, yet to be explored by man. Unruly winter seas usually limit diving to the spring and summer months. Runs to prime diving grounds are long and visibility is limited, but when you do get down, be ready for a thrill. Fish are large and abundant, turtles plentiful and shelling superb. Both ledge reefs and wrecks support a profusion of large, colorful sponges and gorgonians. The large jewfish colonies that inhabit area wrecks and ledges are impressive.

NO. 1. BLACK HOLE
Location: 27 miles southwest of Gordon Pass.
The circular entrance to this large 'drowned' sink is 100 feet in diameter. The rim is in 65 feet of water and plunges to a 215 foot depth. The limestone shaft takes on an hourglass shape at 115 feet. Fish life is plentiful with large jewfish and grouper common. Many sea turtles frequent the area. Several sponge-covered ledges can be found nearby.

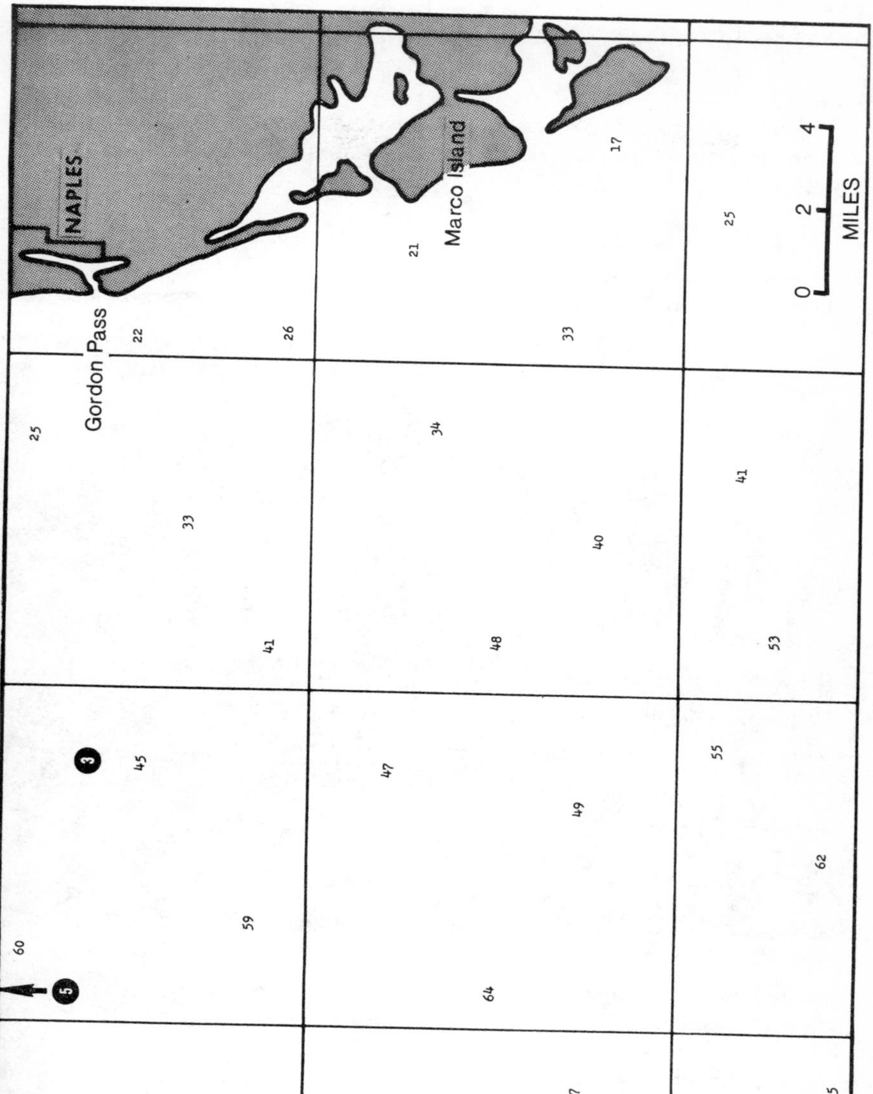
NAPLES
Gordon Pass
Marco Island
Gulf of Mexico
N
0
2
4
MILES
1
2
3
4
5
17
21
25
22
26
33
25
34
41
33
40
41
48
53
45
47
55
49
62
59
60
64
68
70
67
65
70
75
76

NO. 2 HOUSE BOAT WRECK
Location: 27 miles southwest of Gordon Pass, or about 4 miles north of the Black Hole.

This is a great spot to observe large jewfish. Many make their homes in and around the 50-foot wreck. The boat remains are intact and rest upside-down in 70 feet of water.

NO. 3 MINE SWEEPER
Location: 11 miles west of Naples.

The vessel is mostly broken apart. Water visibility is generally less here

Wreck diving in the Gulf.

than at other area sites, but the large concentration of gamefish make it a prized dive for local spearfishermen. Depths are to 45 feet.

NO. 4 NAPLES LEDGES
Location: 30-40 miles west of Naples.

Several ledge lines run parallel to one another for miles. Depths rang from 70 to 80 feet. Many virgin areas can still be found along the line, an several varieties of snapper and grouper inhabit the seven-to eight-foo high ledges.

NO. 5 CRATER
Location: 22 miles northwest of Naples.

The Crater resembles a large bowl on the ocean floor. The 15-fo depression is brimming with gamefish, making it a spearfisherman delight. 'Cuda and snapper abound.

JACKSONVILLE

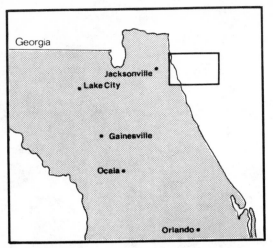

Offshore Diving Locations

1. Rabbit's Lair
2. Nine Mile Reef
3. Paul Main's Reef
4. Ponte Vedra Ground
5. Southeast 16-17
6. Tanzler Waters Reef
7. East Eighteen
8. Blackmar's Reef
9. *Casa Blanca*
10. East Fourteen (Gator Bowl)
11. Clayton's Holler

Area Information

Offshore Jacksonville has long been the center of diving activities along the northeast Florida coast. The best conditions are found during the summer months when the water is warm and visibility averages 30 feet. Pick a calm day, since the best diving locations are well offshore and require rather long boat rides. Spearfishing and lobstering are popular and usually rewarding.

NO. 1 RABBIT'S LAIR

Location: On a 58° course, 12.4 miles from the Mayport jetties and marked by two RL buoys.

Rabbit's Lair consists of a long series of ledges reaching a maximum height of ten feet and depths to 80 feet in some areas. Many different species of bottom and surface fish can be found. Grouper, ranging in size from five to 20 pounds, are the most abundant bottom dwellers. Snapper

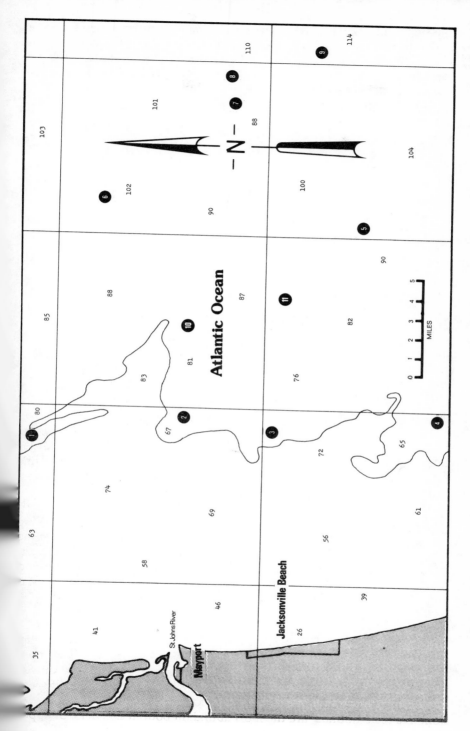

151

can be found along the ledges or over the sandy bottom. Large schools of sheepshead and spadefish are common. Lobster are frequently found under the ledges or hiding in nearby holes. Surface fish found in the area include jacks, barracuda, cobia and kingfish. This is a good spot for spearfishing, sightseeing and underwater photography. It harbors many tropical fish and has an average visibility of 30 feet.

NO. 2 NINE MILE REEF

Location: On a 90° course, 10.4 miles from the Mayport jetties.

Nine Mile Reef is a series of ledges and broken bottom. Visibility averages 20 feet; depth to 65 feet. The reef rises six feet off the bottom in some areas. There are good opportunities for spearing grouper and small red snapper. Tropical fish are plentiful.

NO. 3 PAUL MAIN'S REEF

Location: On a course of 111°, 9.9 miles from the Mayport jetties.

Three large tugboats (up to 90 feet) and a barge were sunk in this area to build an artificial reef. All are intact and in upright positions. Many large jewfish, grouper from five to 20 pounds, and snapper inhabit the wrecks. Jacks and barracuda are abundant. In addition to the wrecks, there is a long ledge averaging three feet in height. Many tropical fish, grouper, snapper and some lobster are found here. Photography can be good when visibility allows. The average visibility is 20 to 25 feet.

NO. 4 PONTE VEDRA GROUND

Location: 16 miles southeast of the Mayport jetties.

This large ledge averages four to five feet in height. The area is covered with broken bottom and harbors many grouper, small snapper and tropical fish, but few lobster. It is common to see nurse sharks resting under the ledge. This area is generally good for spearfishing.

NO. 5 SOUTHEAST 16-17

Location: Approximately 22 miles east-southeast of the Mayport jetties.

Many grouper, large mangrove snapper (up to 15 pounds), and lobster are found here. Depths average 95 feet to a broken bottom. This area is good for spearfishing, shelling and some photography.

NO. 6 TANZLER WATERS REEF

Location: On a course of 70°, 22 miles from the Mayport jetties.

This area is an artificial reef (tugboat) with natural ledges. Large jewfish can be seen around the wreckage. Spearfishing is mostly for grouper and snapper. Lobster, tropicals and shells can be found around the ledges. Depths are up to 102 feet, with average visibility 40 feet. Many surface fish are found around the wreck. This is a great dive for sightseeing and photography.

AQUIFER
DIVE CENTER

Scuba Instruction
Sales, Service, Repairs

Offshore Diving Charters

ABOARD *The Unwinder*

- New 39' Custom Dive Boat
- Full Day Charters
- Only 6 Passengers
- Spearfishing & Wreck Diving Classes

4564 Atlantic Blvd.   A.C. (904)
Jacksonville, FL 32207   398-1274

NO. 7 EAST EIGHTEEN

Location: On a 95° course, 25.2 miles from Mayport jetties.

The area is made up of broken bottom and ledges, with an average depth of 80 to 85 feet. Visibility usually remains pretty good throughout the year, averaging 30 feet. This is an excellent area to spearfish for grouper and snapper, and lobsters are common. Shelling is also a popular activity.

NO. 8 BLACKMAR'S REEF

Location: On a 95° course, 25.2 miles from the Mayport jetties. Marked with BR buoys.

Blackmar's Reef is composed of a combination of broken bottom and artificial reef made up of three wrecks—a tugboat, a barge and a ferry boat. All were sunk intact and settled in an upright position. Depths range to 110 feet. Many surface fish, jacks, barracuda, and an occasional cobia are found swimming about the wreckage. The visibility is good, averaging 40 feet. Spearfishermen find grouper, snapper and large jewfish inhabit the area. Sightseers and photographers enjoy good visibility and large schools of fish found around the wrecks. Shelling is also good on the sandy bottom.

NO. 9 *CASA BLANCA*

Location: On a 63° course, 4.6 miles from Blackmar's Reef.

LST landing craft is intact and sitting upright on the bottom at *Casa Blanca*. The wheelhouse and upper deck of the ship start 65 feet below the

Underwater Designers Company
Manufacturers Outlet

- High Quality Equipment & Clothing
- Open Tuesday – Saturday
  10 a.m. – 6 p.m.
- U.D.C. Name Brands
- Sales & Service for
  25 years
- National/International N.U.E.
  Certification & Master Scuba
  Instructor
- 4 classrooms & indoor heated pool
- Most major credit cards accepted

13637 Beach Blvd., Jacksonville, FL 32224 (904) 246-6729

surface, with the bottom of the ship resting in 112 feet of water. This allows divers to explore the wheelhouse and deck area with more bottom time. Many large jewfish and grouper inhabit the ship. Snapper and shells can be found in the sand surrounding the wreck. The landing craft offers very good sightseeing and photographic possibilities.

NO. 10 EAST FOURTEEN (GATOR BOWL)
Location: On a course of 90°, 15 miles from the Mayport jetties.

Six large structures from the old Gator Bowl press box were dropped on a prominent ledge formation. Although all the sections were scheduled to be placed together, they ended up in two groups situated about a quarter of a mile apart. Spearfishing along the ledges and around the broken rubble is quite good.

NO. 11 CLAYTON'S HOLLER
Location: 16.3 miles from the Mayport jetties on a course of 106°.

This is an area of natural ledges complemented by two sunken tugs. The larger tugboat is sitting upright a short distance from the main ledge. It is constantly surrounded by thousands of cigar minnows, which lend to it an eerie effect of motion. Mangrove and red snapper are thick on its deck, while grouper hide in the washed-out crevices under the hull. The entire area is good for spearing, shelling and lobstering. The deepest spot is 95 feet.

AQUATIC'S UNLIMITED

11300 Beach Blvd. Jacksonville, FL 32216
904-642-3073

Indoor heated pool • International certification
• Small personal classes • Day, night or private classes
• Steak dinner graduation party • Tropical salt water dives

Condition your body
Get more fun out of life
Stay healthier too

INSTRUCTION SAFETY National Association of SCUBA DIVING SCHOOLS SPORT INTEGRITY

DAYTONA BEACH

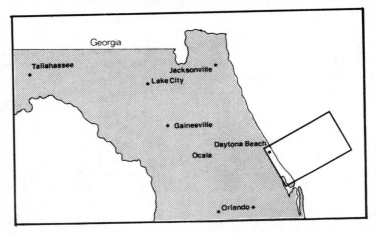

Offshore Diving Locations

1. North Jetty
2. Nine Mile Hill
3. North East Grounds
4. Party Grounds
5. East Eleven

6. Turtle Mound
7. East Ridge
8. Twelve Mile Wreck
9. Twin Airplane Wreck
10. Freighter Wreck

Area Information

The waters off Daytona Beach offer a variety of challenging diving experiences, from spearfishing and "bug snatchin'" to wreck diving of WWII planes and Liberty ships. They even have an old 19th Century Spanish-American War gunrunner. Water temperatures vary from the low 50s in winter to the high 70s in summer. Visibility is best during the summer months, averaging 25 feet. Diving charters run to the wreck nearly every weekend. Check with local dive shops for information.

NO. 1 NORTH JETTY (Beach Dive)
Location: Runs approximately one mile out into the Atlantic Ocean from the north shore of Ponce Inlet.

Large numbers of fish, stone crabs and some lobster inhabit this artificial reef. No spearfishing is allowed. Follow A1A south from highway 92

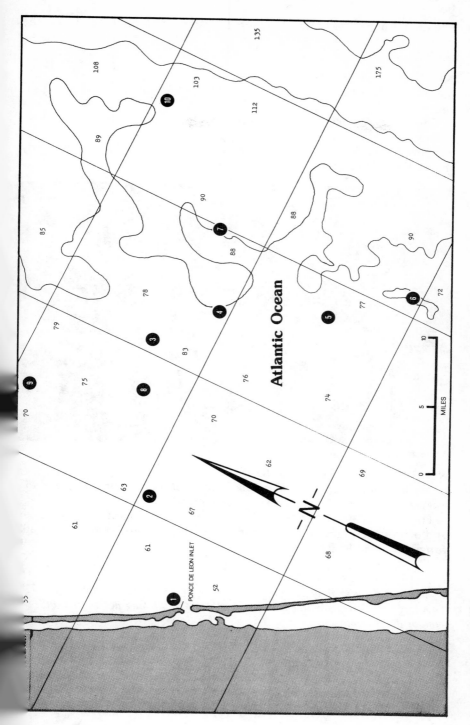

Atlantic Ocean

PONCE DE LEON INLET

-N-

MILES
0   5   10

135
175
108
103
112
89
90
88
90
85
78
88
77
72
79
83
76
74
75
70
70
69
63
67
62
61
61
68
52
55

1
2
3
4
5
6
7
8
9
10

Daytona Beach for ten miles to where it dead ends. Turn left and go to the beach. Then turn right and go one half mile and you'll see the granite jetty. Seek local advice about currents before diving.

NO. 2 NINE MILE HILL
Location: Go approximately 9 miles from the sea buoy at Ponce Inlet on a 43° course.

This is a large artificial reef composed of old cars, tires and concrete pilings. There is also some natural reef in the area with four-foot ledges. However, it is difficult to locate. The artificial part of the reef is clearly marked with two large orange balls, one at each end.

A tiny arrow crab makes his home in a sponge.

NO. 3 NORTH EAST GROUNDS
Location: Approximately 14 miles from Ponce Inlet sea buoy on a course of 45° marked by a black flag with markings NE on float.

The North East Grounds is a good area for large snapper, sheepsheac and octopus. Ledges of two to four feet are typical, and depths generall run about 80 to 85 feet.

NO. 4 PARTY GROUNDS
Location: Approximately 24 miles from Ponce Inlet sea buoy on a course of 72 This large reef area is marked with a north and south flag designated with th symbol PG on floats.

This area is good for grouper, snapper, cobia and lobster. The reef rur northeast and southwest, and has depths from 80 to 95 feet. Visibili ranges from 15 to 80 feet, but is usually at least 20 feet plus.

NO. 5 EAST ELEVEN
Location: Approximately 25 miles from Ponce Inlet sea buoy on a course of 9

This is a large reef with eight- to ten-foot ledges and depths from 66 to 75 feet. Large numbers of fish and some lobster are found here. There's also excellent shelling and tropical fish collecting. Visibility usually averages 20 to 30 feet.

NO. 6 TURTLE MOUND

Location: Approximately 27 miles from Ponce Inlet sea buoy on a course of 103° (no markers).

This is another large reef with ten- to 12-foot ledges and depths of 60 to 70 feet. There are large numbers of fish, and visibility usually runs from 15 to 80 feet.

NO. 7 EAST RIDGE

Location: Approximately 28 miles from the Ponce Inlet sea buoy on a course of 62°.

East Ridge is an excellent dive spot, with ten- to 14-foot ledges and numerous small caves. Large grouper, snapper and lobster inhabit the area. It is also excellent for photography, especially during the summer months. Seek local advice before attempting to locate East Ridge, as it is not marked.

NO. 8 TWELVE MILE WRECK

Location: 14 miles from Ponce Inlet sea buoy on a course of 52°. Marked by a black flag during the summer.

This wreck sank during the 1800s, and is reported to be an old Spanish-American War gunrunner, deduced from the large amounts of Gatling ammunition found around it. Large jewfish inhabit the area along with giant amberjacks and vast numbers of spadefish. This is an unusually beautiful dive during the summer when the water is clear. Local guides must be contacted for assistance in locating this small wreck.

NO. 9 TWIN AIRPLANE WRECK

Location: 16 miles from the Ponce Inlet sea buoy on a course of 25°. Local guides should be contacted for exact location.

This is an area where two TB-M torpedo bombers crashed during WWII. The wrecks are located approximately 200 yards apart, in 71 feet of water. Excellent spearfishing is to be had here, with many snapper and large sheepshead. This is also a good area for artifact hunting. There are still machine guns and shell casings aboard the two aircraft.

NO. 10 FREIGHTER WRECK

Location: Approximately 50 miles offshore of Daytona on a course of 60° from the Ponce Inlet sea buoy. Seek the assistance of local guides for exact location.

This is a Liberty ship that's loaded with jeeps and other war materials. It was torpedoed during WWII. Its remains are scattered over a large area of bottom, and many artifacts can be found. Spearfishing is great here, but the current is often strong (one to three knots).

VERO BEACH

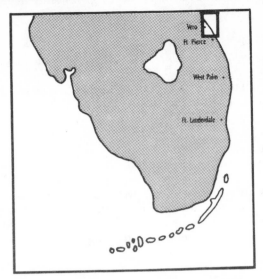

Offshore Diving Locations

1. *El Capitana* and McLarty Museum
2. Wabasso Beach
3. Indian River Shores
4. Tracking Station
5. Jaycee and Conn Way Beaches
6. *Breconshire* Wreck (Boiler Wreck)
7. Humiston Beach
8. Riomar Reef
9. Sandy Point
10. Round Island
11. The Pines

Area Information

The Vero Beach area offers a rarity of Florida—good beach divin Although the clear waters of the Gulf Stream course well offshore, insho visibility of up to 25 feet can be expected during periods of calm sea Spearing, lobstering, tropical fish collecting and relic hunting are favor underwater activities.

A stellar attraction of the area is the scattered remains of cannon a ballast from the ill-fated 1715 Spanish Silver Plate Fleet. Violent hurrica winds forced ten treasure-laden ships onto inshore reefs. A pounding s quickly broke the wooden vessels apart, scattering their valuable carg silver and gold. It was not until the late '50s that the wreck site v discovered and salvaged. The excavated riches produced one of

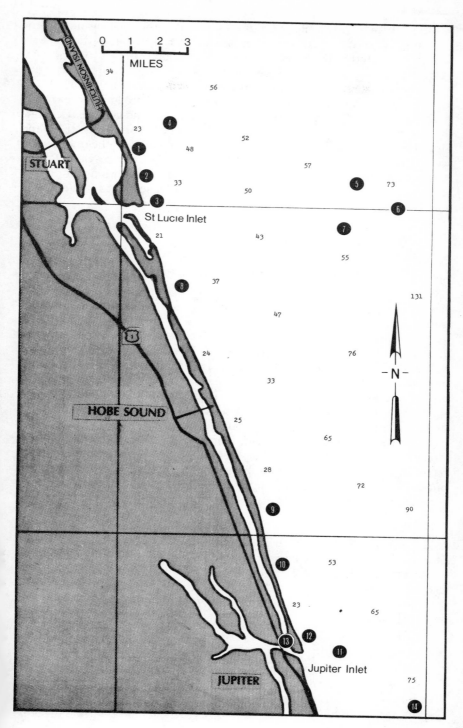

HUTCHINSON ISLAND

0   1   2   3
MILES

STUART

St Lucie Inlet

HOBE SOUND

JUPITER

Jupiter Inlet

- N -

34
56
23   48   52
33   57
50   73
21
43   55
37
47
24   76
33
25
65
28
72
90
53
23   65
75

world's greatest underwater treasure finds. Today, the exciting story of the treasure fleet and the recovery of her precious cargo are told at the McLarty Museum, located in the Sebastian Inlet Recreational Area. An occasional cannon or ballast pile can still be spotted by divers on local reefs.

Offshore rock reefs run for miles parallel to the many beaches. There are four reef lines. The first (closest to shore) and second are low and partially covered with sand. A variety of tropicals, soft corals and sponges decorate the outcroppings. Approximately 200 to 400 feet offshore lie the third and fourth reefs, their depths varying from ten to 30 feet. Here, the underwater scenery is bolder, with high ledges often undercut by deep crevices. Rough seas not only limit water visibility, but create unsafe conditions for diving. However, when the conditions are right, you will discover a real underwater treat in the beach diving off Vero.

NO. 1 *EL CAPITANA* AND McLARTY MUSEUM (Beach Dive)
Location: From the intersection of SR 60 and A1A, go north on A1A for 11 miles,
OR
1 mile south of the Sebastian Inlet Bridge to the Sebastian Inlet State Recreation Area.

The *El Capitana* is one of the ten treasure galleons that were driven onto local reefs by violent weather in 1715. A few cannon and hundreds of ballast stones are scattered across the reef. The large reef area starts 20 feet offshore. Depths range from two to 20 feet. Because of the shallow depth, entries and exits can be hazardous during periods of rough surf.

Divers will be interested in visiting the state-run McLarty Museum which is located in the park. It is situated on the site of the salvage camp used by the survivors of the fleet. The exciting history of the fleet, its violent fate and the recovery of its fabulous wealth of gold and silver are recounted at the museum. It is open to the public Wednesday through Sunday from 9 a.m. to 5 p.m. Admission to the recreational area, including a visit to the museum, is 50¢.

NO. 2 WABASSO BEACH (Beach Dive)
Location: Go east from the intersection of SR 510 and A1A.

Wabasso Beach area is a large public park with plenty of parking and easy access to the beach. The reef starts 75 feet from the shore. Depths range from six to 15 feet. There are many ledges inhabited by an abundance of marine life.

NO. 3 INDIAN RIVER SHORES (Beach Dive)
Location: From the intersection of SR 60 and A1A, go north for 5 miles. There are two access roads to the beach within 1 mile of each other.

A long section of ledges run parallel to the beach, 150 feet offshore. Depths vary from ten to 20 feet. Fish and lobster are abundant in the area.

NO. 4 TRACKING STATION (Beach Dive)

Location: Travel 2 ½ miles north on A1A from the intersection of SR 60 and A1A. The beach access is located between a 7-11 and an Eckerd's drugstore.

Tracking Station is located at a large public beach with plenty of parking. The reef line starts about 200 feet off the beach. Depths range from ten to 20 feet. The bottom is quite rocky, with piles of large stone slabs forming the reef.

NO. 5 JAYCEE AND CONN WAY BEACHES (Beach Dive)

Location: Go 1 mile north from SR 60 on Ocean Drive.

This large public beach area is over one-mile long. Beach entries can be made anywhere. There are four distinct reef lines starting 200 feet from shore. Depths average 20 feet. There are numerous ledges, eight- to ten-feet high. Many are undercut with intersecting caves.

NO. 6 *BRECONSHIRE WRECK* (BOILER WRECK) (Beach Dive)

Location: At the end of SR 60 (east), 150 yards east of the Ocean Grill Restaurant, a section of the boiler protrudes from the surface, making her exact location easy to spot.

This 200-foot steel ship went down on April 30, 1894. She rests in 15 to 20 feet of water. A conglomerate of marine growth covers her twisted

THE PERSONAL SERVICE SHOP

DEEP **6** DIVE SHOP INC. VERO BEACH, FLORIDA 562-2883

INSHORE REEFS WHICH PROVIDE

BEACH DIVING LOBSTERING SPEAR FISHING WRECKS

TRIPS REPAIRS RENTALS CLASSES

OPEN 7 DAYS

1550 Old Dixie, Vero Beach, Fl. 32960 (So. of 16th St.) (305) 562-2883

remains. Natural reef ledges surround the site. Good lobstering and spearfishing are found here.

NO. 7 HUMISTON BEACH (Beach Dive)

Location: From the end of SR 60, go south on Ocean Drive for ¼ mile.

Humiston is a large public beach area with ample parking, restrooms and showers. Beach lifeguards can point out the better entry points for the reef. The first of four reef lines start 100 feet from the shore. The last line is 400 feet off the beach.

NO. 8 RIOMAR REEF (Beach Dive)

Location: From the 17th Street Bridge, go north on A1A for 1 mile. Turn east on Riomar Drive. Public parking is located at the end of the road. Public access is next to the Riomar Beach Club.

This is a large expanse of reef that sweeps in an arc   from ten to 500 feet off the beach. Depths vary from three to 20 feet. A few cannons from the 1715 fleet are located in the area.

NO. 9 SANDY POINT REEF

Location: The reef can be reached only by boat due to the lack of public access from shore. It is situated 250 feet due east of the Moorings Development water tower.

Sandy Point consists of some nice ledges in ten to 20 feet of water, where there is good spearing and lobstering. Cannons from the 1715 fleet are in the area.

NO. 10 ROUND ISLAND (Beach Dive)

Location: 5 miles south of the 17th Street Bridge on A1A. Look for the entrance sign on the east side of the highway.

Round Island is another large public beach with easy access to the water. The reef is 150 feet offshore, in 15 feet of water. Good fish life and a few lobster inhabit the area.

NO. 11 THE PINES (Beach Dive)

Location: From the 17th Street Bridge, go south on A1A for 7 miles. Look closely for a small gravel drive-through in a large cluster of pine trees. Or, go ¾ of a mile north of the Bryn Mawr Camp Ground. Be careful not to get your car stuck in soft sand pockets on the road. Walk 300 feet north for water entry to close-in section of reef.

This is not a public beach, but it is open to the public. The reef starts 200 feet from the beach. Depths range from ten to 20 feet. The Pines is one of the better sites for spearing and lobstering.

DINGO
"The Choice of Professionals"

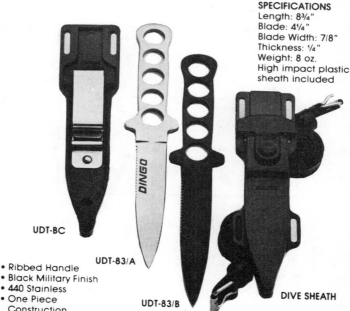

SPECIFICATIONS
Length: 8¾"
Blade: 4¼"
Blade Width: 7/8"
Thickness: ¼"
Weight: 8 oz.
High impact plastic
sheath included

UDT-BC

UDT-83/A

UDT-83/B

DIVE SHEATH

- Ribbed Handle
- Black Military Finish
- 440 Stainless
- One Piece Construction
- Fully Guaranteed
- Includes Sheath Straps
- Bootclip Sheath $4.95
- Leather Bootclip $5.95

UDT-83/A	$31.95
UDT-83/B	$34.95
UDT-BC	$4.95
DIVE SHEATH	FREE
S/H/I	$3.00
FOREIGN	$6.00

TO ORDER CALL TOLL FREE
1-800-874-8499
(Florida, Hawaii, Alaska Call [904] 376-2220)
Visa/MasterCard or send check/money order to
DINGO CUTLERY CO.
4509 NW 23 AVE. #8
GAINESVILLE, FL 32606
*Please add $3.00 S/H/I to your order (Foreign add $6.00)
DEALER INQUIRIES WELCOME

FT. PIERCE

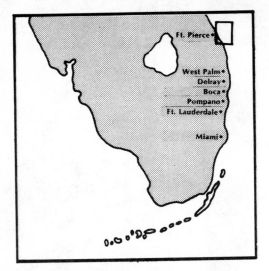

Offshore Diving Locations

1. Paddle-Wheeler Wreck
2. Pepper Park
3. Inlet Park
4. Jaycee Park
5. South Beach Rocks
6. Old South Bridge
7. The Fingers
8. Independence Reef
9. The Horse Shoe
10. *Amazon* (12A Wreck)
11. Halsey (Southeast Wreck)

Area Information

A Spanish treasure fleet, the Civil War, WWII and Mother Nature have all contributed to the adventure and beauty that is Ft. Pierce diving. For years, the region has been known as a spearfishing and bull lobster haven, but today it is being acclaimed as Florida's newest up-and-coming sport diving center. Clean sandy beaches provide easy access to several good dives within a short distance of shore. Add to this an excellent, protected, deepwater inlet for quick boat trips to the deeper reefs and wrecks, and it's a wonder that Ft. Pierce wasn't discovered years earlier. Motels and hotel rooms are plentiful, as is evening entertainment. With a small town flavor and big city conveniences, Ft. Pierce is ready to greet adventurers of the '80s.

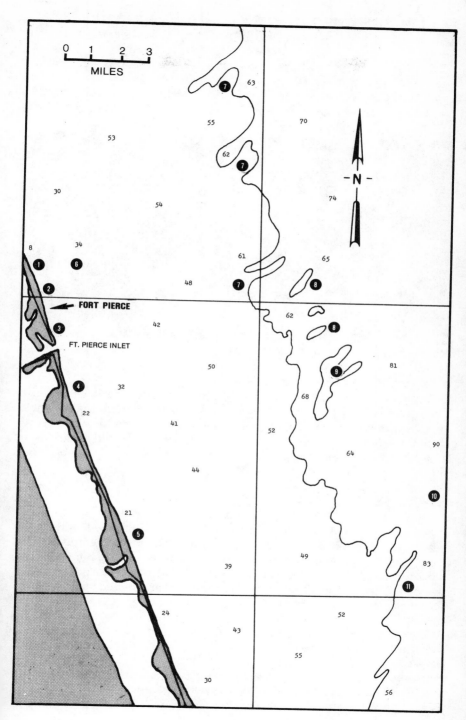

NO. 1 PADDLE-WHEELER WRECK (Beach Dive)
Location: .9 of a mile south of Bryn Mawr Camp Grounds entrance on A1A north.

The remains of a Civil War-era paddle-wheeler lie 100 yards off the beach. The ship rests on clean sand and can be seen easily from shore on calm days. Thousands of tropicals make their home among the broken ribs and boiler. Depths vary from 15 to 20 feet.

RICHARD COLLINS

Wrecks abound from Ft. Pierce through the Keys.

NO. 2 PEPPER PARK (Beach Dive)
Location: On north A1A, approximately 2 miles north of the Ft. Pierce Inlet.

This is an all-time favorite of area divers. The formations begin as close as 100 yards from the beach, and are great for both skin and scuba diving. Depths range from 15 to 30 feet. There is good lobstering, but spearfishing is prohibited because Pepper is a municipal park. The park provides showers and other excellent facilities.

NO. 3 INLET PARK (Beach Dive)
Location: Just off A1A at the southern point of Ft. Pierce Inlet.

A large variety of rock formations and ledges stretch the length of the beach. Some are as close as 75 yards from shore. Depths range from 15 to 30 feet. This is a great spot for lobstering and tropical fish hunting. The remains of a small net fishing boat can be found a quarter of a mile north of the Inlet. The facilities at Inlet Park are excellent, and include picnic tables, showers and restrooms. The entrance fee is 50¢.

NO. 4 JAYCEE PARK (Beach Dive)
Location: On A1A, 1½ miles south of the Inlet. Use the large water tower as a marker.

The ledges of the south beach area are a continuation of the chain of ledges that run from Ft. Pierce. There are three sets of ledges: at 15 to 20 feet; 25 to 30 feet; and 55 to 60 feet. Spearfishing is good and shelling is excellent. It is also a good location for lobster early in the season. Inshore diving ranges from 100 yards to 300 yards out from the beach, making Jaycee Park an ideal area for inflatables.

NO. 5 SOUTH BEACH ROCKS (Beach Dive)
Location: On A1A south, at the first turn-off after the St. Lucie Nuclear Power Plant.

Marine life is plentiful and spearfishing is hot at South Beach Rocks. Barracuda are commonly sighted. While depths range from ten to 18 feet, this area is not recommended for novices. Care should be taken to stay clear of the intakes of the nuclear power plant. Currents can be treacherous. Enjoy this dive, but use caution.

NO. 6 OLD SOUTH BRIDGE
Location: 1 mile north of the Inlet.

The broken rubble from the Old South Bridge was dumped in 30 to 40 feet of water to create a fish haven. Bottom fish are plentiful, but lobsters are scarce. This is a good spot for the tropical fish collector. The fish haven has proved so popular that plans are underway to develop the area further by placing a tire reef nearby.

NO. 7 THE FINGERS
Location: Follow a 60° heading from the Ft. Pierce Inlet for about 12 miles.

DIXIE DIVERS INC.
A FULL SERVICE PROFESSIONAL DIVE STORE

SPECIALIZING IN DIVING INSTRUCTION

- Instruction from Beginner to Master Diver
- PADI International 5-Star Training Facility
- Over 90 brands sold & serviced
- Trips & Tours
- Air to 5000 psi

OPEN 7 DAYS   MAJOR CREDIT CARDS ACCEPTED

1717 South U.S. Hwy 1
461-4488
Ft. Pierce, FL

1843 S.E. Federal Hwy.
283-5588
Stuart, FL

The Fingers stretch for ten miles north and run at depths ranging from 45 to 66 feet. They are teeming with marine life, and seem to be a combination of beautiful Keys diving and true wilderness. Many snapper and grouper can be spotted roaming around the ledges. The beauty and marine life found here make this a must for the underwater photographer. Lobstering and spearfishing are good. Brightly colored tropicals are plentiful.

NO. 8 INDEPENDENCE REEF
Location: Approximately 7 miles due east of the Ft. Pierce Inlet.

This spot is difficult to find, but because of that, it harbors an abundance of marine life. Its ledges rise three to ten feet off the bottom, and lie in 55 feet of water.

NO. 9 THE HORSE SHOE
Location: Approximately 10 miles east of the Ft. Pierce Inlet.

Depths range from 55 to 65 feet. A wide variety of fish can be found at this site. Grouper, well over 15 pounds, are abundant. Tales of large lobster are commonly associated with this area. In addition, the colors found at The Horse Shoe are beautiful. This dive is a must.

NO. 10 *AMAZON* (12A WRECK)
Location: 16 miles east-southeast of the Ft. Pierce Inlet.

A large freighter torpedoed during WWII rests in 100 feet of water. Her several large parts are host to hundreds of large gamefish.

NO. 11 HALSEY (SOUTHEAST WRECK)
Location: Approximately 13 miles east-southeast of the Ft. Pierce Inlet.

Halsey consists of two large freighters sunk two days apart during WWII. They lie on a sandy bottom, about three miles apart. Over the years, they have attracted an abundance of sea life, creating one of the coast's most prolific fish havens. They are a favorite of divers and bottom fishermen alike. Divers should show courtesy to fish charter captains. Also, be aware of frequently strong currents in the area.

UNDER SEA WORLD
FULL SERVICE PRO DIVE SHOP

- PURE AIR
- INDOOR POOL
- TWIN COMPRESSORS

- CHARTERS
- REPAIRS
- RENTALS • SALES

521 NORTH U.S. 1   FORT PIERCE, FL **(305) 465-4114**

STUART-JUPITER

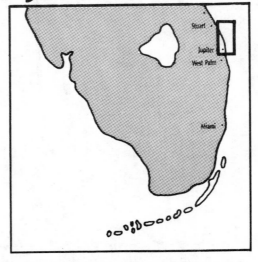

Offshore Diving Locations

1. House of Refuge-Old Schooner Wreck
2. Bathtub Reef
3. North Jetty Reef-St. Lucie Inlet
4. Toilet Bowl Reef
5. Six Mile Reef
6. LST-St. Lucie Inlet
7. Tire Reef
8. Pecks Lake and Kingfish Hole
9. Gulf Pride
10. Blowing Rocks
11. Jupiter Reefs and Grouper Hole
12. Carlin Park
13. South Jupiter Island Bridge
14. Jupiter High Ledge

Area Information

The Atlantic reefs from Jupiter through Stuart are generally continuations of the rock ledges that parallel the West Palm coastline. However, there are two major differences: water visibility is less here, and there are fewer divers exploring these waters.

The Florida peninsula inclines gradually westward as it proceeds north of West Palm. Reefs following the contour of the land are abandoned by the Gulf Stream's clear water as it continues its northerly flow. Murky outflow

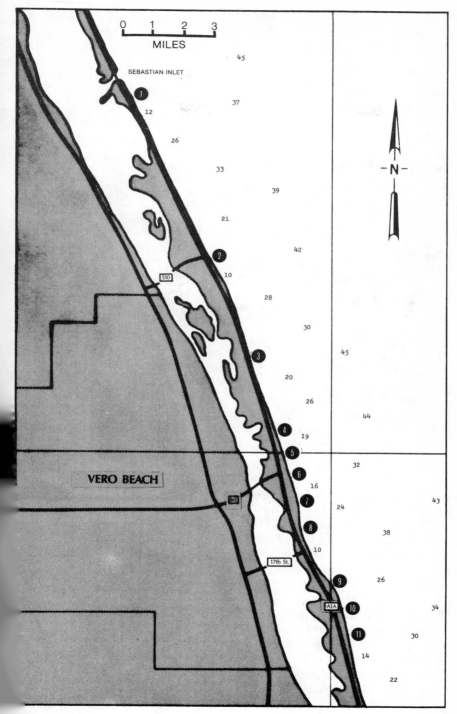

0 1 2 3
MILES

SEBASTIAN INLET

45

37

12

26

33

39

21

42

510

10

28

30

45

20

26

44

19

32

VERO BEACH

50

16

43

24

38

10

17th St.

26

34

A1A

30

14

22

-N-from rivers and water periodically released from Lake Okeechobee also limit visibility. Summer diving is considered best. Then, calm and clearer waters usually prevail. Diving during winter months is more demanding but offers a greater variety of fish and more lobster.

Fewer divers mean more and larger lobster and lobsters are what make local waters famous! Dixie Divers' Annual Lobster Hunt brings divers down from all over the southeast to try their hand at grabbing record size "bugs" for prizes. The top ten finishers are all between eight and 13 pounds!

Warm South Florida waters nourish creatures such as this feather duster.

Because they are dived less, the rock reefs of the area are not as easily identified as those to the south. They are, however, quite large and extensive, sometimes running continuously for miles. Prominent reefs begin three miles offshore in 60 to 65 feet of water. The outer ledges are impressive but deep. They are in 120 to 160 feet of water. Divers accustomed to the shallower reefs in southern Palm Beach County find the northern reefs more sparse in terms of marine life such as sea fans and gorgonians. They more than redeem themselves with their abundance of larger species (grouper, amberjack, turtles, and, of course, lobster).

NO. 1 HOUSE OF REFUGE—OLD SCHOONER WRECK (Beach Dive)
Location: Just off A1A at the south end of Hutchinson Island.

The House of Refuge is an old life-saving station, the last of its kind. Now a museum, it is well worth a visit to see the displays and the turtles that are raised there. The turtles are kept until they are big enough to have an increased chance of survival; then released to the oceans.

The ribs of an old schooner can be found by swimming 100 yards straight off the south end of the concrete block wall in front of the museum. Sand dollars are sometimes found on the sandy flats that lead to the schooner.

NO. 2 BATHTUB REEF (Beach Dive)
Location: On Hutchinson Island, travel south on MacArthur Blvd. to the public beach at the end of the road.

This is a popular snorkeling site. The best diving is at high tide on the shallow rock reefs that parallel the beach.

NO. 3 NORTH JETTY REEF/ST. LUCIE INLET (Beach Dive)
Location: From the tip of the north rock jetty at the St. Lucie Inlet, head due north toward the Bathtub Reef area.

This is a good drift dive over rock ledges in four to 20 feet of water. Be sure to look for large snook hiding under the reefs. Early in the season, many lobster of legal size and a few nice size stone crabs are in residence. Make sure they are in season, though, as the Florida Marine Patrol diligently protects this area.

NO. 4 TOILET BOWL REEF
Location: From the St. Lucie Inlet, travel 3 ½ miles on a 10° course, or about 2 miles due east of the House of Refuge.

DIXIE DIVERS INC.
A FULL SERVICE PROFESSIONAL DIVE STORE

SPECIALIZING IN DIVING INSTRUCTION

- Instruction from
  Beginner to Master Diver
- PADI International 5-Star
  Training Facility

- Over 90 brands
  sold & serviced
- Trips & Tours
- Air to 5000 psi

OPEN 7 DAYS   MAJOR CREDIT CARDS ACCEPTED

1717 South U.S. Hwy 1
461-4488
Ft. Pierce, FL

1843 S.E. Federal Hwy.
283-5588
Stuart, FL

175

The area is aptly named because this artificial reef was formed by the dumping of old toilets. The depth is 60 feet. It will certainly be a memorable dive and it might be possible to "flush" out a fish or lobster.

NO. 5 SIX MILE REEF
Location: From the St. Lucie Inlet, travel 6 miles on an 80° course.

This reef includes a nice ledge in 75 to 80 feet of water. Many gray grouper are found in the area. A current is usually running to the north.

NO. 6 LST—STUART
Location: From the St. Lucie Inlet, travel 6½ miles due east.

A recently sunk LST rests in an upright position in 85 feet of water. It was stripped and then sunk by blowing two holes in her bottom.

NO. 7 TIRE REEF
Location: From the St. Lucie Inlet, travel 4 miles on a 115° course.

This artificial reef project has been underway for several years. The old tires form excellent habitats for marine life. Its depth is about 60 feet.

NO. 8 PECKS LAKE AND KINGFISH HOLE
Location: 3 miles south of the St. Lucie Inlet, adjacent to Pecks Lake in the Intracoastal Waterway.

The Kingfish Hole is about 900 yards offshore in 34 feet of water. Lobster abound in this area. Depths vary from two to 20 feet. This is an excellent place to free-dive when the weather is clear.

NO. 9 GULF PRIDE
Location: 4 miles due north of the Jupiter Inlet.

A victim of a collision during WWII, the *Gulfland* tanker burned and split into two sections. Today, the wreckage supports a huge variety of marine life, ranging from swarming schools of baitfish to large barracuda and grouper. Because of its close proximity to the beach (about one mile offshore) it should only be dived during periods of calm seas when there is clear water. She rests in 40 feet of water.

NO. 10 BLOWING ROCKS (Beach Dive)
Location: 2 miles north on A1A of Jupiter Inlet, at the beachfront on Jupiter Island. The area is called the Blowing Rock Preserve. The reefs begin just about where the condos end and continue north to Hobe Sound.

A very craggy, rocky shoreline (footwear is recommended) that extend below the surface of the water in the form of holes and ledges that ar favorite haunts of snook and other schooling fish. This area can be roug to dive when the surf is up, but on calm days it is an excellent spot. Ther is plenty of parking available.

NO. 11 JUPITER REEF AND GROUPER HOLE
Location: 1½ miles due east of the Jupiter Inlet on the first reef line.

The reef parallels the shoreline and runs north. Depths range from 70

80 feet. Surrounding waters can be very clear on calm days. Deep, tunneled ledges about five feet in height make ideal havens for grouper during their annual winter migration. Some areas of the reef have back openings or "blow holes" which divers can swim through.

NO. 12 CARLIN PARK (Beach Dive)
Location: A county park on the beach just south of the Jupiter Hilton.

A good snorkeling and diving spot with crumbled rocks extending out to about 15 feet of depth. The surf can be rough here, but on calm days the water clears quickly. Many tropicals adorn the rocks. The park provides excellent parking and picnic facilities.

NO. 13 SOUTH JUPITER ISLAND BRIDGE (Beach Dive)
Location: On the south end of Jupiter Island, take the bridge over the Intracoastal just north of the Coast Guard Station. The road is marked as A1A or SR 707. Go down the dirt road on the bridge's left bank.

Dive at high, slack tide for the best visibility and least current. Stay out of the Intracoastal channel and fly a dive flag. The depth near the bridge footings just off the beach is approximately 25 feet. There are many tropicals here, with some stone crabs and lobster early in the season.

NO. 14 JUPITER HIGH LEDGE
Location: A northern extension of the Juno Ball Reef (No. 2 in the next chapter) 3 to 4 miles offshore and virtually in the Gulf Stream. It runs to the Jupiter Inlet.

A spectacular dive for more experienced divers. This is the highest relief of any Palm Beach County reef, 90 feet in the sand at the base and 65 to 70 feet at the top of the reef. A huge, stepped ledge includes crumbled boulders and crevices galore. This ledge lends itself to drift diving. Due to its sheer mass and myriad hiding places, the reef supports an abundance of marine life in many sizes, shapes and species. Schooling snapper, amberjack and grunt can be so thick that they occasionally obscure the reef from view. Grouper, lobster, moray eels and tropicals lurk about the shadowy holes and crevices.

SCUBA SPORTS INC.

JUPITER TEQUESTA
SCUBA SPORTS
150 US HWY 1 TEQUESTA
TEQUESTA FASHION SQUARE
746-1555

Stop in and talk diving.

• SALES • REPAIRS • AIR STATION
• REEF TRIPS • INSTRUCTION
• MARINE EQUIPMENT
• GEAR & WETSUIT RENTALS

WEST PALM BEACH
RIVIERA BEACH

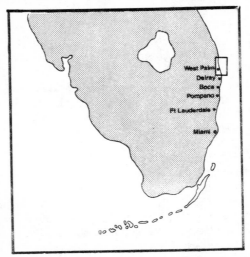

Offshore Diving Locations

1. The Cave
2. Juno Ball Reef
3. Sea Shell City
4. Koller's Reef
5. Valley Reef
6. *Mizpah*
7. *Amarilys*
8. The Barge

9. North Cove
10. Rock Piles
11. Breaker's Reef
12. The Trench
13. Cable Crossing
14. The Cove
15. Paul's Reef
16. Horseshoe Reef

Area Information

Diving the reefs along the shores of the Palm Beaches provides a sensational sense of exploration and discovery. Local divers refer to themselves as "Palm Beach Divers" because of their pride in the rugged, untamed beauty that envelops the reefs. Palm Beach diving has an advan-

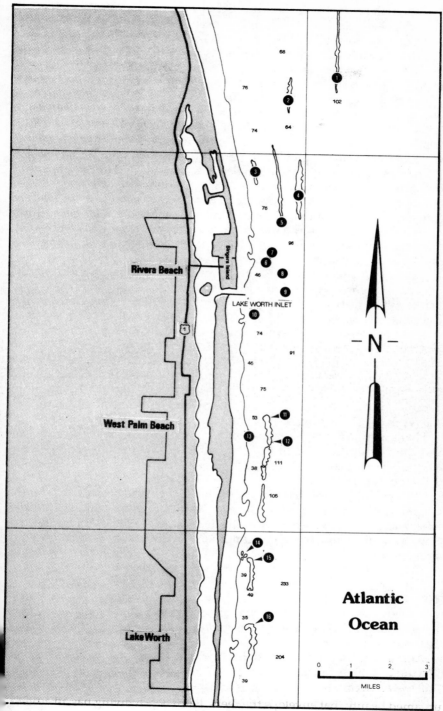

Rivera Beach

West Palm Beach

Lake Worth

LAKE WORTH INLET

Atlantic Ocean

-N-

0   1   2   3
MILES

tage over all other diving locations because of one main factor—the Gulf Stream. This warm current swings closer to shore here than anywhere else along the coast of Florida. The result is warm water diving year 'round and unbelievably clear, clean water that is continually feeding and refreshing the reefs, keeping them well-stocked with beautiful tropicals, lobster, huge game fish, sea fans and corals. The gentle currents let divers experience drift diving, and enables them to explore miles of beautiful reefs with little swimming effort! One of the great conveniences of Palm Beach diving is that all the reefs, ranging in depth from 30 to over 100 feet, are well within two miles of land and close to the inlet. The Palm Beach Inlet is wide and deep, making boating quite easy and safe even for beginners.

The diving facilities of the Palm Beaches offer vacationing divers everything they could ask, making trips exciting, convenient and diverse. Reef trips for single or two-tank dives are available. The diving operations are complete facilities, supplying guide services, sales, rentals, instruction, repairs, photo services and air. Marinas and boat ramps are located only minutes from the Palm Beach Inlet. The Palm Beaches is a vacation resort offering a wide variety of motels, fine restaurants and beaches.

A year 'round look at Palm Beach diving shows that the summer months of May through September offer the calmest seas, ranging anywhere from flat as a lake to two to three feet on average. From September through December, the weather is changeable. Seas can still be flat, but may increase to three to five feet depending on the South Florida weather picture. From January through March, temperatures from the low to mid-60s can be expected at night, with 75° to 85° as daytime highs. Charter boats still run trips when the seas are five to six feet for the hardy divers. The possibility of flat seas, however, exists year 'round. For those on vacation, good diving can be guaranteed some time, some place, during the week. April weather starts changing again to summer conditions.

There is always a great abundance of marine life for the avid spearfisherman, tropical fish collector, shell collector, photographer or sightseer. Visibility is normally 50 feet plus, though it is not uncommon to get 80- to 100-foot visibility.

The general attitude of the boat captains in the Palm Beach area is one of cooperation and safety-mindedness toward all divers coming into the area. Feel free to stop by at any of the dive shops that charter for information on local diving areas and conditions. It should be a must on your agenda.

NO. 1 THE CAVE
Location: 3½ to 4 miles offshore, and approximately a 45-minute boat ride from the Palm Beach Inlet. This dive site is located on the outside ledge of a reef that runs north and south.

Among the most awesome sights available to the underwater observer, the top of this reef is in 120 feet of water, its sides plunging downward to 160 feet. The cave, actually better described as a tunnel, cuts into a corner of this drop-off and elbows right back out again. The tunnel is big enough to drive two semis, side by side, all the way through. The floor of the cave is at 140 feet. The inside of the tunnel is full of ledges where 300-pound jewfish, 45-pound snappers and 50-pound grouper park themselves. The lobster are big enough to scare you. No lights are necessary. Once you enter the tunnel, you can see the huge exit. The length of the tunnel is approximately 60 to 80 feet. Schools of fish such as mackerel, tuna and amberjack whisk past the opening, waiting to catch glimpses of divers. This dive is for experienced divers only. Strong currents and sharks are common.

NO. 2 JUNO BALL REEF

Location: Approximately 3 miles from shore, and a boat ride of 45 minutes from Palm Beach Inlet.

This reef has a spectacular drop-off which starts in 65 feet of water and plummets to 85 feet. This ledge is ideal for drift diving, and includes a flagstone design of corals on the wall. You can float down the wall, drifting with game fish and sea turtles. Juno Ball Reef is also great for lobstering.

NO. 3 SEA SHELL CITY

Location: Approximately 3 miles north of Palm Beach Inlet. The boat ride is about 15 minutes.

This reef consists of a series of hills with smooth sloping sides that are covered with huge basket sponges and soft corals. Along the valley of

DIVE PALM BEACH!
ON BOARD THE BEST

Koller's Reef Scuba Charters

Get wet on a fabulous driftdive along coral reefs and wrecks teeming with sea life.

Our 37 foot, 20 passenger boat is equipped with fresh water showers, experienced dive guides, C.G. certified and located at marina, hosting fantastic restaurant, hotel, pool and docks. Also see turtle foundation.

11408 83rd Lane North, Lake Park, FL 33410 • 305-626-5537

these hills there are two-foot ledges with deep cracks and crevices, often crowded with fish and sometimes with lobster. This reef is fantastic for the observant shell collector and has rendered many a rare prized specimen, hence its name, Sea Shell City. Depths range from 65 to approximately 75 feet in the valleys.

NO. 4 KOLLER'S REEF
Location: Approximately 3 miles northeast of Palm Beach Inlet. Boat ride is about 15 minutes.

West Palm's waters are renowned for wrecks.

   Depths at Koller's Reef range from 75 to 85 feet. If you wish, you can drift dive the area, following the reef out to 125 feet. This is a very winding reef which meanders north and south. Sea turtles are quite commonly sighted, and they have no fear of divers, often coming in close to have their pictures taken. Spearfishing is great in this area, as it is on most of the northern reefs, which are heavily populated with red snapper and grouper. These rock ledges are covered with corals and, in combination with the many colorful tropicals, lend intricate beauty to the reefs.

NO. 5 VALLEY REEF
Location: Approximately 2 ½ miles from shore and a boat ride of 15 minutes from Palm Beach Inlet.

This reef is great for a "quickie" dive because it is so close to the Inlet. It runs north and south, making it another terrific drift dive possibility. There is a ledge on both sides of the diver, creating a valley effect down the middle. The depth in the valley is 75 feet, and the walls of the ledges vary between three and ten feet in height. A diver can drift this reef for a full 40 minutes bottom time and never run out of reef. Shelling is great, and the reef is abundant with game fish and tropicals.

NO. 6 *MIZPAH*
Location: Approximately 1 ½ miles from shore and about a ten-minute boat ride from Palm Beach Inlet.

The *Mizpah* is an old Greek luxury liner, 185 feet long and completely intact, lying in 90 feet of water. The *Mizpah* was sunk there about 14 years ago to serve as an artificial reef and fish preserve. Therefore, spearfishing, shell collecting and lobstering are prohibited. Lying next to the *Mizpah* is a patrol craft. The two ships rest on the bottom, side by side, right sides up. This dive site makes getting into wreck diving easy, safe and fun. No lights are needed throughout most of the wreck because it is well-exposed to light. All the doors have been removed and there are no loose cables. This has been done for the safety of divers. The wreck houses tons of fish and corals. The stern section of the patrol craft lies approximately 100 yards

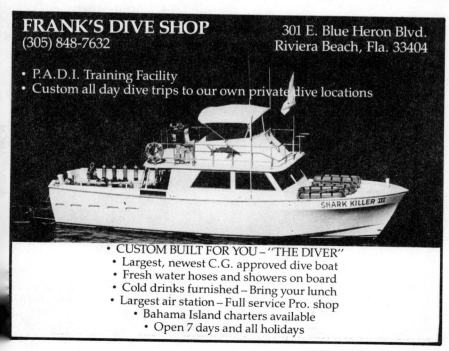

FRANK'S DIVE SHOP
(305) 848-7632

301 E. Blue Heron Blvd.
Riviera Beach, Fla. 33404

- P.A.D.I. Training Facility
- Custom all day dive trips to our own private dive locations

SHARK KILLER III

- CUSTOM BUILT FOR YOU – "THE DIVER"
  - Largest, newest C.G. approved dive boat
  - Fresh water hoses and showers on board
  - Cold drinks furnished – Bring your lunch
  - Largest air station – Full service Pro. shop
    - Bahama Island charters available
    - Open 7 days and all holidays

northeast of the *Mizpah.* Both sections of the wrecks abound with marine life as well as an impressive collection of the rare spiny oyster.

NO. 7 *AMARILYS*
Location: This wreck is located just 300 yards northeast of the Mizpah, *a short distance from Palm Beach Inlet.*

The *Amarilys* is approximately 300-feet long. Only its hull and lower deck remain. Because the wreck lies out in open sand, it has become a home for all the fish and marine life of the vicinity.

Diver explores a typical Palm Beach reef community.

NO. 8 THE BARGE
Location: 2 miles from shore and a ten-minute boat ride from Palm Beach Inlet.

When people think of Palm Beach wreck diving, this little barge doesn't always come to mind because of her competitors, the *Mizpah* and the *Amarilys.* As a result, large game fish constantly surround the barge and never hesitate to greet a diver. Everything on the barge is huge: there are morays, tropicals, 50- to 100-pound grouper, and, occasionally, a 300- to 400-pound jewfish. Shelling is quite good and a few rare specimens have been found. The barge is also full of spiny oysters. Depths range from 65 to

75 feet. Unlike the other wreck sites, the barge is surrounded by natural reefs.

NO. 9 NORTH COVE
Location: Approximately 1½ miles straight out the Palm Beach Inlet, ten minutes from the dock.

North Cove is an inside ledge in 65 to 80 feet of water, with a 15-foot drop. There are some game fish, lobster, and excellent shell collecting. Jewfish and pigmy angels are commonly sighted. If you drift 100 yards to the north, you'll find yourself atop a yellow blanket made up of literally thousands of porkfish. This site has, for obvious reasons, been named "Porkfish Hole." A number of such holes exist throughout the Palm Beach area.

NO. 10 ROCK PILES
Location: A large spoil area approximately half a mile in diameter, lying a short distance southeast of the south jetty of Lake Worth Inlet.

These large rock piles consist mainly of rubble from the dredging of the Inlet and turning basin. Depths range from 50 to 70 feet. The many rock piles are spaced ten to 50 feet apart. The location of the Rock Piles protects them from winds that might disturb other diving areas. The area has become a home to many forms of marine life. Tropical fish collecting is considered excellent, and lobster can be found during most of the year.

Ocean Realm Visors

$3.95

Ocean Realm Visors 2333 Brickell Ave., Miami, Fl. 33129

NO. 11 BREAKER'S REEF

Location: Approximately a half-hour boat ride from the Inlet and 1 mile from shore, straight out from the Breaker's Hotel.

Breaker's Reef is very long and runs north and south, twisting occasionally. Depths range from 45 to 60 feet at the bottom. Because it is extremely craggy, this reef is loaded with fish of all kinds. It also makes a splendid home for the Florida spiny lobster. Because the reef is so long and diversified, the diver will find he is on the verge of discovery with every bend he turns. Huge schools of harmless, friendly barracuda are one of the great sights, as is the abundance of sea turtles.

NO. 12 THE TRENCH

Location: Approximately 1 mile south of the Breaker's Reef.

The Trench is a man-made cut lying in an east-west direction through a natural reef. One hundred yards in length, the trench is about 20 feet across and has a ten-foot drop on both sides. A virtual aquarium in 45 to 55 feet of water, the Trench is abundant with spadefish and porkfish. If the timing is right, you may come up with a bagful of lobster. On every dive, giant turtles are spotted and an occasional nurse shark can be found sleeping under a ledge. This dive is ideal for both novice and experienced divers.

NO. 13 CABLE CROSSING

Location: Approximately ¼ of a mile offshore, following a half-hour boat ride south.

Having decided to protect this area so that all divers could share in its beauty, the Palm Beach divers have left sea fans and corals to grow unmolested. As a result, divers will witness a most colorful reef full of juvenile tropicals, purple sea fans, meandering rock ledges full of corals and sponges, many rays and, occasionally, some huge tarpon wandering through. Because of its shallow depth of only 30 feet, there is never any current and one can enjoy this area with only snorkel gear.

NO. 14 THE COVE

Location: Approximately a 45-minute boat ride from the dock, this area is jus northwest of Paul's Reef.

This is a natural coral arch through the reef which leads into a fishbow environment called The Cove. Large holes honeycomb the reef, providin an abundance of hiding places for large snapper and grouper. In the fa and winter months, large numbers of 15- to 20-pound gray grouper can b seen off in the sand. Huge green parrotfish pose for photographers. Th Cove lies at a depth of 40 to 50 feet.

NO. 15 PAUL'S REEF
Location: Approximately 4 miles south of Breaker's Reef.

Paul's Reef is the north end of a small reef formation, with a depth of 45 feet at the top of the reef and 60 feet at the sand bottom. The reef is noted for the large blue parrotfish that seem to be found around every turn. The reef is overgrown with soft corals, sea fans and hard corals, all exposing their feather-like polyps to the soft currents, even during daylight hours. Drift diving is excellent over the white sand bottom surrounding the reef, where sand dollars, fighting conchs and helmet shells can be found.

NO. 16 HORSESHOE REEF
Location: The northern tip of an extensive reef formation that parallels the coast in a southerly direction. Horeshoe Reef lies about 1 mile northeast of the Lake Worth pier.

Depths on Horseshoe Reef vary from 40 feet at the top of the reef to 55 feet in the sand. The inner ledge is a ten-foot vertical drop undercut in many areas by small caves and ledges. The reef is covered with a beautiful array of sponges and soft corals. Rays, barracuda and amberjacks are common. Many brightly colored tropicals can be seen darting in and out of the undercuts.

GULF STREAM DIVER SCUBA CHARTERS

THE BEST of "PALM BEACH" and "THE BAHAMAS"
2 NEW USCG CUSTOM DIVE BOATS

GULF STREAM DIVER III

- DAILY REEF AND WRECK TRIPS
- BAHAMA TRIPS, GROUP AND CUSTOM CHARTERS
- GUIDES ON EVERY DIVE
- RENTAL EQUIPMENT AND MOTEL RESERVATIONS
- PROFESSIONALLY RUN CHARTERS

WITH FIRST CLASS SERVICE
- 38' GULF STREAM DIVER II UP TO 24 DIVERS
- 41' GULF STREAM DIVER III UP TO 24 DIVERS (10 TO BAHAMAS)
- 4 AND 5 DAY BAHAMA TRIPS
- COMPRESSOR, GENERATOR, FULL ELECTRONICS

2315 CAROMA LANE
WEST PALM BEACH, FL 33406   (305) 965-7878

LAKE WORTH DELRAY BEACH

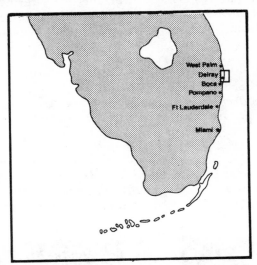

Offshore Diving Locations

1. Hogfish Reef
2. Lynn's Reef
3. Boynton Ledge
4. Fingers
5. Delray Ledge

NO. 1 HOGFISH REEF
Location: Approximately 2½ miles north of the southern Lake Worth Inlet.

The rolling contoured bottom is covered with large growths of grass th
shelter an abundance of tropicals and lobster. Depths vary from 45 to
feet. Low-profile patch reefs are located just to the west, where dept
range around 35 feet. The small reef heads support a community of s
corals and basket sponges. Hogfish are uncommonly plentiful. This is
excellent area for spotting large sea turtles.

NO. 2 LYNN'S REEF
*Location: The northern tip of the Boynton Ledge, a little over a mile south of
southern Lake Worth Inlet.*

Depths vary from 75 feet in the sand to 40 feet at the top of the reef. T
is one of the most popular diving locations in the area; weekend boat tra
is sometimes heavy, calling for caution. Fly your dive flag! Atlantic sea

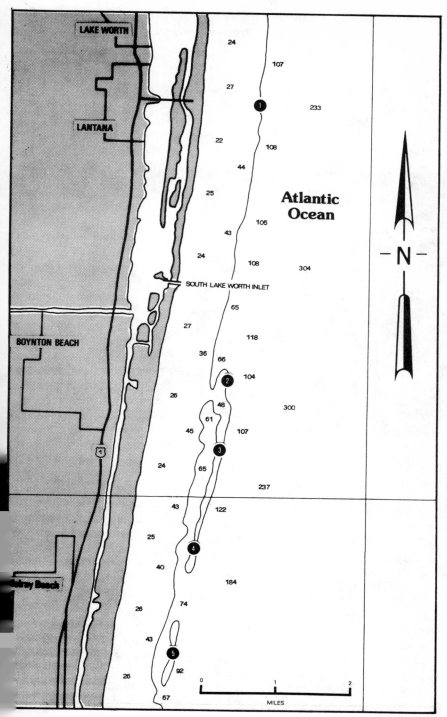

LAKE WORTH

LANTANA

BOYNTON BEACH

Delray Beach

SOUTH LAKE WORTH INLET

Atlantic
Ocean

– N –

24

107

27

233

1

22

108

44

25

105

43

108

304

24

65

27

118

36

66

2

104

26

48

61

45

107

300

3

24

65

237

43

122

25

4

40

184

26

74

43

5

92

26

67

0   1   2

MILES

189

is at its best here, allowing the underwater explorer to spend hours and never uncover all the varieties of tropicals and game fish that inhabit the area.

NO. 3 BOYNTON LEDGE

Location: This ledge is a continuation of Lynn's Reef.

Depths range from 50 feet on top of the reef to 65 feet in the sand. The inside of the ledge is honeycombed with holes, caves and crevices. Both hard and soft corals are plentiful. This is a great location for an exciting drift dive. Barracuda, grouper, snapper and amberjack are common.

A popular beach dive, the Delray wreck is profuse with marine life.

NO. 4 FINGERS

Location: The south end of the Boynton Ledge.

Six or seven major outcroppings project seaward at depths ranging from 45 feet on top to 80 feet in the sand. The Fingers are undercut by caves and ledges. Sea whips, sea fans and corals cover the reef, forming an abundance of hiding places for a large variety of tropicals and game fish.

NO. 5 DELRAY LEDGE

Location: About 1½ miles south of the Fingers.

Dramatic underwater scenery is at its best here. The almost vertical ledge is more profound than anywhere else along the "third reef." Large sections have broken from the main reef, forming narrow tunnels and passages. Caves and overhangs filled with sea life are waiting to be explored. The crown of the reef supports an outstanding growth of sponges and soft corals. Snapper, grouper, grunts and tropicals are common. An occasional nurse shark can be spotted hiding under the protection of an overhang. Depths range from 50 to 65 feet in the sand.

UNDERWATER FLORIDA

BOCA RATON TO HILLSBORO INLET

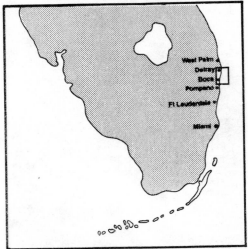

Offshore Diving Locations

1. Delray Wreck
2. Jap Rock
3. Boca North Beach Ledge
4. Westervelt's Ridges
5. Grouper Hole
6. Boca Artificial Reef Ledge
7. Separated Rocks
8. Hillsboro Ledge
9. Labonte Reef

NO. 1 DELRAY WRECK (Beach Dive)

Location: ¼ mile off the south end of Delray's public beach.

This steel-hulled freighter, sunk in the 1920s, has become a very popu diving location. Excellent for the beginner, the ship has broken into th distinct parts. Many varieties of soft and hard corals have taken over remains of the ship, which rests in 22 feet of water. Photography, sp fishing and lobstering are among the activities divers enjoy on the wr Sometimes crowded on weekends, this dive should be on every visi diver's list. It has also become a very popular night diving location. Be to fly your dive flag! This is a very busy boating area.

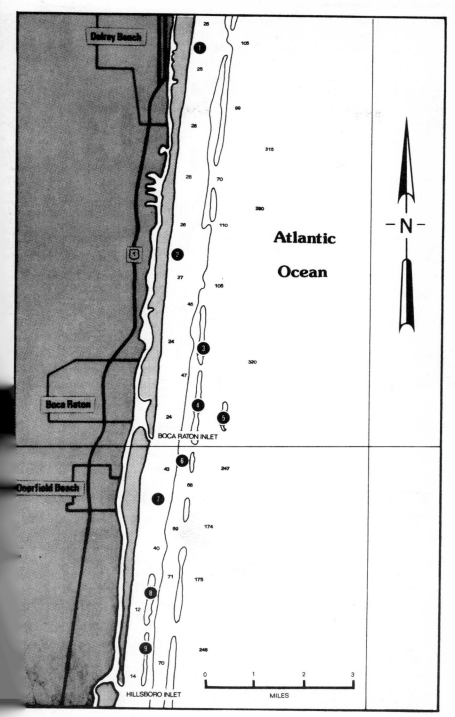

Delray Beach

Boca Raton

Deerfield Beach

Atlantic

Ocean

BOCA RATON INLET

HILLSBORO INLET

—N—

26
105
25
99
26
315
26
70
290
26
110
27
105
46
24
320
47
24

43
247
66
69
174
40
71
175
12
246
70
14

0   1   2   3

MILES

NO. 2 JAP ROCK (Beach Dive)
Location: North end of Boca Raton public beach.

This is a good reef for snorkelers. Its shallow rocks are full of tropicals and an occasional lobster. While it is excellent on calm days, on rough days this reef can be hazardous to your health! Waves breaking on the rocks (which make the site easy to locate) can cut the unprotected diver. This is also an unprotected section of beach. Watch for rip currents and check with local dive shops for conditions.

NO. 3 BOCA NORTH BEACH LEDGE
Location: Seaward of Boca Radar Tower, about 1 mile north of the Boca South Beach Pavilion.

The North Beach Ledge is ten- to 15-feet long, in 60 feet of water. Sea whips, sea fans, sponges and hard corals top the ledge, while caves and overhangs provide food and cover for marine life. Moray eels grow to six feet here, and lobster abound during the winter months. Anchor on the edge, go north, and return to anchor. Fly your dive flag here!

NO. 4 WESTERVELT'S RIDGES
Location: Approximately 3/4 of a mile due east of Palmetto Park Beach Pavilion.

Westervelt's is a 15-foot-high ledge that drops on the outside to 70 feet. Overhangs and caves are common. Lobster, grouper and hogfish are abundant. This reef is noted for moray eels and the caves they hide in while awaiting prey. One tame moray, six feet long, can be hand-fed, providing you know a safe way to approach a six-foot moray! Check with a local dive shop that is familiar with this reef.

NO. 5 GROUPER HOLE
Location: Approximately ½ mile north of the Boca Inlet, about 1½ miles offshore.

This reef lies in approximately 140 feet of water and, on an incoming tide, has visibility which can exceed 100 feet. Jewfish and groupers frequent this reef during the winter months. Drift diving will provide access to Grouper Hole. Be ready for the large critters! Lobsters grow to around ten pounds at this site.

NO. 6 BOCA ARTIFICIAL REEF LEDGE
Location: Just south of Boca Inlet, approximately 3/4 of a mile offshore.

A popular artificial reef area adjacent to natural rock ledges. Depths the sand are 70 feet. The landward side of the reef has a ledge approximately ten to 15 feet high, running north and south. Visibility on a incoming tide can be from 50 to 100 feet. Fifty to 75 feet east of the ledge is small artificial reef composed of erojacks stacked in piles. This is excellent diving and fishing locale, which includes rockfish and midwat sport fish. Currents are often strong here!

NO. 7 SEPARATED ROCKS
Location: South of Deerfield pier off the south end of the public beach.

From a depth of 40 to 45 feet in the sand, these large blocks of coral rise five to seven feet. These blocks provide excellent cover for lobster. Because this reef is on the southernmost tip of the artificial tire reef, you can drift for over two miles on an incoming tide. This reef can be reached only by boat, since it is too far a swim from the beach. Check with your local dive shop about conditions and trips to the reef.

NO. 8 HILLSBORO LEDGE
Location: ½ mile south of the last rock pile on Deerfield Beach.

A five- to ten-foot coral ledge in depths of 34 to 40 feet, this is an excellent reef for the beginner. There are numerous tropicals to photograph or collect. Lobsters are scattered in rocky sections of the reef. Because of its location just outside the inlet, there is not a long wait between suiting up and diving.

NO. 9 LABONTE REEF
Location: Seaward of Hillsboro Landmark Condo, 1 mile north of Inlet.

The top of this reef is in 35 feet of water and reaches to a sandy bottom at 45 feet. This is a nice beginner's reef since it is relatively close to shore, easy to find, and contains an excellent variety of fish and invertebrate life. The inside edge is full of holes. Lobster, snapper and grouper can be found. Because this reef is too far to swim to from the beach, local dive shops run daily trips to Labonte.

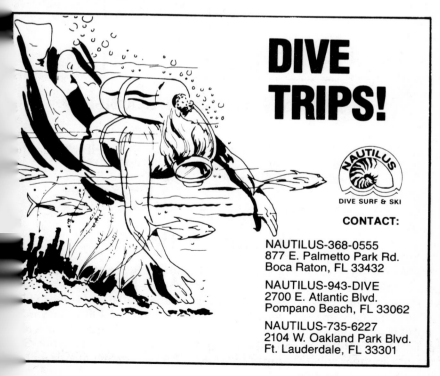

DIVE TRIPS!

NAUTILUS
DIVE SURF & SKI

CONTACT:

NAUTILUS-368-0555
877 E. Palmetto Park Rd.
Boca Raton, FL 33432

NAUTILUS-943-DIVE
2700 E. Atlantic Blvd.
Pompano Beach, FL 33062

NAUTILUS-735-6227
2104 W. Oakland Park Blvd.
Ft. Lauderdale, FL 33301

POMPANO BEACH/FT. LAUDERDALE

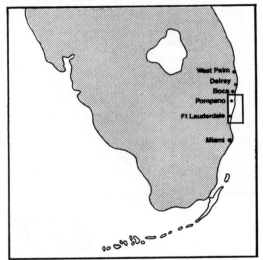

Offshore Diving Locations

1. Suzanne's Reef
2. Third Reef Ridge/Pompano
3. Pompano Drop-off
4. Lauderdale-by-the-Sea Pier Reef
5. 82' Yacht *Monomy*
6. Osborne Reef
7. Yankee Clipper Erojack Reef
8. Spotfin Reef
9. Barracuda Reef
10. Dania Erojacks

Area Information

All of the popular diving spots from Pompano Beach through the F Lauderdale area are found on three distinct reef lines called the firs second and third reefs. These reefs generally run parallel to the shorelin

The distance from the beach to the first reef varies from 100 to 300 yard Depths range from ten to 15 feet. The reef reaches a depth of 30 feet in a fe spots. These patches of natural reef support a variety of marine life. S fans and sponges cover the top of the ridge. This is an excellent area for t

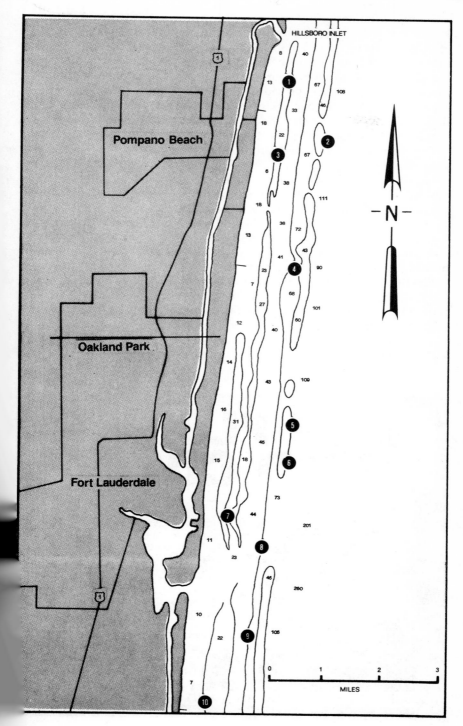

novice scuba diver and is a delight for the free-diver. Scuba diving is not allowed off the beach south of Oakland Park Boulevard, but snorkelers can make beach entrances anywhere along the beach. Few large game fish are found this close to shore, but multicolored tropicals are found by the thousands. The first reef provides excellent lobstering during the season. Many divers have grabbed their first bug from the pockets along the reef line. Visibility is not always the best, depending on the weather. Strong winds will kick up the sand in the shallow waters.

The second reef lies about a mile offshore in most areas. Depths vary from 40 to 50 feet. Visibility is better than on the first reef and is nearly always good. A large selection of sea life can be found along the ten- to 15-foot ledges. Hard and soft corals and many varieties of sponges make up the reef. You not only find an abundance of tropicals, but large schools of grunts, spades, goatfish and yellowtails as well. The underwater photographer will be able to find more than enough beautiful scenery for outstanding shots. The white sand that surrounds the reef is a prime hunting ground for shell collectors.

The third reef starts about a mile offshore and runs at depths from 60 to 100 feet. Because of the depths and sometimes strong currents, this reef should be explored by the more skilled diver. Larger game fish make this area their home, and provide excellent spearfishing opportunities. Both the hard and soft corals are larger and more abundant in the deeper waters. The visibility is nearly always outstanding.

DIVE FLORIDA
GOLD COAST

OVER 50 REEFS AND WRECKS.

■ ANCHOR DIVING AND U.W. PHOTOGRAPHY OR DRIFT DIVING AND LOBSTERING.

■ OPENWATER AND ADVANCED DIVING CERTIFICATIONS AVAILABLE.

■ INTRODUCTORY RESORT COURSES AND 5 DAY CERTIFICATION CLASSES.

Palm Bch.
Ft. Lauderdale
Miami

Professional Diving Schools of Florida
Bahia Mar Yachting Center (A1A)
P.O. Box 3030
Ft. Lauderdale, Florida 33316
305-761-3413

A P.A.D.I. 5 STAR TRAINING AND RESORT FACILITY.

The summer months of May through September offer the best visibility and, of course, the warmer water temperatures. Several outstanding diving businesses are located in the South Florida area. They will be more than happy to provide interested divers with information about diving conditions and to arrange diving charters.

NO. 1 SUZANNE'S REEF

Location: On the first reef line, about a ½ mile offshore and 3/4 of a mile north of the Pompano pier.

Depths vary from ten to 20 feet on Suzanne's Reef, with the ledge from one to five feet in height. There is good shelling on the sand flats inside the ledge. Tropicals are numerous and lobstering can be good during certain times of the year. The rock ledge is pocketed with small crevices, while soft corals and sponges grow on top of the reef.

NO. 2 THIRD REEF RIDGE/POMPANO

Location: 1½ miles east-southeast of the Pompano pier.

Depths on the third reef average 70 feet and the visibility is usually good along the outside edge of the reef line. The 12- to 15-foot-high outside wall is very scenic and therefore a popular area for underwater photography. Basket sponges line the top of the ridge, while multicolored sea fans, sea whips and other soft corals cover the outer edges. Grouper, barracuda and

DIVERS UNLIMITED

in Hollywood, Florida
*invites you to visit the largest training facility in the U.S.; awarded
"#1 Training Facility" by PADI.*

- Monthly PADI Instructor courses.

- Instruction from entry level through Instructor.

- Complete travel agency within the store for domestic & foreign destinations.

- VID charge accounts available

DIVERS UNLIMITED

6023 Hollywood Blvd.   Hollywood, FL (305) 981-0156   800-327-2740 (outside Florida)

chubs swim through the undercuts. This area can be subject to strong currents at times, so use caution.

NO. 3 POMPANO DROP-OFF
Location: About ½ mile due east of the large blue water tower on Pompano Beach.

This large, flat, rocky reef starts just 15 feet below the surface, and drops to just over 30 feet on the outside. Like in most of the areas close in to shore, visibility is usually poor, but there is little problem caused by currents. There are few large fish, but good tropical fish collecting.

NO. 4 LAUDERDALE-BY-THE-SEA PIER REEF
Location: A little over a mile due east of the Lauderdale-by-the-Sea pier.

The top of this third reef area is in 45 feet of water and drops to a white sandy bottom at 65 feet. This area is popular for spearfishing. It also contains good hard and soft coral growth on the rough ledge. Be cautious of currents here.

NO. 5 82' YACHT *MONOMY*
Location: About 1¾ miles due east of Sunrise Boulevard.

An old wooden yacht lies on its side in 55 feet of water on the outer edge of the third reef. Most of her portholes and brass fittings have been removed, but it is still fascinating to explore her broken remains. The yacht has become an artificial reef, and is in an advanced stage of development. Spearfishing is rated good. Snapper, barracuda, jacks and other mid-water sport fish are commonly sighted. The depth of the surrounding reef ranges from 45 to 70 feet.

NO. 6 OSBORNE REEF
Location: On the third reef, about 1,000 yards south of the Monomy.

BLUE WATER DIVE CENTER

FULL SERVICE PRO SHOP   DIVE TRIP SERVICES

AIR • SALES • INSTRUCTION
RENTALS • TRAVEL
One Year Warranteed Regulator Repairs

4429 HOLLYWOOD BLVD. **963-4760**
HOLLYWOOD, FL 33021

OPEN 7 DAYS

INSTRUCTION
National
Association of
SCUBA DIVING
SCHOOLS
SAFETY SPORT
INTEGRITY

This large, artificial reef is made up of the wreckage of old barges, tires and concrete. Osborne is an excellently developed and maintained artificial reef that supports an almost unbelievable abundance of fish life. Depths vary from 70 feet in the sand to 60 feet on top of the reef.

NO. 7 YANKEE CLIPPER EROJACK REEF
Location: About 300 yards due east of the Yankee Clipper Hotel.

Huge piles of concrete jacks provide a home for a multitude of sea life in 15 to 25 feet of water. An advanced life-cycle has developed within the rubble, creating a most interesting dive.

NO. 8 SPOTFIN REEF
Location: 2,000 yards from the beach on the third reef, ¾ of a mile north of Port Everglades Inlet.

This is a very pronounced ledge starting in 50 feet of water and dropping to 65 feet in the sand. The ledge is picturesque, undercut in many places with caves and crevices. The area is covered with a large variety of soft and hard corals and is good for spearfishing and tropical fish collecting.

NO. 9 BARRACUDA REEF
Location: About 2,000 feet from the beach and 1½ miles north of the Dania pier.

This is a large section of the second reef with pronounced ledges dropping from 20 feet on the top to 36 feet in the sand. It harbors typical second reef sea life, with many large basket sponges.

NO. 10 DANIA EROJACKS
Location: About 1,000 yards offshore and just north of the Dania pier.

A mixture of natural and artificial reefs support a variety of interesting coral polyps. Depths range from ten to 20 feet.

YOUR FULL SERVICE DIVE
SHOP IN FT. LAUDERDALE

Daily local reef trips. Dive travel tips and reservations.

Certified instruction YMCA – NAUI – PADI

U.S. reservation hdqt. for Bimini Undersea Adventures)

And you can charge it to your
ISA * MASTERCARD * AMERICAN EXPRESS

UNDER SEA SPORTS INC.
Village Shoppes
1525 N. Federal Hwy.
Ft. Lauderdale, Fl. 33304
(305) 564-8661

MIAMI

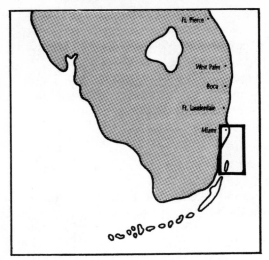

Offshore Diving Locations

1. Haulover Shallow Rocks
2. The Crane Wreck
3. Harbor House Reef
4. Eighty-Eighth Street Reef
5. Deep Freeze
6. The Cuban Hole
7. Schooner Wreck
8. Key Biscayne
9. Emerald Reef
10. Captain Dick's Wreck
11. Biscayne Wreck/Banana Freighter
12. *South Seas* and Cluster of Small Vessels
13. *Arida*
14. *Lakeland*
15. *Orion*
16. Hopper Barge
17. *Blue Fire*
18. *Almirante*
19. Fowey Rocks
20. Brewster Reef
21. Star Reef
22. Mystery Reef
23. Triumph Reef
24. Long Reef
25. Ajax Reef

Area Information

Miami's offshore waters have long been a delight to water sportsme. For years the city has been the center of many water-related activitie. Sport diving, of course, is no exception.

Recent artificial reef construction projects by the Dade County Enviro mental Resources Management office (DERM), Dade Sportfishing Cou cil and private concerns have produced some of the state's most drama

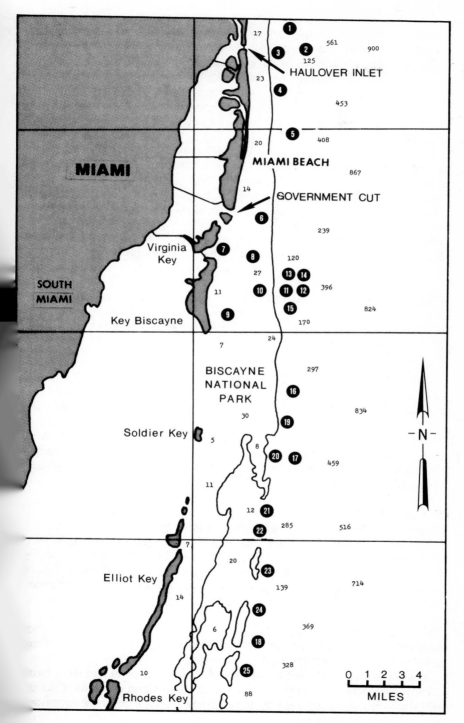

MIAMI

HAULOVER INLET

MIAMI BEACH

GOVERNMENT CUT

SOUTH MIAMI

Virginia Key

Key Biscayne

BISCAYNE NATIONAL PARK

Soldier Key

Elliot Key

Rhodes Key

– N –

0 1 2 3 4

MILES

diving sites. Large derelict ships have been purchased, cleaned and towed to specially permitted sites where they were sunk. The large structures quickly attract myriad sea life, bountiful for fishermen and thrilling for divers to explore. Because of the clear waters that bathe Miami's wrecks, their visual impact is startling. Water visibility varies, depending on the caprice of the Gulf Stream. Days with 100 feet of visibility are not uncommon. Windy periods seem to have only marginal effect, but water run-off from Miami's street system after heavy rains can drop visibility considerably.

Depths vary from a few feet at shallow-water reef areas to several hundred feet only a few miles offshore. The wrecks are all relatively deep—from 70 to 200 feet. Those wishing to visit these sites should be experienced open-water divers. Although spearfishing is now allowed on wreck sites, county ordinances banning such activities will probably be implemented in the near future.

Natural rocks and coral reefs are prevalent from North Miami south through the Biscayne National Park. The southern reefs are as lovely as any found in the Caribbean. Acres of antler corals teeming with schooling fish lie in wait for visitors.

Some of the nation's oldest and best operated diving stores and charter boats operate in the Miami area. They know the surrounding waters well and are always ready to provide sport divers with assistance in discovering Miami's spectacular underwater world.

NO. 1 HAULOVER SHALLOW ROCKS
Location: Directly east of 158th Street and the beach. If you run a north an *south course, you will pass over a covered discharge pipe with an elevation of 1* *to 15 feet.*

The area has scattered coral formations on a white sand bottom th varies in depth from 30 to 40 feet. Grouper and small snapper are commor The rocks that cover the discharge pipe are a protective haven for an arra of colorful tropicals. The best diving in the area is at high tide.

NO. 2 THE CRANE WRECK
Location: 2 miles east of the 7th building south of Haulover Cut.

The wreckage of an old steel crane rests on a sand bottom in 80 feet water between coral fingers. Visibility is usually between 30 and 40 fe Spearfishing is common in the area due to the depth and expansive r formations. Diving is exciting and challenging. The area is not reco: mended for inexperienced divers.

NO. 3 HARBOR HOUSE REEF
Location: Straight out from the Harbor House (first large apartment comp *south of the Haulover Inlet on Miami Beach).*

The reef starts in 45 feet of water and rapidly drops to 85 feet. The system supports numerous varieties of soft corals and sponges. This i: excellent area to photograph grouper, turtles and large green morays

T·M·S·P ENTERPRISES

SPECIALISTS IN
VIDEO PRODUCTIONS — PHOTO DECOR
(for Resorts, Travel Agencies — Manufacturers) (for all occasions)

944-1754

BROCHURES
CATALOGS—ANNUALS

ADVERTISING

Tom Mount — Underwater Photography College
Patti Schaeffer's Underwater Modeling School

A/V PRODUCTIONS — SURVEYS

14875 N.E. 20th AVE. NORTH MIAMI, FLORIDA 33181

om Mount's Underwater Photography College
nd Patti Schaeffer's Underwater Modeling Schools held at:
askin in the Sun, Haiti, — Spanish Cove, Grand Cayman,
alkers Cay, Bahamas, — Anthony's Key, Roatan,
amingo Beach, Bonaire. — Miami, FL.

Or Travel with
Tom and Patti to
The Red Sea
Galapagos
The Philippines
The Coral Sea

NO. 4 EIGHTY-EIGHTH STREET REEF
Location: The reef lies about ¾ of a mile due east of the Holiday Inn on 88th Street and Collins Ave.

Coral formations are found at a depth of 35 to 40 feet. The site abounds with tropical fish and is a favorite with fish collectors. On the deeper side of the reef, larger fish and lobster can be found among the bigger coral heads. Always fly a divers' flag, since this is a heavy boat traffic area.

NO. 5 DEEP FREEZE
Location: About 5 miles north-northwest of the Government Cut jetties in the Pflueger Artificial Reef Site.

A 210-foot freighter is resting east to west on her keel in 135 feet of water. Her top deck is at 100 feet. She has been down since October 1976, and is covered with algae and corals. All the companionways are open, but be careful of the fine silt on the deck. Be sure to carry a sharp knife on this and all wreck dives in case of fishing line entanglement. This ship is host to many large fish including grouper, jacks and barracuda. Moray eels and a large colony of Atlantic spiny oysters can be seen.

NO. 6 THE CUBAN HOLE
Location: 2½ miles east of the Government Cut jetties near the south outer marker of the ship channel.

A rock bottom with coral formations offers shelter for grouper and other game fish, providing good hunting for the spearfisherman. The depth ranges from 40 to 60 feet and the water visibility is usually good. Because of tricky currents, the area is recommended for experienced open-water divers only.

NO. 7 SCHOONER WRECK
Location: 75 yards northwest of the red marker on the south side of the Bear Cut channel near Key Biscayne.

This is a great place for the inexperienced diver to visit a wreck. The wreck lies in ten feet of water on a smooth grassy bottom.

NO. 8 KEY BISCAYNE
Location: Just east of Key Biscayne, starting about a mile south of Government Cut.

This is a large area of patch reefs and coral mounds scattered over a sandy bottom varying in depth from 15 to 40 feet. The clarity of the water usually allows you to easily spot the darker coral heads contrasted against the white sand bottom.

Because of the generally calm waters and varieties of depths in this locale, both experienced and novice divers will find this area suited to their talents. Sea fans and gorgonians are plentiful. Tropicals as well as game fish are common.

NO. 9 EMERALD REEF

Location: On the Atlantic side of Key Biscayne, toward the south end.

This is by far the most beautiful shallow reef group in the Miami area. The patch reefs are in 15 to 20 feet of water. Many of the better spots are difficult to locate but well worth the effort. Colors here in the shallow, clear water are truly breathtaking. Sponges in every color predominate. They are complemented by delightful patches of living coral. Every coral head and sponge teems with juvenile tropicals in the spring and summer. There are also many larger fish including parrotfish, grouper and hog snapper.

NO. 10 CAPTAIN DICK'S WRECK

Location: About 2½ miles east of Key Biscayne, in 60 feet of water.

This is a large wreck, about 150 feet in length, lying east to west on a white sand bottom. There is no superstructure, but the hull is intact, allowing the diver to explore the cargo holds and engine room. The wreck supports an extensive marine ecosystem. Grouper, amberjack and parrotfish are common.

NO. 11 BISCAYNE WRECK/BANANA FREIGHTER

Location: The wreck is 4½ miles east of Key Biscayne in the midwestern sector of the Department of Environmental Resources Management (DERM) Key Biscayne Artificial Reef Site.

A 120-foot freighter once used for hauling bananas from Central America sat derelict in the Miami River until 1974 when she was sunk to form an

ALL MAJOR BRANDS AT DISCOUNT PRICES

NEW ENGLAND DIVERS

NEW ENGLAND DIVERS INC.
WORLD'S LARGEST DIVING RETAILERS

TRIPS
SALES
RENTAL
SERVICE
INSTRUCTION

*MENTION THIS AD FOR FREE DIVE DECAL

PADI TRAINING FACILITIES

2945 N.E. 2nd Ave.
Miami, FL 33137
573-4600

9820 S. Dixie Hwy.
Kendall, FL 33156
667-4622

MIKE STEWART

The Lakeland, *one of a growing number of artificial reefs off Miami.*

artificial reef. She rests in 55 feet of water and has a 15-foot relief. This is a very popular wreck dive because of the rather shallow depths and the breathtaking concentration of fish life constantly moving about her structure. At times, the baitfish schools are so numerous and immense that they shroud her from view. This is a fine place for a "fantasy" night dive.

NO. 12 *SOUTH SEAS* AND CLUSTER OF SMALL VESSELS
Location: Found in the Key Biscayne Site, about 150 yards east of the Biscayne Wreck.

This is a cluster of seven vessels in 85 to 100 feet of water. The *South Seas* was a sister ship to Hitler's personal yacht. Her 175-foot steel hull rests in 73 feet of water among the following wrecks: *Sarah Jane*, a 65-foot wooden boat; a 100-foot steel barge; a 60-foot wooden drift boat; a 40-foot steel houseboat; and a 35-foot fiberglass boat. The maximum relief is about 12 feet. Baitfish, jacks and grouper abound among the broken wreckage.

NO. 13 *ARIDA*
Location: In the northwest corner of the Key Biscayne Artificial Reef Site.

The 165-foot *Arida* was an old LCT later converted into a freighter. She is resting on her side in 88 feet of water, with a 25-foot relief. Grouper and other large fish inhabit her remains.

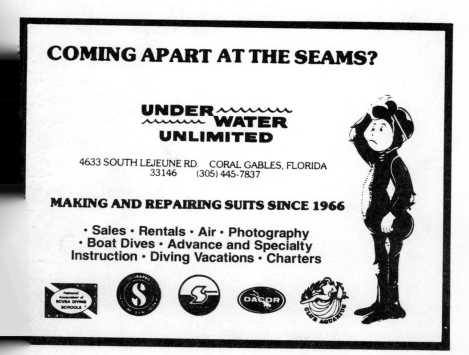

COMING APART AT THE SEAMS?

UNDER WATER UNLIMITED

4633 SOUTH LEJEUNE RD.   CORAL GABLES, FLORIDA
33146   (305) 445-7837

MAKING AND REPAIRING SUITS SINCE 1966

- Sales • Rentals • Air • Photography
- Boat Dives • Advance and Specialty
Instruction • Diving Vacations • Charters

Miami's 118-foot steel tug, the Orion.

NO. 14 *LAKELAND*
Location: On the outside of the Key Biscayne Artificial Reef Site.

The 200-foot steel freighter lies east to west in 126 to 140 feet of water. She is keel-up, resting on her superstructure with a 30-foot relief. Her decks are filled with baitfish, barracuda, grouper and, occasionally, a shark.

NO. 15 *ORION*
Location: The southwest corner of the Key Biscayne Artificial Reef Site.

The 118-foot steel tug once operated in the Panama Canal. She now rests in 95 feet of water with her twin sets of engines and ten-foot propellers intact. Since she sank in 1981, she has been one of Miami's most popular wreck dives. With stacks rising 30 feet and superstructure in place, she casts a haunting spirit over all visitors.

NO. 16 HOPPER BARGE
Location: About 5 miles southwest of Key Biscayne in the center of the R.J. Diving Ventures Artificial Reef Site.

The 150-foot New York garbage barge sits on her side. She has a 40-foot-plus relief off the 163-foot bottom. This is a popular fishing site because of the concentration of large fish that always seem to be about. A huge school of jacks is never far away.

Ocean Realm Tees

$4.95

Ocean Realm Tees 2333 Brickell Ave., Miami, Fl. 33129

NO. 17 *BLUE FIRE*
Location: West of Brewsters Reef, in the North Dade Sportfishing Council Site.

The *Blue Fire* is a 175-foot freighter seized by the Coast Guard during the Mariel boat lift. She was sunk in 110 feet of water in January 1983. Her relief is over 30 feet off a beautiful white sand bottom covered with soft corals and large sponges. Intact and bearing full superstructure, except mast, this is indeed a wreck divers' wreck. It is easy and safe to penetrate her inner structure. The site has become home to a large number of midnight parrotfish, jacks and cobia. Don't miss this one!

NO. 18 *ALMIRANTE*
Location: Found in the South Dade Sportfishing Council Site, halfway between Long and Ajax Reefs.

This is a 210-foot island freighter that sat for years in the Miami River. She was sunk in April of 1974 in 122 to 132 feet of water. She sits upright with her bow facing southeast. It is a 110-foot dive to her main deck. Because of her long stay underwater, her structure has attracted a wide variety of marine life. Her sides are covered with brilliant red soft coral and graced by schooling fish, creating a beautiful seascape for underwater photography. Jacks and barracuda are prevalent and occasional jewfish are spotted. Visibility is always good here, averaging at least 50 feet and often in excess of 100 feet.

NO. 19 FOWEY ROCKS
Location: 11 ½ miles south of Government Cut; marked by a 110-foot lighthouse.

This is a large area, as shallow as ten feet and dropping to depths in excess of 100 feet. There is an abundance of angelfish, soft corals and some elkhorn coral. The entire area is enjoyable. It is a good spot for a repetitive dive after exploring the deeper nearby wrecks. Fowey Rocks is the start of a broken, shallow reef line that runs south into John Pennekamp Coral Reef State Park. Most of the site shares the same topography and marine life. The charm of Fowey Rocks lies in the abundance of fish life, living

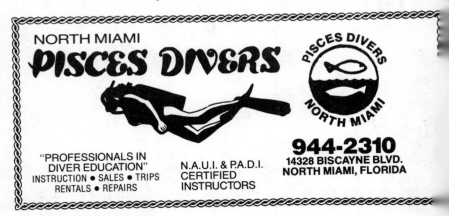

NORTH MIAMI

PISCES DIVERS

PISCES DIVERS NORTH MIAMI

944-2310
14328 BISCAYNE BLVD.
NORTH MIAMI, FLORIDA

"PROFESSIONALS IN DIVER EDUCATION"
INSTRUCTION • SALES • TRIPS
RENTALS • REPAIRS

N.A.U.I. & P.A.D.I.
CERTIFIED
INSTRUCTORS

coral gardens, clear water, their sheer size and the fact that they are less often dived than the Keys' reefs just to the south. Much virgin bottom still remains to be discovered. This and all the following reefs are located in the protected boundaries of the Biscayne National Park. The eastern boundary of the park extends to 60-foot depths. Its southern parameters join those of Pennekamp Park. Fishing, lobstering, conching and spearfishing are allowed. However, collection of tropical fish and relics is not permitted. Stated simply, take nothing that can't be eaten.

NO. 20 BREWSTER REEF

Location: 2 miles south of the 110-foot steel lighthouse on Fowey Rocks. The reef is less than one mile west of the Blue Fire *wreck site.*

This is another large reef area with depths from 25 to 75 feet. Scattered coral heads, soft corals and sponges dot the sand floor. Visibility is usually good, but is best at high tide. Some scattered wreckage can be found along the deep outside edge of the reef in 70 feet of water. This is a good location for the experienced as well as the novice diver.

NO. 21 STAR REEF

Location: 4½ miles south of the 110-foot steel lighthouse on Fowey Rocks and slightly east of the general reef line.

Star is considered to be a favorite reef by many Miami divers. Its rugged bottom is always teeming with marine life. It seems that something unusual can always be found among the coral heads. Depths can be as shallow as 12 feet.

NO. 22 MYSTERY REEF

Location: A small reef area situated halfway between Star and Triumph Reefs, 2 miles west of the Biscayne Monument's North Marker.

This is a beautiful patch reef area with magnificent stands of elkhorn coral. Schooling fish are dominant. There are also many large puffers in the area.

WRECK DIVE MIAMI

Come Dive aboard the 31 ft. custom dive boat "Native Diver."
Will accommodate up to 12 divers.

Native Diver
6492 Miami Lakes Dr. E
Miami Lakes, FL 33014 (305) 558-8217

NO. 23 TRIUMPH REEF

Location: 8 miles south of the 110-foot steel lighthouse on Fowey Rocks, on the same reef line as Brewster, Star and Mystery Reefs. There is a red marker near the outside edge of the reef.

This is another patch of scattered coral heads. Depths on top of the reef are only ten feet. The best diving is in the 40- to 60-foot range, but good diving can be found as deep as 120 feet. Because of exceptionally clear water and rugged underwater terrain, this has long been a popular site.

The Almirante, *a 210-foot freighter sunk off Miami as an artificial reef.*

NO. 24 LONG REEF

Location: 10 miles south of the 100-foot steel lighthouse on Fowey Rocks, less than a mile west of the Almirante *wreck.*

This is a large reef area running south for over two miles. There is a lot of fish activity here. This site has long been used for checkout dives because of its gently sloping bottom, making it ideal for multi-level dives.

NO. 25 AJAX REEF

Location: Ajax Reef and her sister reef, Pacific, are the southernmost reefs in the Miami area. Ajax is actually a continuation of Long Reef. It is about 13 miles south of the Fowey Rocks lighthouse.

These are the last reefs in the Biscayne National Park area. Both have vivid coral structures and offer diving ranging from snorkeling depths to over 100 feet. The continuation of the reef line takes you into Pennekamp Park. The boundary line between the Biscayne National Park and Pennekamp is prominently marked by three pilings displaying warning signs. Of course, there is no spearfishing allowed within the Pennekamp boundaries.

FLORIDA KEYS

Area Information

The Florida Keys are a string of more than 200 islands that extend the length of the Florida peninsula for 180 miles to the sea. From Jewfish Creek to Key West, the island chain is connected by the longest overseas highway in the world—a 108-mile span that links 31 islands with 40 bridges.

The islands separate the shallow flats of the Gulf of Mexico from the Florida reef that lies on the edge of the Gulf Stream in the Atlantic. The reef, which parallels the entire length of the Keys, is the only living coral reef on the North American continent. It is the home of one of the ocean's greatest underwater ecological systems.

Diving Services

Probably no other place provides better services to the sport diver than the Florida Keys. Sales, rentals, equipment repairs, air, diving instruction, boat charters and rentals, fast film processing, information and helpful advice—virtually everything you will need for a successful diving vacation can be found throughout the islands.

Reef trips lasting from half a day to a week are available on fast, modern boats designed for diving. The captains know the waters and what the diver wants. They operate their charters to see that you get the most out of your dive. Above all, you are always treated like a diver—never like a tourist—while visiting the Keys.

Weather

Mild, subtropical weather has long been a trademark of the Keys. Trade winds from the Gulf Stream keep the air warm in the winter and cool in the summer. In the winter, the average temperature is 71 degrees with occasional extremes in the low 40s. Even during cooler periods, it is usually mild and clear during the day. The summer is hot with temperatures ranging in the lower 90s. Rain squalls are frequent during midday in the summer and early fall. The winter months are relatively dry. From November through March, the water temperature is 70 degrees, requiring the use of a wetsuit top. From April through September, the water temperature rises into the lower 80s creating nearly perfect diving conditions.

A Short History

The powerful history of the Florida Keys comes from the sea, and today much of it still remains hidden under miles of clear water and white sand.

For years, historians have studied archives and compared their findings with the glorious relics that adventurous men have brought to shore as prizes from the past. Each piece fits into an exciting story.

The Early Inhabitants

The early Indian tribes of the area were the fierce Vescaynos and Matecumbeses who lived by the sea. Having no permanent villages, they moved from island to island in their piroques, living on fish, turtles and manatees. They became rich from salvaging ships of the first Spaniards who fell victims to the miles of treacherous reefs. By the 1570s, these tribes had given way to the invasion of bearded men.

The remainder of Indian history in the Keys was centered around the strong, tall Caloosas who remained until the 1800s. They befriended the Spaniards, and became notorious only after the Spanish departed and were replaced by settlers from the Bahamas. The Caloosas had to fight for survival. In 1840 they ended their reign in desperation with a savage massacre of the settlement on Indian Key. Afterward, when they fled north, they were followed and wiped out by Col. Wm. S. Harney near Lake Okeechobee.

Pirates

Wherever ships sailed carrying rich cargo, pirates flocked. The waters of the Keys soon became a favorite hunting ground for these ruthless free-loaders. They would hide in their small, fast brigs waiting for an opportune moment to swoop down on an unsuspecting galleon. They would take whatever they wanted; then kill all passengers and crew, and burn the ship to leave no trace of their deed.

Black Caesar, Gasparilla and Blackbeard were a few of the most feared names of the pirate era. A legend as black as his skin has been built from tales of the runaway Haitian slave, Black Caesar. "Dead men tell no tales," was the creed that he lived by. The channel between Old Rodes and Elliott Key today bears the name, Caesar's Creek, because it is believed that this is where he lay in wait for his victims. There is legend of stolen silver bars still buried in the mangrove swamp around his camp.

Wreckers

From the first years that ships sailed the Florida Straits riding the Gulf Stream, sailors have cursed the Florida reefs. Vessels of nearly every description have become victims of the huge coral heads that loom upward from the white sand. From Miami to the Dry Tortugas, it is almost impossible to dive an area without discovering traces of ships that have met violent ends and become part of the reef. Ballast rocks, brass spikes, steel plates and cables lie encrusted in coral or buried under the sand.

Recovering the cargoes of the many ships that broke open on the reefs became the profession of a group of men called "wreckers." They were skilled sailors who, time and time again, risked their lives during violent weather, recovering victims and salvage from disabled ships.

The wreckers centered their operations in two sectors, Key West, 150 miles from the mainland, and Indian Key. By 1850, Key West was the richest city in Florida due to the thriving business of wrecking. Soon afterward, the U.S. government began construction of lighthouses in strategic locations to warn ships of the more dangerous reefs. Wrecking continued, however, until the early 1900s when it became no longer profitable.

Lighthouses

Many of the most beautiful outer reefs you will dive while in the Keys are the very reefs that were most dangerous to early sailing ships. Today they are studded with towering steel-framed lighthouses that serve as a warning to modern shipping. The early galleons and schooners were warned of the hazardous areas only by crude charts and word of mouth.

As early as 1835, a Key West newspaper started crusading for the construction by the U.S. government of permanent lighthouses on the more hazardous reefs that skirt the island's sea lane. It was 17 years later before the first lighthouse was completed on Carysfort Reef. Some of the earlier lights constructed, with the date of completion, their locations and heights are:

Carysfort	1852	12 miles off Elliott Key	100 ft.
Sand Key	1853	8 miles SW of Key West	109 ft.
Sombrero	1858	6 miles S of Knight Key	142 ft.
Alligator	1870	4 miles E of Upper Matecumbe	136 ft.
American Shoal	1880	7 miles S of Sugarloaf Key	109 ft.
Rebecca Shoal	1886	27 miles W of the Marquesas	66 ft.

Overseas Highway

After the 1935 hurricane, the Overseas Road and Toll Bridge District purchased the right of way from the ruined FEC and started construction the final bridges to link Miami with Key West. Many of the bridges and s of the old railroad were used in the project that covered 108 miles from fish Creek to Key West, and connected 31 islands with 40 bridges. On rch 28, 1937, the highway was opened to traffic. By 1954 enough toll had n collected to pay off the bonds, and the road has been free to travelers r since.

LENGTHS OF
BRIDGES OF THE OVERSEAS HIGHWAY

Jewfish Creek — 223 ft.	Vaca Cut — 120 ft.	Park — 779 ft.
Key Largo Cut — 360 ft.	7-Mile - 35,716 ft.	North Harris — 390 ft.
Tavernier Creek — 133 ft.	Little Duck-Missouri — 800 ft.	Harris Gap — 37 ft.
Snake Creek — 192 ft.	Missouri, Ohio—1,394 ft.	Harris — 390 ft.
Whale Harbor — 616 ft.	Ohio—Bahia Honda — 1,005 ft.	Lower Sugarloaf — 1,210 ft.
Tea Table Relief — 226 ft.	Bahia Honda — 5,356 ft.	Saddle Bunch 2 — 554 ft.
Tea Table — 614 ft.	Spanish Harbor — 3,311 ft.	Saddle Bunch 3 — 656 ft.
Indian Key — 2,004 ft.	North Pine — 620 ft.	Saddle Bunch 4 — 800 ft.
Lignum Vitae — 790 ft.	South Pine — 806 ft.	Saddle Bunch 5 — 800 ft.
Channel 2 — 1,720 ft.	Torch Key Viaduct — 779 ft.	Shark Channel — 1,989 ft.
Channel 5 — 4,516 ft.	Torch-Ramrod — 615 ft.	Rockland Channel — 1,230 ft.
Long Key — 11,960 ft.	Niles Channel - 4,433 ft.	Boca Chica — 2,573 ft.
Tom's Harbor 3 — 1,209 ft.	Kemp's Channel — 992 ft.	Stock Island — 360 ft.
Tom's Harbor 4 — 1,395 ft.	Bow Channel — 1,302 ft.	Key West — 159 ft.

FROM MIAMI TO:
...Tavernier — 67 miles
...Marathon — 111 miles

...Key Largo — 58 miles
...Islamorada - 76 miles
...Key West — 159 miles

PUBLIC BOAT RAMPS IN THE KEYS

CROSS KEY . . . . Little Blackwater Sound, Bayside
TAVERNIER . . . . Harry Harris Park, Oceanside
Tavernier Creek at Bridge
BAHIA HONDA KEY . . . . Oceanside
BIG PINE KEY . . . . Bahia Honda State Park, Bayside
LITTLE TORCH KEY . . . . Old Wooden Bridge Marina
WEST SUMMERLAND KEY . . . . Bayside
CUDJOE KEY . . . . Little Torch Marina, Bayside
Mid-key, Bayside
Bow Channel, Bayside

ISLANDS CROSSED BY THE
OVERSEAS HIGHWAY

Key Largo	Conch Keys	Missouri Key	Cudjoe Key
Plantation Key	Duck Keys	Sunshine Key	Sugarloaf Key
Windley Key	Grassy Key	Bahia Honda Key	Saddlebunch Key
Upper Matecumbe	Crawl Key	West Summerland Key	Big Coppit Key
	Fat Deer Key	Big Pine Key	Rockland Key
Lower Matecumbe	Vaca Key	Little Torch Key	Boca Chica Key
	Knight Key	Middle Torch Key	Raccoon Key
Fiesta Key	Pigeon Key	Ramrod Key	Stock Island
Long Key	Little Duck Key	Summerland Key	Key West

coral cave.

PENNEKAMP PARK

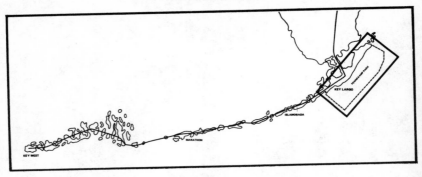

Diving Locations

1. Carysfort Reef
2. The Elbow
3. Christ of the Deep
4. Grecian Rocks
5. French Reef

6. Molasses Reef
7. *Thiorva*
8. HMS *Winchester*
9. *Benwood*
10. *Windless* Wreck

Area Information

Encompassed within the 75 square miles of Pennekamp State Park a
some of the world's most beautiful living reefs. It must be the dream
every serious diver to explore these fascinating coral formations that ha
made Pennekamp underwater park world-famous.

The best thing about the park—besides its outstanding coral reefs a
clear water—is that this area has been preserved for you by law si
December 10, 1960. This has permitted the coral and associated marine
to flourish in the midst of thousands of divers and sportsmen who er
these waters each year.

The park is named for John Pennekamp, a Miami newspaperman
conservationist whose efforts, combined with those of many intere:
and dedicated citizens, have turned a dream into reality.

Guidelines have been established for the park and are enforced by l
the Florida Department of Natural Resources and the Marine Patrol.
regulations are intended to protect the local sea life while provi
maximum use by the public. Spearfishing is illegal within the park,
the possession of spear guns, gigs or bangsticks is prohibited. Th

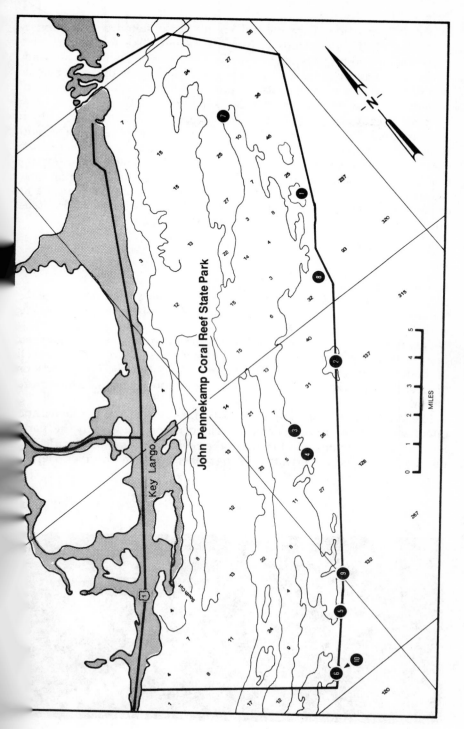

John Pennekamp Coral Reef State Park

moval or destruction of any natural feature is prohibited, and any collection of scientific specimens requires a permit. The wrecks are also protected and nothing should be removed from them. Fishing is allowed, but only by hook and line. The diver begins to appreciate the implementation of these rules after he visits the park and observes the abundance of protected marine life thriving within its boundaries.

There are many outstanding diving businesses on Key Largo which serve the area. They make both half- and full-day reef trips available, and have complete diving operations, supplying guide services, sales, rentals, instruction, repairs, photo services and air for their customers. Camping facilities with marinas, ramps and boat rentals are located along boat channels that lead to the park. These facilities offer an economical and convenient way to visit the reefs. There are also many motels and restaurants. You will spot their signs as you travel along US 1.

NO. 1 CARYSFORT REEF

Location: About 12 miles northeast of the South Cut, or 8 miles northeast of the North Cut off Key Largo on the outside edge of the park. The reef is plainly marked by a 100-foot steel light tower.

Carysfort is one of the outstanding dives in Pennekamp Park. Located east-northeast of the tower is "Carysfort Wall," a beautiful cascading wall of staghorn coral dotted by heads of brain and sheet corals. The wall drops 65 feet to a sandy bottom, and is a good dive for those who like a little more depth.

The south ledge of the reef extends two miles south of the tower and offers some of the most spectacular elkhorn coral ledges in the park. Several small canyons wind through the reef. There is a wide variety of marine life for the underwater photographer and fish observer. Depth

20% DIVE DISCOUNT

DIVE PENNEKAMP WITH

DIVERS' WORLD KEY LARGO, FLA.

P.O. BOX 1663
KEY LARGO, FLA. 33037
PHONE—305- 451-3200

DIVE DISCOUNT APPLIES TO REEF TRIPS AND RENTAL GEAR. YOU MUST BRING THIS AD WITH YOU IN ORDER TO RECEIVE THE DISCOUNT.

"VALID MONDAY THRU FRIDAY"

Florida Keys' ONLY
Complete Dive Resort

- LOCATED IN ONE MODERN CONVENIENT LOCATION FEATURING SCUBA & SNORKEL TOURS TO THE PRISTINE WATERS OR PENNEKAMP PARK

- DIVE LODGING PACKAGES WITH PORT LARGO VILLAS & HOLIDAY INN

- EQUIPMENT RENTALS & SALES

- RESTAURANT ON PREMISES

- RESIDENT U/W PHOTO PRO.

- SCUBA INSTRUCTION & RESORT COURSES

- BOAT RAMP & FUEL

P.O. Box 1113
Key Largo, FL
33037
305/451-1113

P.O. Box 19A
Key Largo, FL
33037
305/451-3737

- STOCK PHOTO SALES

- DAILY FILM PROCESSING

- ADVERTISING & DESIGN CONSULTATION

- UNDERWATER CAMERA RENTALS AND SALES

- PHOTO INSTRUCTION WITH ONE OF THE NATIONS TOP UNDERWATER PHOTOGRAPHERS (PADI U/W PHOTO SPECIALTY CERTIFICATION)

Stephen Frink
Photographic

Complete U/W Photo Service

vary from two to 20 feet.

Four hundred yards north-northwest of the tower, in 25 to 40 feet of water, are two large anchors, possibly from an old sailing frigate of the 1800s. Large schools of blue tangs and grunts are common and can be easily approached by the diver.

NO. 2 THE ELBOW

Location: About 8 miles east-northeast of the South Cut, or 5 ½ miles southeast of

COME VISIT THE SMILIN' ISLANDS & DIVE ABOARD THE 48′ "GOOD TIME CHARLIE"

Charters – Rentals – Instruction

Let our friendly professional staff
introduce you to the wonders of
Pennekamp's living coral reef

Tropic Isle Dive Shop
Box 755 Key Largo, FL 33037
MM 103.5 (305) 451-1063

the North Cut off Key Largo. The area is marked by a 36-foot light tower with #6 on it.

The Elbow, or the "wreck reef" as it is commonly called, is littered with the bones of various ships. 20 yards east-southeast of the tower, in 20 feet of water, lies the *City of Washington*, a large steel freighter that went aground in 1791. This is a beautiful snorkeling spot. About 150 yards east-northeast of the tower lie the broken remains of a steel ship, in 18 to 25 feet of water. About 80 yards west of the steel ship lies the "Civil War Wreck," consisting of large piles of timbers and metal.

About 50 yards east-southeast of the tower are beautiful finger reefs made up of elkhorn coral, ranging in depths from six to 20 feet. Here, hundreds of damselfish and angelfish make their home.

NO. 3 CHRIST OF THE DEEP
Location: About 6 miles east-northeast of the South Cut on Key Largo, and

*SPECIAL
WEEKDAY
RATES.

We've never
forgotten that
Diving is Fun!
This is a
people
business.

SEA
DWELLERS
SPORTS CENTER

MM 100
Key Largo
FL 33037
305/451-3640

DIVE THE BEST OF THE FLORIDA KEYS WITH...

REEF RAIDERS
and
Capt. Billy

Key West
305-294-0660

BUDDY'S DIVE SHOP
Bud 'n Mary's Marina
ISLAMORADA, FLA. KEYS
664-4707

Quiescence
DIVING   SERVICES
Key Largo, Fl.
451-2440

P.O. BOX 409 ISLAMORADA, FL 33036

DIVE PENNEKAMP

aboard the Keys

Premier Fleet!

• Scuba • Snorkle • Glassbottom Boat Tours •
• Complete Pro Dive Shop and Facility •

Capt. Slate's Atlantis Dive Center, Inc.

51 Garden Cove Drive MM 106½   Key Largo, Florida 33037
(305) 451-3020/451-1325
(see back cover for complete information)

marked by a 3-foot white buoy.

Christ of the Deep, also referred to as Christ of the Abyss, is a replica of "Il Cristo Degli Abissi" located in the Mediterranean Sea near Genoa. The 4,000 pound, 11-foot statue of Christ with His arms raised upward was created by Italian sculptor Guido Galletti. In 1961, another statue was cast from the same mold for Egidi Cressi, a European industrialist who presented it as a gift to the Underwater Society of America. After much deliberation, the Society decided to place the statue in the clear water off the Florida Keys. Today, the statue graces the Pennekamp Park Coral Reef State Park at Key Largo, where thousands of divers visit it each year.

About 300 yards around the edge of the reef, to the northwest (inland side), the water is 20 to 25 feet deep and calmer in rough weather. The area is covered with a large variety of tropicals. Skates and leopard rays are commonly sighted in the white sand around the coral.

Anchor in the sand around the edge of the reef, a short distance east of the buoy. The statue stands in 28 feet of water and is surrounded by coral cliffs and several huge heads of brain coral. The statue and its surrounding waters create a dramatic setting for underwater photography and sightseeing. There is good snorkeling in the area behind the statue, with an average depth of five to ten feet.

NO. 4 GRECIAN ROCKS

Location: About ¾ of a mile south-southwest of Christ of the Deep. Grecian Rocks is marked by a 3-foot wide buoy.

Boaters should be cautious in this reef area during the low tide. Parts of the reef are awash.

Grecian Rocks provides some of the best snorkeling in the park. It covers an area approximately a half mile long (running north to south) by 150 yards wide. It is a beautiful area with one of the largest varieties of tropical fish to be found. Many are so accustomed to divers that they can be handfed. An old Spanish cannon lies about 25 yards south of the buoy. The reef is made up of elkhorn, staghorn and brain corals, which can be found in 25 feet of water at the southern tip of the reef. During choppy weather, the

"AFTER YOU DIVE THE KEYS

"STOP AT GINNIE AND WASH OFF THE SALT"

Complete Dive Shop—
5000 PSI

*(See our ad in the Fort White-
High Springs section)*

Rt. 1, Box 153 High Springs, Fl. 32643
(904) 454-2202   1-800-874-8571

inland side of the reef provides the best diving because its waters are protected.

NO. 5 FRENCH REEF

Location: About 4½ miles south-southeast of South Cut off Key Largo, or about 1 mile northeast of the steel tower on Molasses Reef. The reef is marked by a black piling. Anchor in 30 feet of water about 150 yards off the piling.

French Reef is one of the most exciting dives in the park, with its large coral formations creating many canyons, ledges and caves. Exploring with an underwater light, the diver discovers many forms of marine life hidden under the dark ledges and inside the coral caves. The bold coral cliffs and crevices are filled with fish and make dramatic settings for underwater photography. Macro-photography is also good, since there is an abundance of small tube worms and polyps scattered over the coral heads.

NO. 6 MOLASSES REEF

Location: Located 5 miles south of the South cut off Key Largo at the southern end of the park. It is marked by a 45-foot steel light tower. Anchor in the sand on the southeast side of the tower.

Molasses is one of the most popular diving areas in the park, with its beautiful coral formations and fish life. Depths range from five to 40 feet. Broken wreckage of a schooner lies in 25 feet of water, about 30 yards due east of the tower. This is a good area for underwater photography, with many varieties of fish common and macro subjects plentiful. Night diving at Molasses is popular because it is one of the easier areas to locate.

NO. 7 *THIORVA*

Class: Schooner
Date: Unknown
Location: North end of Turtle Reef.

The broken wreckage lies scattered among the coral. Nothing of value has been recovered from the area, but many relics remain encrusted in the coral and buried beneath the sand.

AIRPORT TRANSFERS

Key Largo — Miami Airport

A COMFORTABLE RIDE TO YOUR HOTEL OR ANY LOCATION IN THE UPPER KEYS

CALL COLLECT (305) 451-4607

SERVICE PROVIDED THROUGH

Bali Tours

P.O. BOX 2029 KEY LARGO, FL 33037
Reasonable Rates Advance Reservations requested

NO. 8 HMS *WINCHESTER*
Class: British Ship of the Line
Date: 1695
Location: Southeast of Carysfort Light, on a direct line between Carysfort and the Elbow, in 28 feet of water.

Much of the *Winchester* is encrusted with coral, making it hard to locate. During World War II, many cannons were taken from the area for scrap iron.

NO. 9 *BENWOOD*
Class: Freighter
Date: 1942
Location: From the pile on French Reef, travel northeast toward a Red Nun buoy (difficult to see on the horizon) for approximately 1½ miles. The ship lies almost halfway between and on a direct line with the pile and buoy. Look closely for the dark outline of the ship on the white sand bottom.

During World War II, the freighter M.V. *Benwood* was torpedoed off the Florida Keys by a German submarine. As she limped toward shallow

Sandy ravines and coral caves make up spectacular Keys scenery.

water to go aground for easy salvage, she was rammed by a friendly ship. Later, five shells exploded amidship, finishing her off and sending her to the bottom. She now rests at the edge of the park. Her hull was later used for bombing practice, and the bow was dynamited because it was a hazard to navigation.

The *Benwood* is about 285-feet long, and lies in a northeast line. Her bow is in 25 feet of water, and the depth increases to 55 feet at the stern. An eerie underwater setting is created by the huge aft section that looms sharply upward off the ocean floor. The maze of steel wreckage provides a haven for large numbers of fish, from small tropicals to large grouper and snook.

NO. 10 WINDLESS WRECK
Class: Schooner
Date: Unknown
Location: In 25 feet of water, 30 yards due east of Molasses tower.
   Broken remnants lie buried in the sand between coral heads.

—reck of the Benwood, *a highlight of Pennekamp.*

UPPER KEYS

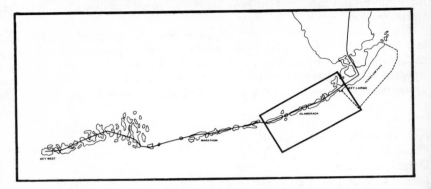

Diving Locations

1. Conch Reef
2. Davis Reef
3. Crocker Reef
4. Hens and Chickens Reef
5. Islamorada Coral Gardens 2
6. Beans Reef
7. Islamorada Coral Gardens 1
8. Alligator Reef
9. Matecumbe Drop-off
10. Fish Hole
11. South Coral Gardens

12. *Infante*
13. *San Jose*
14. *El Capitan*
15. Brick Barge
16. *Chaves*
17. *Herrera*
18. *Tres Puentes*
19. USS *Alligator*
20. *San Pedro*
21. *Lerri*

Area Information

Diving experiences in the Upper Keys range from snorkeling ov
exquisite coral gardens to plunging down the sides of underwater dr
offs. The sunken remains of some of the richest treasure galleons e
discovered rest in these waters. Over the last few years, the huge piles
egg-shaped ballast stones have given up thousands of silver coins and ra
artifacts to hardworking treasure hunters. Much treasure still lies hidd
under the sand and in acres of grass beds.

Diving guide services to the Upper Keys reefs and wrecks are found
Windley Key and Lower Matecumbe. The region also boasts several re
motels that cater to divers. There is a pro underwater camera shop,
diving charters to the Cay Sal Bank operate out of Windley Key.

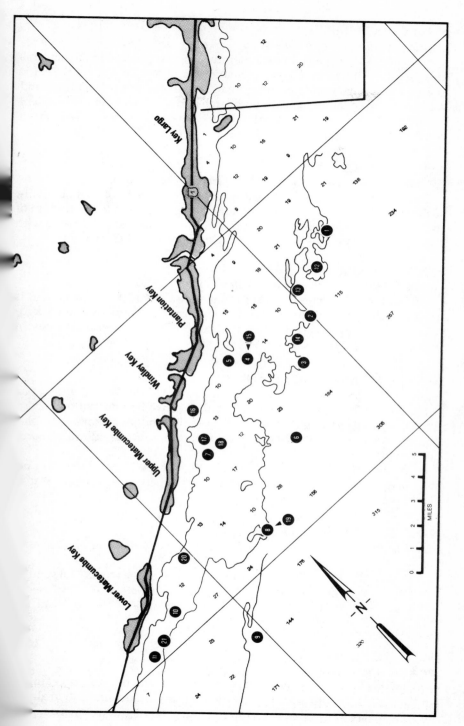

NO. 1 CONCH REEF
Location: 8 miles east of Windley Key, marked by two piles.

A rugged, sloping terrain with depths ranging from 15 to 20 feet, this area is full of interesting coral formations and sea fans. Conch Reef is known for its outstanding visibility year 'round, and its great mounds and valleys. This reef abounds with both large and small fish, and is excellent for the collector. The area is bordered by thousands of conch shells, from which the name of the reef is taken.

NO. 2 DAVIS REEF
Location: 3 miles east-southeast of Hens and Chickens Tower.

Davis is an outer reef known for its giant schools of fish. Literally, "schools of thousands" of tiny fish, all moving in unison to the rhythm of the sea, accent this beautiful reef. Striking stands of coral are covered with a multitude of sponges and sea fans. Depth averages 35 feet.

NO. 3 CROCKER REEF
Location: 5½ miles southeast of Windley Key.

One of the outer reefs, Crocker ranges from 35 to 100 feet deep and is graced with beautiful formations of staghorn coral and swaying gorgonians. This is a paradise for the tropical fish collector, with an array of multicolored sponges and varying sea life.

NO. 4 HENS AND CHICKENS REEF
Location: 3 miles east-southeast of Windley Key. Marked by a 35-foot tower

Hens and Chickens Reef abounds with massive boulders of brain coral which reach up to 20 feet in height. Here, the underwater photographer can find settings of iridescent tropical fish swimming amid multicolored gorgonians.

At the north end of the reef lies the wreck of the "Brick Barge," an old steel barge that went down after being torpedoed during World War II. Depths range from 20 to 28 feet.

NO. 5 ISLAMORADA CORAL GARDENS 2
Location: 2½ miles due east of Windley Key, about ¾ of a mile off Plantation Point.

A beautiful underwater coral garden that provides a wonderful sight for snorkelers in water just eight to 12 feet deep. The bottom is comprised of soft coral and sea fans. This is a good area for shelling, tropical fish collecting, lobstering or just plain exploring.

NO. 6 BEANS REEF
Location: 4 miles southeast of Windley Key.

Beans Reef is a bit deeper than most of the reefs, but just as beautiful. Starting in 45 feet of water, you can descend an underwater hill to almost 110 feet, where you will find gigantic grouper and hogfish. Down deep the fish are blue until you hit the shutter release of your camera and your fish lights up a rainbow of colors that is breathtaking. Spotted rays with wingspans of more than 15 feet can be seen gliding effortlessly toward the open sea. Everything here is majestic, making a day on Beans Reef a total diving experience.

NO. 7 ISLAMORADA CORAL GARDENS 1

Location: 3 miles south-southwest of Windley Key, or 1 mile directly off Upper Matecumbe.

A picturesque setting for the photographer, these coral gardens contain large mounds of brain coral and a wide variety of soft corals. An excellent reef for snorkeling, and a good place for beginners, this reef averages 12 feet in depth.

NO. 8 ALLIGATOR REEF

Location: 6 miles south-southwest of Windley Key. Marked by a 136-foot tower.

Named after the USS *Alligator,* a U.S. warship sunk in 1825, this reef is one of the largest in the Upper Keys. The deep coral crevices and ravines have made this a popular area for underwater exploration. Here, the diver will find all types of coral, both hard and soft, as well as numerous tropical fish and shells. The broken remains of the warship can be found a few hundred feet on the ocean side of the light. Depths range from eight to 40 feet.

NO. 9 MATECUMBE DROP-OFF

Location: Located between, and on the line with, the 136-foot tower on Alligator Reef and the 49-foot tower on Tennessee Reef.

The good areas on this drop-off are hard to find without a guide or depth sounder. This area provides a lot of excitement for the more experienced divers. The drop-offs vary in depths, but usually run from 35 to 135 feet. The greater depths offer a variety of marine life unlike that found in the shallows.

NO. 10 FISH HOLE

Location: 1 mile off the center of Lower Matecumbe.

Small coral heads are scattered across a white sandy area. Depths average 12 feet. This is a good close-in area for shell and tropical fish collecting.

NO. 11 SOUTH CORAL GARDENS

Location: 1 mile directly offshore from Caloosa Cove Marina.

The Coral Gardens is an impressive dive with its many stands of brain, lettuce and star corals. Underwater photography is excellent and the reef fish are friendly. Depths vary from five to 18 feet, providing good snorkeling and shallow scuba. This is also an excellent area for night diving.

UPPER KEYS WRECKS

On September 15, 1733, a strong hurricane engulfed the famous Spanish fleet as it skirted the Florida reefs riding the Gulf Stream toward Spain. Twenty-one galleons were driven over the dangerous reefs by the high winds and scattered from Key Largo down the chain of islands to Key Vaca. Today, large piles of ballast are all that remain to mark their final resting place.

The wrecks were first salvaged by the Spaniards. Centuries later, modern treasure hunters brought their airlifts and carefully combed the areas of ballast for hidden silver and rare relics. However, much of the treasure is buried there today under the ever-shifting sands. The sport diver can still be rewarded by patiently fanning the sands around the wrecks. Small pieces of pewter and pottery are common, and an occasional piece of coral-encrusted silver is discovered.

NO. 12 *INFANTE*
Class: Galleon
Date: September 15, 1733
Location: 75 yards north of Little Conch Reef in 25 feet of water.

A large pile of ballast stones mark this site. The wreck is known for unique silver coins with special edge markings called pillar dollars. Hundreds of them were recovered from the area. Supposedly, the *Infante* was carrying the first such coins minted in the New World.

NO. 13 *SAN JOSE*
Class: Galleon
Date: September 15, 1733
Location: In 35 feet of water, about 1 mile east of Little Conch Reef.

The *San Jose* is still producing treasure. In March of 1973, a new section of the wreck, located not more than 50 yards from the main wreck, produced $30,000 in gold and silver on the first day of salvage. The ribs and keel are exposed, creating an exciting setting for underwater photographers.

NO. 14 *EL CAPITAN*
Class: Galleon
Date: September 15, 1733
Location: In 20 feet of water, 6 miles east-southeast of Windley Key.

This wreck, marked by a huge ballast pile, has been the source of untold amounts of fascinating relics, as well as real treasure. Much remains!

NO. 15 BRICK BARGE
Class: Barge
Date: Modern
Location: On the north end of Hens and Chickens Reef.

This is a very scenic steel wreck lying among picturesque coral heads

NO. 16 THE *CHAVES*
Class: Galleon
Date: September 15, 1733
Location: Just off Windley Key, south of the entrance to Snake Creek.

The *Chaves* rests in one of the many sand pockets in a grass bed in around ten feet of water. This small ballast wreck still yields relics to patient divers.

NO. 17 *HERRERA*
Class: Galleon
Date: September 15, 1733
Location: About 2½ miles south of Snake Creek Bridge.

The ballast piles of *Herrera* lie in a grass bed in 18 feet of water. Many interesting relics have been recovered from this area, including small clay figurines of animals and fish.

NO. 18 *TRES PUENTES*
Class: Galleon
Date: September 15, 1733
Location: In 20 feet of water, about 3½ miles south-southeast of Snake Creek Bridge.

This area has produced quite a bit of silver. There is still some good relic hunting on the ocean side of the ballast pile.

NO. 19 USS *ALLIGATOR*
Class: Man of War
Date: 1822
Location: Between coral heads on the ocean side of Alligator Light.

In 1822, this ship was returning to Key West after a skirmish with pirates which left her commander, Lieutenant W.H. Allen, critically wounded. She now rests on the reef that bears her name.

NO. 20 *SAN PEDRO*
Class: Galleon
Date: September 15, 1733
Location: This wreck lies on one of many sand pockets of a large grass bed about 1¼ miles due south of Indian Key.

Many coins have been recovered on the ocean side of this wreck.

NO. 21 *LERRI*
Class: Galleon
Date: September 15, 1733
Location: 20 feet of water, ¾ of a mile off Lower Matecumbe.

The huge 150-foot ballast pile hasn't produced much treasure, but many interesting relics have been recovered. This wreck provides a setting for some interesting photography.

MIDDLE KEYS

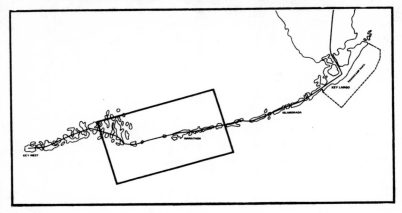

Diving Locations

1. Coffins Patch
2. East Washerwoman
3. Delta Shoals
4. Sombrero Reef
5. G Marker
6. Looe Key

7. Looe Key Drop-Off
8. *Ignacio*
9. Delta Shoal Wreck
10. Ivory Wreck
11. HMS *Looe*
12. Fish Market
13. Pillars

Area Information

The heart of the fabulous Florida Keys' diving lies in the Middle Keys. This is the location of Sombrero Reef and Looe Key, two of the most magnificent coral reefs in the Atlantic. Days could be spent exploring these reefs, but there is much more to do and see in the surrounding waters. Deep drop-offs bathed by the Gulf Stream challenge the experienced open-water divers, while acres of living reefs afford hours of shallow-water snorkeling enjoyment.

NO. 1 COFFINS PATCH

Location: A large reef area running about 1½ miles northeast and southwest located 3½ miles southeast of Key Colony Beach.

Coffins Patch offers several exciting scuba diving and snorkeling areas with depths varying from ten to 15 feet.

On the southwest end, a six-foot piling sticks out of the water. Anchor 5 yards east or west of the pile. This is a very colorful area that is a thrill t dive. Large 20-foot brain corals, fire coral and staghorn corals provic homes for an abundance of marine life. Spanish lobster and small spir

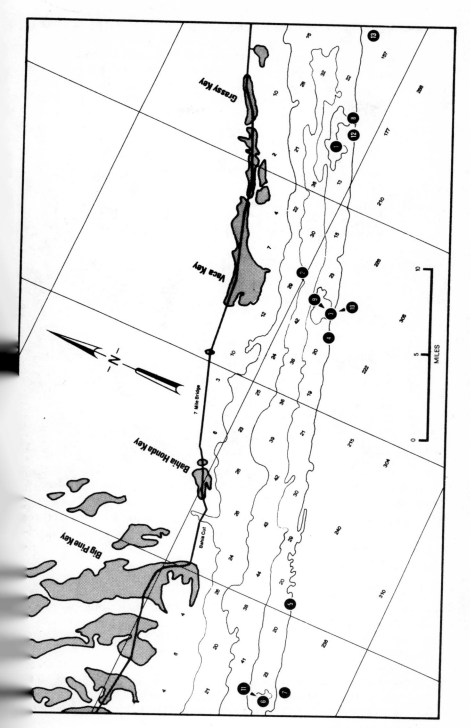

rock lobster can be found hiding under small ledges, and large schools of French grunts and mutton snapper are everywhere.

If you line up the pile with the Sombrero light and go 1¼ miles northeast, you will be over another beautiful reef with some of the largest heads of brain coral to be found in the Keys. This is a good spot for underwater photography, with many ledges alive with fish. Several large French angelfish will follow you around, waiting for a handout.

Continuing on the same line with the pile and light tower for another

Beach camping in the Keys.

200 yards, you will find another exceptional diving location covered wi brain and staghorn coral. There is even more 300 yards to the south.

NO. 2 EAST WASHERWOMAN
Location: About 6 miles southwest of Key Colony Beach.

Marked by a 36-foot tower, this is a good area for snorkeling, w depths from ten to 18 feet. Many varieties of coral, including rose, mid brain, star and staghorn dot the bottom. Sea fans and sponges common.

NO. 3 DELTA SHOALS
Location: About 1½ miles east-northeast of Sombrero light.

This area is easily sighted when approached. The shoal runs for h mile, east and west, with depths from ten to 20 feet. The best diving i the scattered coral heads near the outside. The remains of several wrecks lie in the coral fingers on the ocean side of the shoal. The broken remains of an old slaver that went aground in the 1850s can be found buried in the sand between the coral fingers. She is called the "Ivory Wreck" because of the elephant tusks that have been recovered from her. No treasure was discovered on any of the wrecks, but many unique relics still remain hidden under the sand.

NO. 4 SOMBRERO REEF

Location: About 8 miles southwest of Key Colony Beach. The reef is marked by a 142-foot light tower. The best diving is on the south side (ocean side) of the light. Anchor between the light and the coral heads.

The moment you leave your boat and start gliding down through the clear water surrounding the light, you'll realize the magnificence of Sombrero Reef. Several huge fingers of coral, covered with a stunning variety of gorgonians and brightly colored tropicals, run over the white sand bottom toward the ocean. A diver can easily use several tanks in the area and never fully explore all the ravines, ledges and archways formed by the large coral outcroppings. Cudas are large and plentiful and add to the bold setting created by the reef. Many varieties of coral are present, with large stands of brain coral and lettuce coral common.

The underwater photographer will need to load his camera with a 36-exposure roll instead of 20, because he will find many interesting settings

Looking for the ultimate experience in Keys vacation diving?

With over 10 years of Keys diving experience, Hall's has been taking divers to those hard to find spots that make a dive vacation unique and forever interesting.

- **Fully equipped 40' Dive Boat with daily trips to:**
  SOMBRERO, DELTA, COFFIN'S PATCH, LOOE KEY plus WRECKS, CAVES, DROP-OFFS, DAY or NIGHT
- **Dive classes start every day:**
  SCUBA CERTIFICATION, LOBSTERING, U/W PHOTOGRAPHY, SPEARFISHING
- **Diving Leadership Training:**
  DIVE MASTER, ASST. INSTRUCTOR, INSTRUCTOR, all NAUI-CMAS APPROVED
- **Complete vacation resort facility**
  RESTAURANTS, COCKTAIL LOUNGE, ENTERTAINMENT, SWIMMING POOL, MARINA, CHARTER BOATS, ACCOMODATIONS

- •LESSONS•TRIPS
- •GROUP RATES
- •PACKAGE RATES
- •COMPLETE DIVE SERVICES

HALL'S ® **DIVING CENTER & COLLEGE**

CALL OR WRITE FOR INFORMATION:

CALL 305-743-5929

**Mile Marker 48
1688 Overseas Highway
Marathon, Florida Keys 33050**

bursting with nearly every color and shape a reef can display.

NO. 5 G MARKER
Location: From the Bahia Honda Cut, go 5 miles south-southwest to a 36-foot tower.

This is a large, flat area with depths from 15 to 40 feet. Small scrub corals and sponge formations dot the white sand floor. Many large fish prowl the area, including plentiful schools of jacks. The area around the tower is a favorite haunt for large barracuda.

NO. 6 LOOE KEY
Location: From the Bahia Honda Cut, go 5 miles south-southwest to a 36-foot tower called G Marker. Line up this tower with the 109-foot light tower on American Shoal. Travel 5 miles west-southwest on the imaginary line until you spot a piling with a triangular sign.

Looe Key is one of the most impressive reefs in the Keys, with huge fingers of living coral that jut out to sea. The area was named after the HMS *Looe*, a ship that ran aground on the sharp coral heads in 1744 while escorting a captured French ship to South Carolina.

The open, V-shaped shoal is completely awash and varies in depth from two to 40 feet. Shallow flats sprinkled with assorted shells lie inshore, and coral fingers hundreds of feet long and up to 25 feet high slope off southward into 40 feet of water. There are many large overhangs on the coral heads, and grouper and barracuda warily swim through the sand filled valleys. There is also an abundance of marcro subjects to keep the underwater photographer busy.

NO. 7 LOOE KEY DROP-OFF
Location: About ¼ mile south of Looe Key.

This deep reef lies on the edge of the Gulf Stream, near Looe Key. There the bottom profile drops almost vertically from 50 to 90 feet. The steep gradient consists of large rocks and clefts inhabited by very large fish, and the rarer varieties of mollusks, crustaceans and corals. It is literally untouched by local divers. However, there are strong currents to contend with, and the depths border on the realm of decompression, so exploration of the deep reef is best conducted on professionally organized diving charters.

NO. 8 *IGNACIO*
Class: Galleon
Date: September 15, 1733
Location: 100 yards east-southeast of the old beacon on Coffins Patch Reef.

As the *Ignacio* was carried over the reef by high winds, her bottom broke open and her cargo, including much silver, was scattered for hundreds yards over the flat grass bed.

NO. 9 DELTA SHOAL WRECK
Class: Schooners and Galleons

Date: Unknown
Location: Between the coral fingers of Delta Shoals.

The broken wreckage of several ships lies hidden in the sand between the coral outcroppings. Remnants of both schooners and galleons have been recovered from this area.

NO. 10 IVORY WRECK
Class: Schooner
Date: 1850s
Location: Between the coral fingers of Delta Shoals.

There isn't much to see of this slaver, which went aground on Delta Shoal in the 1850s, but many interesting relics have been recovered from the sands around her broken remains. Elephant tusks were found, helping to establish her as a slaver and giving the wreck the local name, "Ivory Wreck."

NO. 11 HMS *LOOE*
Class: Frigate
Date: 1742
Location: On and between coral fingers on the ocean side of the reef.

The British frigate HMS *Looe* went down in 1742 under curious circumstances. Some sources have it that she had under tow the disguised French ship, *Snow,* while other references are unclear on this point. The *Looe*

SUMMERLAND

DIVE SHOP

(305) 745-1890

DIVE LOOE KEY

SALES • PADI TRAINING FACILITIES • SERVICE • CHARTERS • RENTALS • AIR

M.M. 24½ • Oceanside • P.O. Box 321 • Summerland Key, FL 33042

Diver explores a Keys coral community.

burned to the water line and her prize, if indeed under capture at the time, joined her on the bottom. Many old commercial sailing vessels and rum rummers have since broken their keels on the massive coral ridges. An old anchor from one of the ships runs through one of the coral fingers that has since grown around it. Ballast piles from assorted eras are scattered along the reef, including some 50-pound iron ingots visible in the vicinity of the third coral finger.

NO. 12 FISH MARKET
Location: 4 miles southeast of Key Colony Beach.

This is a large, broken reef area that runs for over a mile in 50 to 70 feet of water. The beautiful heads of living coral rise 15 to 20 feet from the white sand. Fish life, like the reef's name indicates, are the main attraction. Thousands of schooling fish roam through coral gardens, while larger grouper and hog snapper hide in the shallow undercuts. Lobster are common.

NO. 13. PILLARS
Location: 8 miles east-southeast of Key Colony Beach.

Some of the Keys' tallest coral heads loom up 20 to 25 feet from the sea floor. Depths are from 60 to 90 feet. There are plenty of large fish around the beautiful coral spires.

Divers Unlimited invites you to

DIVE MARATHON
Wreck and Reef Diving

Basic Instruction and Advanced Training, Air, Rentals and Service. Two 20 passenger, 40 ft. charter boats.

SPECIAL PACKAGE PRICES
Call Toll Free
(800) 327-2740 (outside FL)

HOLIDAY INN MARINA, MILE MARKER 53½

For additional information, call or write
DIVERS UNLIMITED 6023 Hollywood Blvd.
Hollywood, Florida (305) 981-0156

LOWER KEYS

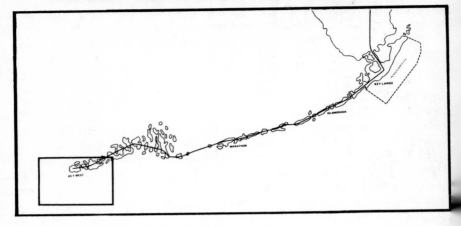

Diving Locations

1. USS *Wilkes-Barre*
2. Pelican Shoal
3. The Sambos
4. *Aquanaut*
5. Ten-Fathom Ledge
6. *All-Alone*
7. #1 Marker Reef
8. Nine Foot Stake
9. Eastern Dry Rocks
10. Eastern Dry Rocks Wreck
11. Rock Key
12. Tile Wreck
13. Sand Key
14. Ten-Fathom Bar
15. Ten-Fathom Ledge off Western Dry Rocks
16. Mallory Square
17. Cottrell Key
18. *Alexander*'s Wreck
19. Smith Shoal
20. *Sturtivent* and Other Freighter
21. Marquesas Keys
22. *Northwind*
23. Marquesas Reef Line
24. S-16 WWI Submarine

Area Information

For years, divers were waylaid by the beautiful reefs of the Upper and Middle Keys and just did not seem to make it to Key West. Today this changed as divers are discovering the virgin reefs of the Lower Ke Starting at Western Sambo and continuing 45 miles westward to Marquesas is a series of spectacular reefs covered with an abundanc sea life. The underwater terrain is dramatic, having towering boulder coral and sudden drop-offs.

Key West also is a point of departure for the Dry Tortugas, Marquesas, and other out islands in the Gulf of Mexico, where s

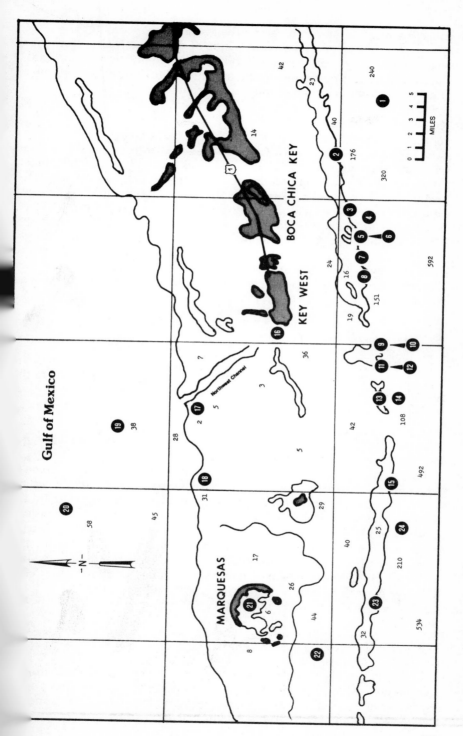

collecting and bug snatching are at their best.

Key West has facilities for many kinds of diving activities. Reef trips, boat rentals, air and complete sales and rentals of diving gear are available. There are two campgrounds on the outskirts of town, and superb motel and hotel accommodations throughout the city.

NO. 1 USS *WILKES-BARRE*
Location: 14 miles west-southwest of the Boca Chica channel.

In 1972, the 610-foot WWII Cleveland Class Light Cruiser *Wilkes-Barre* was sunk to create an artificial reef. The sleek cruiser is completely intact, minus ammo, bunks and fuel. Because of her size, she was placed in 320 feet of water to prevent her from becoming a navigational hazard. She sits on an even keel. The shallowest depth of her superstructure is 140 feet; her deck is at 210 feet. Her massive size has done its job of attracting marine life. She teems with schooling fish as well as large bottom dwellers.

Because of the depths in which she rests, she should be visited only by divers highly experienced in both open-water and deep diving. Local Key West charter boat captains who frequent the site are the only guides who should be considered if you feel yourself capable of making the dive.

NO. 2 PELICAN SHOAL
Location: 7 miles west-southwest of the Boca Chica Channel.

This is part of an extensive coral reef line that runs west into the Sambos. Depths range from ten to 40 feet. Elkhorn and staghorn are the reef's most common corals.

NO. 3 THE SAMBOS
Location: 4 miles south of Boca Chica Channel to black and white buoy #.
Looking due east, a pole can be spotted on the east end of Western Sambo.

The Sambos (Eastern, Middle and Western) are divided by expanses white sand. All sections range in depth from ten to 40 feet. Good diving found all along the reef line. A popular spot is in 25 feet of water on t west end of the Western Sambo section. Here, large fields of branch co grow in profusion. Near this site, at 40 feet, is a series of large, isolat heads covered with sea life. The splendid grouping runs for 125 yards. T grass bed in the shallow water inland from the reefs is good for shelli and lobstering. For best results, maneuver your boat so that it is in 15 f of water over the grass. Let your boat drift with the slow current a snorkel beside it. Be sure to fly a divers down flag.

NO. 4 *AQUANAUT*
Location: ½ mile south of Western Sambo.

This is one of Key West's best and easiest wreck dives. A beautiful foot wooden-hulled tug rests in 75 feet of water. She has been down s 1967. When the Gulf Stream sweeps clear water through the area, the can be seen in its entirety. What a site!

NO. 5 TEN-FATHOM LEDGE
Location: 1 mile southwest of Western Sambo.

Ten-Fathom is a nice ledge in 35 to 50 feet of water. The series of coral ledges is undercut by several interesting caves noted for hiding big grouper. The ocean side drops from 50 feet to 115 feet. This is a great area for a drift dive.

NO. 6 *ALL-ALONE*
Location: On the Ten-Fathom Ledge in 90 feet of water.

The split hull of a 75-foot tugboat rests on the outer edge. There are always plenty of fish around the old wreck, and grouper and snook are common.

NO. 7 #1 MARKER REEF
Location: 4½ miles south of Boca Chica Channel.

This is probably the prettiest shallow reef area off Key West. Fifteen large coral fingers extend out toward the sea.

NO. 8 NINE FOOT STAKE
Location: 1 mile west of #1 marker. Marked by a tall pile.

A nice shallow reef in 15 to 30 feet of water. Because the Navy-Air Development Corp. does its testing in this area, divers make all types of interesting finds.

Quality Inn

KEY WEST PRO DIVE

presents

3 DAYS / 2 NIGHTS

$129⁰⁰ PER PERSON DOUBLE OCC. **DIVING PKG.**

$99⁰⁰ PER PERSON DOUBLE OCC. **SNORKELING PKG.**

- 2 days diving or snorkeling incl. tanks & equip.
- 2 nights deluxe accommodations
- Full breakfast each morning from menu
- Welcoming cocktail

EXTRA PERSON
$90 diving/$62 snorkeling

SINGLE OCCUPANCY
$175 diving/$148 snorkeling

QUALITY INN of KEY WEST 3850 N. Roosevelt Blvd., Key West, FL 33040
(305) 294-6681 • TOLL FREE (800) 228-5151 or Key West Pro Dive Shop
1605 N. Roosevelt Blvd., Key West, FL 33040 • (305) 296-3823

Offer — excluding December 25, 1983–January 4, 1984 — expires December 1, 1984.

NO. 9 EASTERN DRY ROCKS
Location: 2 miles due east of Sand Key and 5 miles south of Key West. Marked in the center by a steel beam.

Large mounds of coral are found southwest of the marker. There is also a wreck on this end of the reef, but it is hard to find due to disintegration of the wood. Divers still find stone ballast and some brass fittings. Lobstering and shelling for conch are good in the shallow water around the marker.

Diver examines a sea fan .

NO. 10 EASTERN DRY ROCKS WRECK
Location: Southwestern end of the Eastern Dry Rocks.

Little remains of this old galleon, but an occasional brass fitting is fou buried in the white sand.

NO. 11 ROCK KEY
Location: 1 mile due east of Sand Key. The area is marked by a steel beam pla in the back center of the reef.

This is a deeper reef with spectacular cracks, some as deep as 20 f and only as wide as a diver. There is also good snorkeling and lobster on the shallow inland side.

Two very old wrecks are located in the area. The first is unidentified. located on the southwest end of the reef in approximately 15 feet of w Among the artifacts recovered are numerous cannon balls and b spikes.

NO. 12 TILE WRECK

Location: Northeast end of Rock Key.

A ship carrying a load of building tiles from Barcelona, Spain went aground on Rock Key. Divers have been digging the tiles out of the sand for years. Other interesting relics which have been recovered include iron ballast, brass spikes and anchor chain.

NO. 13 SAND KEY

Location: 6 miles south of Key West, this reef is easy to find. In the middle of the reef there is a small island with a 110-foot lighthouse.

This peaceful sand island is a great place for *all-weather* diving, as you can always find a lee side with good snorkeling. The best side to dive is the ocean side. When you arrive at the island, go around so that you can see Key West through the lighthouse. Anchor in approximately 15 feet of water and swim toward the island. You will find nice ledges dropping from 45 feet to 70 feet. Numerous grouper are found along the ledges.

NO. 14 TEN-FATHOM BAR

Location: ½ mile due south of Sand Key. Anchor your boat so that the anchor drops over the wall.

This is a spectacular wall dive with the top of the wall in 25 feet of water and dropping almost straight down to 130 feet. Exceptionally clear water flows through this area much of the year. Divers need to be aware of a strong current which will be encountered the first 30 feet of the dive. If you would like to try your hand at feeding large fish, this is the place to do it. Grouper and snapper are very tame, and it is not uncommon to discover a large grouper looking over your shoulder. Schools of rays have been spotted swimming near the bottom of the ledge. You will see corals and sponges that are not found on the shallower reefs. If you have an underwater tow, be sure to use it here: you will be able to explore a great deal more in the limited amount of bottom time you will have.

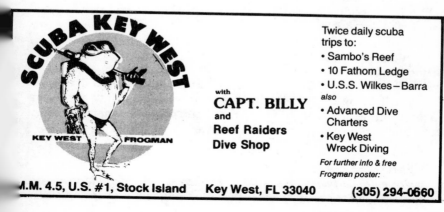

SCUBA KEY WEST

KEY WEST   FROGMAN

with **CAPT. BILLY** and **Reef Raiders Dive Shop**

Twice daily scuba trips to:
- Sambo's Reef
- 10 Fathom Ledge
- U.S.S. Wilkes—Barra

also
- Advanced Dive Charters
- Key West Wreck Diving

For further info & free Frogman poster:

M.M. 4.5, U.S. #1, Stock Island   Key West, FL 33040   **(305) 294-0660**

NO. 15 TEN-FATHOM LEDGE OFF WESTERN DRY ROCKS
Location: 4½ miles west-southwest of the Sand Key Light.

This is the hot-spot in Key West waters for reef diving. Most area diving charters spend a great deal of time exploring the coral caves, ledges and outcroppings. Its close proximity to the Gulf Stream increases the water visibility, creating spectacular vistas of underwater coral gardens. The relatively shallow 40- to 50-foot depths add to the popularity of the site. Schools of fish gather around the higher peaks, while a spectacular array of colorful tropicals dance about the undercuts and soft corals. A large black grouper population is another attraction. This is thought to be one of their spawning grounds. Larger grouper are found from March through June.

NO. 16 MALLORY SQUARE (Beach Dive)
Location: At the north end of Duval Street in Key West, turn left, go one block, and turn right. The dock on which you find yourself is Mallory Square.

This pier is over 100 years old. It is currently used as a dock for large ships. Diving off the pier in 20 to 30 feet of water has produced thousands of old bottles along with various artifacts dating back to the 1800s. Diving should be done only at slack tide as the currents are very strong during tidal changes. Visibility is in the three- to ten-foot range. An underwater compass is a necessity.

NO. 17 COTTRELL KEY
Location: Travel out the Northwest Channel for about 9 miles until you come to the ruins of old Coast Guard lighthouse (only the pilings are standing). Turn west, and run until you are parallel with the first mangrove island on your left. Coast your boat in until you are in 4 to 5 feet of water.

This is a good area for shell collecting. Figs, tuns, milk conch, fighter conch, horse conch, cowries and tulip shells have all been found here. This is also a good area for lobsters. Look for them in the shallow water, hiding in sponges and under rocky ledges.

Cottrell is an old military strafing site. Many shell holes pock the bottom. Artifact hunting is a popular diving activity. Depths range from ten to 15 feet. This is where divers head when the south wind is too strong for good diving on the Atlantic reefs.

NO. 18 *ALEXANDER'S WRECK*
Location: 4 miles west-northwest of Cottrell Key.

The *Alexander* was a 300-foot Destroyer Escort sunk in the Gulf in 1970. She is in half, lying on her side in 40 feet of water. Visibility at the site averages from 40 to 50 feet. The wreck still produces many military artifacts and is the year 'round home of swarming baitfish.

NO. 19 SMITH SHOALS
Location: 12 miles northwest of Key West. Marked by a 47-foot tower.

Visibility limited to about 20 feet is the only thing that prevents this area from being rated an excellent dive. Huge stands of large plate, brain and staghorn corals loom 15 to 18 feet up from the sand bottom just south of the tower. Depths range from 20 to 40 feet.

NO. 20 *STURTIVENT* AND OTHER FREIGHTERS
Location: 7 miles on a 293° course from the Smith Shoals Tower.

The broken remains of a four-stack destroyer rest in 70 feet of water. She was sunk in 1942 by our own mines. You can expect visibility of 25 feet. Several other WWII casualties are located in the same general area of the Gulf. They include the 3,018-ton American freighter, *Luchenbach,* that went down with one-sixth of the world's tungston supply and the Norwegian freighter, *Bosikka,* sister ship to the *Benwood,* which is located in the Pennekamp Park area nearby. The Danish freighter, *Gumbar,* is considered a hot fishing spot. All of these ships were sunk between June and August of 1942. Fish life is prolific at each, with large grouper, jewfish, cobia and snapper.

NO. 21 MARQUESAS KEYS
Location: 25 miles due west of Key West.

The Marquesas are a group of ten mangrove islands surrounded by shallow waters. The area is good for both shelling and spearing. Four miles to the west lies the now-famous Spanish galleon, *Atocha,* successfully salvaged by Treasure Salvors, Inc. of Key West. Ten miles to the west at Halfmoon Shoal, is the broken wreckage of an old island ferry, lying in 15 feet of water. These waters are known locally as the Quicksands. Rip currents are constantly present. For this reason, the area is not recommended for novice divers.

NO. 22 *NORTHWIND*
Location: 3½ miles southwest of the Marquesas.

A large, metal tugboat belonging to Treasure Salvors tragically sank one night. She rests on her side in 40 feet of water, and is inhabited by several large jewfish.

NO. 23 MARQUESAS REEF LINE
Location: A continuation of the Atlantic reef line, running east and west, 6 miles south of the Marquesas.

A long, broken line of coral ledges and caves in 30 to 70 feet of water, some of the Keys' best spearing is found in these waters. Far from land, seldom dived, large snapper and grouper roam freely here.

NO. 24 S-16 WWI SUBMARINE
Location: 14 miles west-southwest of Key West.

The S-16 sub was sunk completely intact in 1945 by the Navy for experimental purposes. She was built in 1919. Her depth of 250 feet makes this a very difficult dive. A few local captains make runs to the area during September or October, when the Keys' weather is at its best.

THE DRY TORTUGAS

The Out Islands of the Keys

The Dry Tortugas is one of the most varied and beautiful diving locations in Florida. Not only are the diving opportunities numerous and rewarding, but picturesque Fort Jefferson also offers 'landlubbers' a chance for adventure and rare sightseeing.

A brief sketch of the colorful history of Fort Jefferson and the surrounding islands will help to familiarize you with the area. The islands were first visited in 1513 by Ponce de Leon, who named the area the "Tortugas" for the great abundance of tortoises he found there. Fort Jefferson stands on Garden Key. Construction was begun on it in 1846 by the U.S. military. The mammoth six-sided, three-tiered fortress was designed for a garrison of 7,500 men and an armament of 450 cannons. Although construction continued for 30 years, she was not completed, and no battle was ever fought from her walls. Following the Civil War, she was turned into a prison. Dr. Samuel Mudd, the physician who set James Wilkes Booth's leg after the assassination of Lincoln, was sent to serve a life sentence at Fort Jefferson after being convicted of conspiracy in the assassination plot. During an epidemic of yellow fever in 1867, the assigned post surgeon was one of the first to die. Dr. Mudd performed admirably by filling in the vacancy, and helped stem the spread of the disease. He was released with full pardon in 1869. His quarters can still be viewed in the fort.

Fort Jefferson covers nearly ten acres. It is approximately half a mile in perimeter, has walls eight feet thick and 45 feet high, and is surrounded by a breakwater moat. Fort Jefferson National Monument, along with the surrounding reefs and islands, was set aside on January 4, 1935 as a national preserve by proclamation of President Franklin D. Roosevelt. It is under the jurisdiction of the National Park Service.

As you stand in front of the fort, the island directly east of you is Bush Key, a rookery for thousands of terns, chiefly noddies, sooties and least terns. Anyone wishing to visit the bird sanctuary must acquire permission from the federal park rangers stationed in Fort Jefferson.

Two and one half miles due west of Garden Key is Loggerhead Key upon which stands the present Coast Guard lighthouse. The lighthouse is 151 feet high. It is the first thing you see as you approach the Dry Tortugas from Key West. The island is almost one mile long and is covered with rugged Australian pines. Just off the beach, on the northwestern side of the island, are beautiful snorkeling areas.

Jefferson Monument, a landmark of the Dry Tortugas.

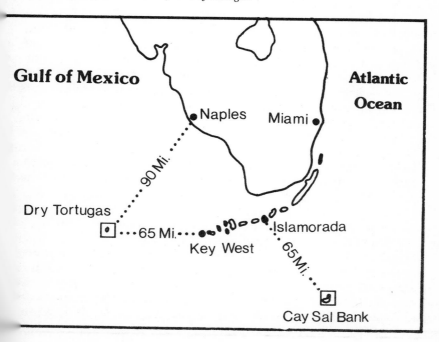

The constant flow of the Gulf Stream current over more than one hundred square miles of living coral reef guarantees visibility in the 80- to 100-foot range year 'round. Ledges that drop 30 to 80 feet, 16 reported wrecks, and miles of shallow snorkeling depths invite all types of reef diving enthusiasts. Relative inaccessibility ensures that the Dry Tortugas will seldom be overrun by boaters or divers. The distance from the nearest populated area (Key West) is 65 miles. It can be reached only by boat or seaplane. There are no commercial facilities in the group of eight islands. Most people either sleep in their boats or camp on Garden Key, where there are barbeque grills for cooking. All food and water must be brought in as there is none available. Also, visitors must transport their garbage away with them.

Among the wrecks in the area, one of the favorites is a 300-foot, steel-hulled wreck, located one mile southwest of Loggerhead Key. It is called the *French* wreck. She is broken in half and lies in 30 feet of water. Many schooling fish make their homes there, among them grunts, snappers, porgies, and thousands of colorful tropical fish. Jewfish may be seen in and under the wreck on almost every dive. Her estimated age is 150 years

Approximately 100 yards off buoy No. 8 is the wreck of a sailing schooner. She is broken up and very old. This is a good place to look fo artifacts. Stone ballast piles lie in 60 feet of water.

A 1971 government survey reported there were 16 wrecks in the area However, the validity of finds would have to be checked with governmer officials.

There is an unidentified wreck on White Shoal halfway between Log gerhead Key and Garden Key, lying in approximately 25 feet of wate Several antique bottles have been found which date from the 1840s.

Spearfishing is prohibited within the boundaries of the Monument. Y may take fish at depths beyond 70 feet, where you will be out of pa limits. Tortugas Bank, seven and a half miles west of Loggerhead Key, good for spearfishing, with average depths of 50 feet. Two lobsters per d per person may be taken during the season. The taking of other shellf and coral is prohibited.

If you plan a trip to Dry Tortugas from Key West in your own boat, sure to check with the National Weather Service in Key West for the la forecast. Usually discouraging to skippers of small boats is the 30-n stretch of deep water between Rebecca Shoals and the reefs of the I Tortugas. Tidal currents, which flow against the prevailing winds, co bine with the Gulf Stream current to make this an especially rough a during periods of strong winds, usually in winter. Once reached, h ever, the harbor in front of Fort Jefferson is well protected.

Dead seashells may be collected when found above the high-water Bush Key is reserved for birds during the nesting season of March thro September. Then, the sooty terns gather by the thousands from the C bean Sea and west-central Atlantic. Their nests are depressions in warm sand and the parents take turns shading their single eggs fror hot sun. Disturbing the birds during this period can result in the dea many of the young. When the babies have finally grown large and strong enough for continuous flight, the entire colony leaves. Brown noddies can also be seen among the sooties, but in much smaller numbers. Frigate birds are sighted in the summer, while blue-faced and brown boobies are sighted only occasionally. Songbirds and migrant birds rest at the islands which lie in their flight path from the United States to Cuba and South America. In winter, gulls, terns of the north, and migratory shore birds find refuge there. All keys except Garden and Loggerhead are closed during the turtle season, May through September 30.

...ndoned now, Ft. Jefferson of the Dry Tortugas.

...exciting way to visit the Dry Tortugas is by five-passenger sea plane ...Stock Island, near Key West. The 35-minute flights leave twice a day. ...pectacular ride takes you over sand flats, grass beds, quicksand and ...drop-offs populated by large fish which are easily spotted from the ...lying plane. Schooling tarpon, sharks, rays, turtles and porpoise are ...d on every flight. Directly under the flight path is the hull of the ...*wind*, Treasure Salvors' ill-fated tug that helped in the salvage of the ...re-laden Spanish galleon, the *Atocha*. The view of the huge fort, ...nded by crystalline blue waters, is worth the trip by itself. Visitors ...en two and a half hours to explore the fort, sunbathe or snorkel over ...allow coral patches west of the fort. The best diving locations are ...d by a convenient buoy system.

THE CAY SAL BANK

The Cay Sal bank encompasses an area roughly 60 miles in diameter, located 65 miles south-southeast of Islamorada, Florida, in the Keys, and 30 miles north of Cuba. The bank is made up of assorted reefs, shoals and scattered cays, and forms the western edge of the Bahama Islands. The only transportation to the area is by boat. The problem of having to check in with Bahamian customs, however, has limited travel to the banks in recent years.

One of the most popular diving spots on the bank is Elbow Cay. This is a barren chain of uninhabited rocks lying in an east to westerly line, roughly one and a half miles in length. The bleak topside scenery contrasts sharply with the compelling underwater beauty here. The Elbow offers a full range of diving activities for divers of any experience level. For snorkeling, there are small, colorful reefs only a few yards off the islands, with depth dropping down to 30 to 35 feet.

The diver will always remember Cay Sal's underwater caves and clear lagoons that are hidden in the rocky cliffs of the islands. Snorkeling through these rugged passages, from air pocket to air pocket, is a real adventure. A number of holes penetrate the surfaces of the islands, allowing bright light to enter through them to the white sand floor of the cave below. At the east end of the Elbow, there is a sandy lagoon connected the outside ocean by a large underwater passage. The lagoon is a refuge for tropicals, leopard rays and loggerhead turtles.

On the western end of the Elbow there are ruins of a British lighthouse. Several of the buildings make for interesting exploration between dives. On the sand bottom, about 100 yards north of the ruins, lie the rusty remains of an old supply steamer. The massive, circular iron frames of paddle wheels are still visible above the sand, making it a good site for hunting and photography.

Off the west end of the cay is a sheer vertical wall that provides spectacular dive location for experienced divers. The depths involved a strong surface current make this a challenging, but very rewarding, From the flat, low coral bottom at the 90-foot level, the wall plunge 1,200 feet. Visibility is usually in the 150- to 200-foot range.

Suspended on the wall in this super-clear water, taking in the fascinating forms of luxurious soft corals, sponges and exotic fish, and feel touch of narcosis, the diver is left with an impression he will not forget. The natural beauty of this untouched area will keep the underwater photographer wishing for more air and film at the end of his all too visit over the wall at Cay Sal.

INDEX
Reefs and Ledges

Springs and Sinks